Dedication

After a long and courageous struggle against cancer Colin Good, one of the authors and editors of this volume, died on 22 November 2000. Even at the advanced stages of his illness Colin retained his unstinting enthusiasm for his profession and worked tirelessly to see this project through to its completion. We will miss him.

Attitudes Towards Europe

Language in the unification process

Edited by
ANDREAS MUSOLFF
University of Durham
COLIN GOOD
University of Durham
PETRA POINTS
University of Durham
RUTH WITTLINGER
University of Durham

Ashgate

Aldershot • Burlington USA • Singapore • Sydney

Published by
Ashgate Publishing Ltd
Gower House
Croft Road
Aldershot
Hants GU11 3HR
England

Ashgate Publishing Company
131 Main Street
Burlington, VT 05401-5600 USA

Ashgate website: http://www.ashgate.com

British Library Cataloguing in Publication Data
Attitudes towards Europe : language in the unification
    process
    1.Public opinion - England 2.Public opinion - Germany
    3.Europe - Foreign public opinion, British 4.Europe -
    Foreign public opinion, German
    I.Good, Colin H.

Library of Congress Control Number: 00-110693

ISBN 0 7546 1431 X

Printed and bound by Athenaeum Press, Ltd.,
Gateshead, Tyne & Wear.

Contents

Contributors

Colin Good is Professor of German at the University of Durham. His research focuses mainly on the application of insights from linguistic theory to political and ideological texts. His other interests include sociolinguistics of German, translation theory and interpreting. He is the author of *Die deutsche Sprache und die kommunistische Ideologie* (1975), *Presse und soziale Wirklichkeit* (1985), *Newspaper German. A Vocabulary of Commercial and Administrative German* (1995).

Dieter Herberg is Professor of German Linguistics at the *Institut für Deutsche Sprache* in Mannheim. His main research interests are in the field of lexicography and orthography of contemporary German. He is co-author of *Schlüsselwörter der Wendezeit* (1997).

Heidrun Kämper is a Researcher at the *Institut für Deutsche Sprache* in Mannheim and visiting lecturer at the *Technische Universität Darmstadt*. Her main research interests are in the areas of historical semantics, the language of National Socialism, lexicography, post war German language and forensic linguistics. She has recently been awarded a major research grant from the *Deutsche Forschungsgemeinschaft*.

Gerlinde Mautner is Professor of Business English at the Vienna University of Economics and Business Administration (*Wirtschaftsuniversität Wien*). Her research interests are in discourse analysis and corpus linguistics, and the genres to which she has applied both methodological frameworks include the discourse of politics, the media, advertising and other forms of corporate communication in the for-profit and non-profit sectors.

Andreas Musolff is Reader in German at the University of Durham. He has published a book and a number of articles on the history and the current use of political terminology and imagery in British and German public discourse.

Petra Points is Course Leader for European Studies and Head of the Language Teaching Centre at the University of Durham, Stockton Campus. Her main research interest is the language of the media and the representations of Germany in the British Press.

Christina Schäffner is Senior Lecturer in the School of Languages and European Studies at Aston University in Birmingham and Co-director of the Institute for the Study of Language and Society. Her main research interests are translation studies, political discourse, textlinguistics, and metaphors. Her publications include Language and Peace (co-edited with Anita Wenden, 1995), Cultural functions of translation (co-edited with Helen Kelly-Holmes, 1995), Conceiving of Europe - Diversity in Unity? (co-edited with Andreas Musolff and Michael Townson, 1996), Translation and Quality (ed., 1997), Translation and Norms (ed., 1999).

Wolfgang Teubert holds the Collins Chair of Corpus Linguistics at Birmingham University, after having headed the Multilingual Reasearch group at the *Institut für Deutsche Sprache* for many years. He is editor-in-chief of the *International Journal of Corpus Linuistics* and has published widely on multilingual semantics and discourse analysis.

Arachne van der Eijk-Spaan studied Classics at Leiden University in the Netherlands. She works as an interpreter and translator in Dutch and German and she teaches Dutch at the University of Newcastle upon Tyne. She is a post-graduate student at the University of Durham.

Ruth Wittlinger is Lecturer in European Studies at the University of Durham, Stockton Campus. Her main research interest is in the area of German politics and in the interdisciplinary study of politics and literature, with particular reference to Britain in the 1980s.

Foreword

HANS-FRIEDRICH VON PLOETZ
German Ambassador to Britain

For over two thousand years the term 'Europe' has been used and discussed, and in this long period it has been applied to the most varied political, ideological and geographical concepts. As long as 'Europe' understood itself as a unity, distict from other philosophical, religious and geographical identities, the term was not particularly controversial.

Today things are more complicated. Christian Europe split into catholic and Protestant, into capitalist and communist; and today we have the Europes of the European Union, the council of Europe and other European organisations, each with its different group of members.

We are, I am glad to say, in the process of overcoming old dividing-lines. The project of EU reform and further development initiated by the Treaty of Amsterdam and to be continued by the Treaty of Niece, expected in autumn this year, provide the basis for an unprecedented enlargement of the EU to the East and South East. A truly historic development which will, step by step, lead to the lasting emergence of a just and peaceful order in all of Europe.

In the last few years there has been a gratifying convergence of ideas in many areas. But the lively discussion on 'Europe' will continue, including, of course, in the domestic political arena. Geography and history contribute to a wide range of views, and sometimes also misunderstandings, about the goals and contents of specific European policies.

Both the German and British governments are committed to the task of shaping a modern and competitive Europe for the age of globalisation, just as their other partners in the EU. By further intensifying our bilateral relations, for example through German-British youth exchange and the promotion of German in British schools and universities, we are making a vigorous contribution to greater mutual understanding and friendship.

With its highly scientific analyses of the way in which the term 'Europe' and related concepts have been used and understood, especially in Britain and Germany during the last decade, this work *Attitudes towards Europe* thus renders a great service at a time of the utmost significance for

Europe. It is instructive not only in order to understand our countries and the political currents within them, but also as an insight into what expectations people have of Europe. Historians of all kinds, but also those who, like myself, are concerned with concrete issues of European policy on a day-to-day basis, will gain much useful information from this study. Its authors deserve the warmest thanks for a work of lasting significance, which I wish every success.

Attitudes Towards Europe - Einstellungen zu Europa

COLIN GOOD, ANDREAS MUSOLFF, PETRA POINTS,
RUTH WITTLINGER

The 'attitudes towards Europe' which are the subject of this volume are obviously broadly determined by the respective national contexts in which they operate and reflect the diversity and complexity of the distinct historical and political experiences of Britain and Germany. There are some very obvious factors which potentially have an impact on collective attitudes towards Europe such as the geographical position of the two countries, for example. Thus, Britain's position on the periphery of Europe is in obvious contrast to Germany's central position on the continent, sharing borders with nine countries. More complex and also more powerful, however, are those factors which are rooted in recent history.

In the post-war period, West Germany's political elites, backed by a popular consensus, consistently showed themselves to be 'good Europeans'. The underlying motive is evident: the most important objective on the agenda of post-war (West) Germany's foreign policy was to gain respectability and prove itself a worthy and reliable member of the international community. The most promising route to achieve Germany's rehabilitation therefore led through a constructive membership of western alliance systems such as NATO and the European Community which offered plenty of scope for multilateral initiatives without requiring or encouraging unilateral German moves. Another positive side effect of closer European integration was the identificatory potential it offered to those Germans who - after the horrendous excesses carried out in the name of German nationalism - still had very ambivalent feelings towards a German national identity and appreciated the opportunity to skip the national level and identify with the supranational entity of Europe. Furthermore, it was the European context, which finally and not without opposition, facilitated German reunification and restored Germany's full sovereignty by providing a structure which helped allay fears of Germany's neighbours about its potential for renewed dominance. Hence, it is quite clear that the German nation-state has benefited from 'the European idea' because it provided a useful way out of a problematic situation after 1945, in practical terms of power politics as well as on the identificatory level.

Britain, on the other hand, has gained the reputation of being 'an awkward partner' (George, 1994) in the context of European integration. In contrast to Germany's case, European integration has never offered similar advantages for Britain. Quite the reverse, it has frequently been perceived as a threat to national identity which has found a powerful expression in the concept of 'Britishness' or 'Englishness'. In addition to this, the transformation from being an imperial power to being a 'mere' member of a community meant a relegation in the international league of nations in terms of status. Accordingly, the issue of sovereignty is of a different quality in these two nation-states. Whereas the European Community provided the framework in which Germany was allowed to regain full sovereignty as a nation-state, British perceptions are strongly influenced by the fear of losing sovereignty.

There are numerous other determinants which are linked to the current political and economic systems of Britain and Germany. Federalism, for example, has served Germany well in its post-war history whereas it is an alien concept for Britain. With regard to the economic systems, the two countries also show a different pattern with different priorities. This becomes more and more obvious, the more 'deepening' policies such as the Economic and Monetary Union and a Common Foreign and Security Policy are pursued. Whereas New Labour, for example, has been careful to exercise frugality in terms of public expenditure and levels of taxation, having by and large adopted the Thatcherite neo-liberal economics of the 1980s, the rhetoric of Germany's new left-of-centre government is, broadly speaking, still more interventionist and less free market. This became very obvious in the debate which erupted within the German Social Democrats after the publication of the joint Blair/Schröder paper which was meant to boost the European Election campaign in 1999. For many German Social Democrats, it contained far too much 'free market speak'.

These examples obviously do not provide an exhaustive list but they do illustrate the complex and diverse issues in terms of 'national baggage' which provide the framework for discourses on European integration. The papers in this volume describe in great detail the operation of these discourses within the general conditions outlined so far.

In a speech given at the Humboldt University of Berlin in May 2000, the German Foreign minister, Joschka Fischer, stated that, almost 50 years after Robert Schumann's announcement of the political vision of a

European Federation, 'History was asking again the question "Quo vadis Europa"'.[1] The answer, he argued, could only be 'onwards to the completion of European integration', for a 'step backwards, even just a standstill or satisfaction with what has been achieved, would demand a fatal price of all EU member states and of all those who want to become members',but especially of the 'people' (*Menschen*), who would experience the consequences of any EU policies in their own lives. Fischer presented his thoughts on the 'finality of European integration' as the opinion of just such a man of the 'people', casting aside 'the mantle of German Foreign Minister and member of the Government'. This diplomatic disclaimer did not, however, prevent Fischer from giving a clear indication of his government's ideas about the 'way' in which the EU should develop, namely as a 'transition from a union of states [in German: *Staatenverbund der Union*] to full parliamentarization as a European Federation [in German: *Föderation*]' with institutions that 'really do exercise legislative and executive power'.

Nor did the 'mantle' of cautious diplomacy slip completely from Mr Fischer's shoulders when he explained the potential misunderstandings between Germany and its partners, specifically: 'not least [...] our friends in the United Kingdom", whom he singled out because he knew 'that the term "federation" irritates many Britons' (in German: 'dass der Begriff "Föderation" für viele Briten ein Reizwort ist', ibid.). He even referred back to a notorious 1994 discussion paper by the then ruling Christian Democrat Parties, which though coming close to his own ideas 'was stillborn, as it were, because it presupposed an exclusive, closed "core"' of an integrated elite group within the EU. Fischer was careful to distance himself from such hierarchical concepts as well as from the ideas of a dissolution of the nation states: even when the Federation is attained, he asserts, 'we will still be British or German, French or Polish' and the 'nation states will continue to exist and [...] retain a much larger role than the Länder have in Germany' (ibid.).

It is hardly surprising, of course, that a German Foreign Minister, when announcing a new initiative in the field of European policy, should take every precaution not to offend partner governments and that he should use the standard devices of diplomatic hedging in order to minimise potential political damage. In fact, it seems astonishing how explicitly and openly he speaks about the different perceptions and opinions held in other EU countries, especially Britain with its sensitivity over the term and concept of a *European federation*. However, a look at the historical background of international disputes over political discourse on Europe, e.g. the 1991 row about the British government's refusal to sign the Maastricht Treaty as long as the Treaty text included the term *federal*, the 1994 debate about the precise meaning of the *core* concept that Fischer mentioned, demonstrates that the debate about European politics has always also been a debate about the linguistic and discursive manifestations of competing concepts of Europe. From the perspective of comparative analysis of political discourse, Fischer's reference to the interpretation problems concerning *federation* are just one of many argumentative attempts made by participants in the international public debate to explain political strategies by way of commenting on semantic and pragmatic contrasts between linguistic expressions used in the different discourse communities, notably the British and German public.

It is this 'interaction' between two national discourses on Europe that is explored in the contributions to this volume. They represent the results of the first phase of a joint project by two research groups at Durham University and at the *Institut für Deutsche Sprache* in Mannheim (Germany) on 'Attitudes towards Europe', funded by the British Council and the German Academic Exchange Service. Further colleagues, from Aston University (Birmingham), the *Wirtschaftsuniversität* at Vienna and Dublin City University, have also participated in the four project workshops that have been held so far,[2] and two of them have contributed to this volume.

By combining research methods of political science, lexicography, critical discourse analysis and corpus linguistics, the project aims to investigate the public debate about the future structure of the European Union in Britain and Germany, with special emphasis on debates about the common currency *Euro* and on further moves towards closer economic and political integration. The objective of the first phase has been to provide comparative accounts of the main strands of the 'Europe debate', as they have developed in the two countries. This is reflected in the structure of the volume, which proceeds from accounts of British discourse about EU politics via studies of German Europe-debates to comparative/contrastive analyses, with two studies concentrating specifically on translation aspects. In the first contribution, *Gerlinde Mautner* explores the discursive representation of British national identity, as seen against the backdrop of an as yet amorphous European identity. Her study is based on a corpus of newspaper articles on Europe dating from the early 1970s to the mid-1990s, and matches the results of statistical concordancing procedures with the qualitative discourse-analytic analyses. *Ruth Wittlinger* investigates the ways in which Margaret Thatcher instrumentalised stereotypes about Germany and the Germans in her political autobiographies, *The Downing Street Years* and *The Path to Power*, as arguments against both German national unification and also against further European integration. *Wolfgang Teubert* presents a corpus of data drawn from British Eurosceptic web sites that deal with the EU. He analyses recurring key terms and explicit comments on such uses in other sources as well as their distribution across text registers as reflections of underlying cultural attitudes towards liberalist vs. paternalistic concepts of state and society.

Introducing the second part of the book, *Heidrun Kämper* looks at the role which the 'idea of Europe' played in post-war political thinking and discourse of West Germany, offering a new basis for national German identity after the catastrophe of nazism. Her chapter focuses on the modification of traditional concepts of 'Europe' as well as on the argumentative exploitation of this concept for a newly 'internationalised' (West) German identity, and the justification of claims to partner status among (West) European nations. Moving on to more recent debates in Germany, *Dieter Herberg* investigates neologisms based on the term *Euro*, which have been coined in the German public debate about the common currency. His analysis, which is based on data from three representative corpora of German press texts in the 1990s, in particular examines the distribution of such terms and their collocations across participants in the public debate and relates them to their specific political attitudes and strategies.

In the opening chapter of part III, *Colin Good* takes issue with the simplifying notion that it is 'false friends' or problematic internationalisms which have hindered the development of a European discourse. Against this, he argues that it seems more plausible to assume that European discourse is hampered by the fact that key words and concepts, as used in parliamentary debates on Europe in Great Britain and Germany, are caught up in the complex conditions of national political debates, which involve rival parties, determined to win out over the opponent by instrumentalising differences in meaning. The respective national public also have deep-rooted views and suspicions about language, which contribute to the communicative difficulty. In the following chapter, *Andreas Musolff* compares the imagery of British and German press texts dealing with EU-politics during the 1990s. He demonstrates that the use of metaphors of Europe as a *train, ship, convoy, car* etc., *travelling at two speeds* in the two national discourses is characterised by systematic differences in argumentative 'bias'. In the German press, Britain is mostly 'cast' as the *late* or unwilling *traveller*, whereas Germany itself used to be depicted as the *driver/locomotive* up to 1997/98; since then, Germany is also perceived as a *problem passenger*. British media share the *journey* scenario but are divided over its political evaluation. Pro-EU voices take a pessimistic view of British *lateness*, whilst 'Euro-sceptic' media paint a picture of the Union *travelling towards disaster*.

In the first of two chapters dealing with the role of translations in cross-national discourse, *Christina Schäffner* focuses on the communicative effects of the translations of two policy announcements, i.e. the aforementioned German Christian Democrats' 1994 discussion paper suggesting the building of an EU *core* group and the proposals for EU-wide tax harmonisation at the 1999 EU summit in Helsinki. In both cases, English translations of statements by German politicians produced an emphatic rejection in the British public, which was certainly not the intended outcome but can be related to the lexical choices and strategies of information selection in the respective translation texts. *Arachne van der Eijk-Spaan* then provides a detailed case study of a change-of-political-message through translation by way of comparing an article by Fredy Gsteiger in *Die Zeit* with its English version published in *The Guardian*. The changes which she observes in the vocabulary, imagery and argumentation of the translation shift the focus from a critical depiction of Germany as an overbearing *schoolmaster* (vis-à-vis the French) into a confirmation of British stereotypes about Germany's role as an *aggressor*.

These contributions cannot and do not attempt to draw a 'complete' picture of the discourse on Europe in Great Britain and Germany; rather they aim at pointing out perspectives for further research into the factors determining the way we conceive of and communicate about European politics across national borders. Obviously, many facets even of the bi-national Euro-discourse remain still to be explored and the Anglo-German 'axis' is, of course, only one perspective in the whole picture of the increasingly internationalised debate about Europe's political, social and economic future. Furthermore, this discourse is continuously developing in unpredictable ways. The contribution of political discourse analysis therefore cannot lie in predicting, even less in prescribing, ways of developing cross-national communication, but rather in identifying and highlighting discourse traditions that may shape the public's perception without being made explicit (and which thus may be instrumentalised by participants in the power-games of European politics) as well as recurrent patterns of communication conflicts - and their solutions - that may inform choices of future communicative strategies. Last not least, it may raise an awareness of the strong influence that stereotypes, prejudices and other nationally established discourse patterns play in what is supposed to be - and hopefully, will become - a truly common (if not 'united' or 'unified') European discourse.

Notes

1   Cf. Fischer 2000. Quotations in English are from the from the official advance text and its translation, both published by the German Foreign Office.
2   For information on membership and workshops of the project cf. Kämper 1999 and the web-site: "www.dur.ac.uk/SMEL/depts/german/euro-arc.htm".

References

Baker, D. and Seawright, D. (eds) (1998), *Britain for and against Europe. British Politics and the Question of European Integration*, Oxford University Press, Oxford.
Fendler, S. and Wittlinger, R. (eds) (1999), *The Idea of Europe in Literature*, Macmillan, London.
Fischer, J. (2000), 'Vom Staatenbund zur Föderation - Gedanken über die Finalität der europäischen Integration'/'From Confederacy to Federation - Thoughts on the finality of European integration', Speech at the Humboldt University in Berlin, 12 May 2000; on web-sites: "http://www.auswaertiges-amt.de/6-archiv/2/r/r000512a.htm" and "http://www.auswaertiges-amt.de/6-archiv/2/r/r000512b.htm".
George, S. (1994), *An Awkward Partner: Britain in the European Community,* Oxford University Press, Oxford.
Good, C. (1996), 'Political communication and Political Culture in Germany and Great Britain: Some Differences and Similarities', in A. Musolff, C. Schäffner and M Townson, 1996, pp. 109-120.
Kämper, H. (1999), 'Haltungen zu Europa - Attitudes towards Europe', *Sprachreport*, 2/1999, pp. 25-6.
Musolff, A., Schäffner, C. and Townson, M. (eds) (1996), *Conceiving of Europe - Unity in Diversity.* Dartmouth Publishers, Aldershot.
Teubert, W. (1998), 'Europäische Herausforderungen', *Sprachreport*, 4/1998, pp. 11-13.
Young, H. (1998), *This Blessed Plot. Britain and Europe from Churchill to Blair.* Macmillan, London.

PART 1: BRITISH DISCOURSE ON EUROPE

1   British National Identity in the European Context

GERLINDE MAUTNER

Introduction

European integration is a multifaceted problem involving not only a variety of political, economic, and legal issues, but also causing disturbances of a less palpable nature, such as clashes of mentalities and crises of identity. The 'hard' factors, such as the introduction of the common currency and the harmonisation of tax laws for example, are all safely in the hands of experts. In those areas, politicians, bureaucrats and academics are continuously engaged in processes of analysis, strategic planning, and policy making. 'Soft' factors, on the other hand, are less obviously amenable to intervention. After all, emotional commitment to Europe cannot be created by decree, and conditions for 'Europeanness', essentially a state of mind, cannot be stipulated, fulfilled or rejected like the Maastricht criteria. Instead, we are dealing with elusive categories such as identity and nationhood, which are expressed through symbols, rituals, beliefs, and discursive practices rather than through material and quantifiable manifestations. Nonetheless there can be no doubt that these intangible issues are having a major impact on the progress, or lack of it, of European integration. 'National identity', Odermatt (1991, p. 220) argues, 'based as it is on us-them divisions, is the biggest stumbling block on the way towards a united Europe'.

It is on this symbolic level that linguistics and specifically discourse analysis, can make a substantial contribution to elucidating the opposing forces that help and hinder the growth of cohesion in Europe. In this struggle between integrationist and isolationist tendencies - present all over Europe, but particularly prominent, perhaps, in Britain - both centripetal and centrifugal forces leave traces in discourse, and it is the aim of this chapter to investigate those that are linked specifically with questions of national identity.

3

This chapter is part of a larger project (Mautner, 1997) on British Euro-Discourse, a study based on about 350 leader articles from four national newspapers (*The Guardian, The Daily Telegraph, The Daily Mirror, The Sun*) and covering the period from the early 1970s to the mid-1990s, as well as a host of supplementary data, such as advertisements and political speeches. The analytical tools used were a combination of critical discourse analysis (CDA) and computer-supported corpus linguistics. The resulting synergies are two-fold: a machine-readable corpus helps broaden the empirical base beyond the limited corpus sizes generally associated with qualitative discourse analysis. In turn, the theoretical framework, analytical categories and interpretative procedures typical of discourse analysis are instrumental in re-embedding the data in the context it has been stripped of by being run through a concordance program. The two-track approach also allows for maximum flexibility, with each track being given more or less salience depending on whether a particular question put to the text lends itself more to in-depth qualitative analysis of small samples of data or to the extraction of quantitative evidence from a larger collection of text. Generally speaking, the more direct the link between lexical patterns and extra-linguistic phenomena – that is, between what is *in* the text and what is *outside* it – the more leverage is to be gained from investigating the collocational profiles of individual items.

Given that the concept of 'national identity' is as complex as its discursive reflexes are elusive, only limited benefits can be derived from looking at the concordances for individual keywords. Accordingly, the present chapter is primarily qualitative in orientation, tracing linguistic manifestations of identities being threatened, clashing, and re-asserting themselves.

National versus European Identities

Why is it that European integration is causing a crisis of identity? The answer lies partly in the ideology of nationalism, which, according to Smith (1991, p.74) is based on the following premises:

1. The world is divided into nations, each with its own individuality, history and destiny.
2. The nation is the source of all political and social power, and loyalty to the nation overrides all other allegiances.

3. Human beings must identify with a nation if they want to be free and realise themselves.
4. Nations must be free and secure if peace and justice are to prevail in the world.

All of the keywords involved here – *individuality, history, destiny, loyalty, identification, freedom,* etc. – do not bode well for the development of cohesion and a sense of common fate among Europeans. The nation, by definition, claims undivided allegiance from its citizens, and it asserts this claim through a variety of institutions, such as parliament, supreme court etc., as well as through official symbols, such as flag, anthem, and currency, to name but a few. The European Union has followed suit, though, creating its own version of all these symbols and thus providing an additional challenge to traditional nation-states, which are already under considerable threat because of the many limitations to their sovereignty imposed by the EU. Traditional nation-states thrive on exclusive and uncompromising identification and allegiance, and this is precisely what 'Europe' is perceived to be interfering in. Identity has become an issue because it is in crisis (cf. Mercer, 1990, p. 43), with uncertainty and a sense of uprootedness easily fostering exaggerated patriotism, prejudice and xenophobia. 'In European culture', Morley and Robins (1995, p. 90) point out, 'the longing for home is not an innocent utopia'. It needs to be borne in mind that, as Billig (1995, pp. 78-79) explains, 'nationalism' is not only 'an ideology of the first person plural, which tells "us" who "we" are' but also 'an ideology of the third person. There can be no "us" without a "them". [...] The national community can only be imagined by also imagining communities of foreigners.

There is no shortage of alternative models attempting to neutralise the apparent incompatibility of national and European identities. The catchphrases bandied about in this context include 'multiple allegiances' (Picht, 1993, p. 84), 'concentric identities' (Garcia, 1993, p. 15), 'fuzzy frontiers' (Cohen, 1994, p. 7), and 'dual loyalties' (Wallace, 1993, p. 101). Schlesinger (1992, p. 321), too, pleads for allegiances to become 'actively multifold'. On paper, both the cognitive and the emotional appeal of such models is considerable. Pitted against the reality of the starkly nationalist mindset, though, none of these conciliatory approaches cuts much ice with the self-proclaimed defenders of national independence.

Even where some allowance is made for the co-existence of identities, a rank order is usually implied, relegating Europeanness to a subordinate position and giving precedence to what are clearly perceived as 'primary' identities rooted in regional and national affiliations. The following letter to the editor of *The Guardian* is a case in point:

> I am Welsh first, British second and European third. [...] I have not forgotten or forgiven the country which was the cause of so much suffering. I resent the future of this country being governed from abroad, and the effect that will have over future years on a way of life which is particular and perculiar [sic] to England, Ireland, Scotland and Wales. Because, while logic and economy seems to lead that way, one's heart wains [sic] otherwise. That is a strong motivation. (*The Guardian*, 17 July 1990, p. 18)

In this extract, four motifs emphasising emotional distance towards Europe co-occur: (1) the ranking of identities, as mentioned above, (2) reminiscences of World War II, highlighting the status of Germany as an enemy, (3) the uniqueness of the regions of Britain and Ireland, and the implication that this is being threatened by Europe, (4) a dichotomy between *logic* and *economy* on the one hand, and the *heart* on the other. The head-versus-heart motif, incidentally, is not restricted to the nostalgic musings of readers writing to their daily paper. John Major, too, once went on record with a similar declaration bearing vivid testimony to his less-than-enthusiastic approach towards European integration:

> I am more a European in my head than in my heart, but I want to see Europe succeed. (John Major in an interview with Hugo Young, quoted in *The Guardian*, 25 March 1994, p. 24)

What is, quite literally, 'half-heartedness' about Europe frequently involves the desire to strengthen the borders, both physical and figurative, around nations, to highlight differences and downplay similarities with one's neighbours. The *us*-versus-*them* distinction, functioning as an elementary bipolar classification scheme (Leggewie, 1994, p. 53), is one of the key argumentative patterns in the construction of the self and the other. A textbook example of this pattern is included in the following statement made by the Conservative MP Bernard Jenkin in a TV debate:

> This goes to the heart of the matter. Because European integration redefines who is we and who is them. And most people in this country regard British people as us and other European countries as friendly neighbours but them. (*The Big Debate*, 4 June 1995, 8 p.m., BBC 2)

Thus, pressure from above to move closer together is answered by counter pressure from below to stay apart, with xenophobia among the more sinister side effects.

The irony, of course, is that attempts to keep Europe at arm's length and assert the independence of nation-states are likely to fail eventually because of the many economic interdependencies created by trade, telecommunications, transnational mergers, and a growing levelling out of differences between formerly distinct cultures, sub-cultures and markets. Interestingly, the unifying impact of globalisation also affects the internal cohesion of nations. As Billig explains,

> The nationally imagined identity is diminishing in importance, as compared with imagined 'life-style' groups of consumers. The result is that the processes of globalisation, which are diminishing differences and spaces between nations, are also fragmenting the imagined unity within those nations. (Billig, 1995, p. 132)

The internal fragmentation caused by globalising forces is yet another reason why nations are in crisis and looking to replace lost certainties by renewed patriotism at odds with pan-European sentiments.

Arguably, none of this is unique to ihe political and cultural landscape of Britain, and indeed, the phenomena described here do occur all over Europe in some form or other. However, there are elements which are characteristic of the discursive construction of a specifically British identity in the European context, and these will be discussed in the sections below.

The Island Myth and Atlanticism

Geographically, the United Kingdom of Great Britain and Northern Ireland is located on a group of islands off the Western Coast of Europe. Under conditions of highly developed transport and telecommunications systems, a country's position on the periphery of a region rather than at its centre would not, as such, have to be of any particular political relevance – if, that is, it weren't for the symbolism that the concept of the island carries. It functions as a metaphor signifying safety, defence against intruders, secludedness and, by implication, difference. As a literary topos it is firmly established in the national consciousness – witness, above all, John of Gaunt's monologue on *this sceptred isle* in Richard II – and thus readily available to be activated as a specifically anti-European motif within the framework of conservative (with a small c) Eurosceptic discourse.

The island myth, though dealt with under a separate heading here, is closely connected with the issue of national sovereignty. As the following extract from *The Daily Telegraph* shows, both concepts play an important role as motifs realising a discursive strategy of differentiation vis-à-vis Europe:

> Why do we seem to be alone in having this problem with sovereignty? Every country has a segment of public opinion that fears giving up national sovereignty, but these misgivings are most widely held in Britain. This has to do with the antiquity of our parliamentary, military and social institutions: most of Europe's have been swept away by wars and revolutions. We also have an island tradition of keeping Europe at arm's length, whereas our partners have been forced by geography to look for a way of living together. (*The Daily Telegraph*, 6 Dec. 1991, p. 17)

Britain's reluctance to give up any of its sovereignty is explained with reference to its uniqueness, and this, in turn, is related to both its *island tradition* and the *antiquity* of its institutions. Britain is shown not only to be different from, but in fact superior to Europe, which, unlike the island fortress, has had its institutions *swept away by wars and revolutions*.

Britain's island status is thus made out to be a barrier against forging closer ties with continental Europe. On the other hand, it is seen to be perfectly in keeping with another aspect of British national identity, namely the image of the sea-faring nation establishing links with countries all over the world rather than just those on the continent of Europe. 'Although we are much reduced', Lord Skidelsky once said in the House of Lords, 'our instinct is still to seek our fortune overseas, not on the continent' (*Hansard / House of Lords*, vol. 532, 25 November 1991, col. 1208). Even with the Empire gone and the Commonwealth reduced to a loose association of member states, both Conservative and Labour politicians continue to define Britain's role from a global rather than a European perspective, emphasising, as John Major once did, 'the UK's interests and responsibilities in the four other continents and the oceans between, because the UK as an island with a trading and seafaring tradition has always looked outwards' (quoted in *The Daily Telegraph*, 30 March 1995, p. 7). And when the Labour Party took over in 1997, one of the first statements that Foreign Secretary Robin Cook went on record with stressed the need for good relations with the US and argued that Britain ought to play a leading role in Europe (cf. *Guardian International Edition*, 13 May 1997, p. 2).

Britain's overseas orientation was one of the factors that made it stand aside from rather than take part in the first phase of European integration in the fifties. Then as now, the political and economic arguments were coupled with 'a popular sentiment that could easily be mobilised in favour of "kith and kin" in the Commonwealth and against "foreigners" in Europe' (George, 1994, p. 16). The United States, in particular, still occupies a privileged position both in the national imagination and in day-to-day politics, in spite of certain economic indicators, such as export volume, already pointing towards the EU as Britain's main international partner.

Even more recently, emotional ties with former colonies, and in particular with English-speaking (and white!) North America, are still called upon to justify anti-European attitudes, as was the case, for example, during a fishing dispute involving Spain and Canada, where British fishermen were siding not with their fellow 'Europeans' but with the Canadians, following a principle which *The Independent* aptly summed up in a headline saying 'Empire Blood Proves Thicker than Water' (14 March 1995, p. 8).

While what is sometimes referred to as *atlanticism* may not be as dominant a force as it used to be, incidents like this show that Britain's overseas ties are clearly still a highly active relic of the nation's colonial past and a powerful ingredient of anti-European rhetoric. Few speakers perhaps go as far as Viscount Tonypandy, a crossbencher in the House of Lords, who once said in a debate, that he 'would rather be the 51st state of the USA than one-twentieth of Europe and would like it to be clearly known that they share our heritage and our language' (*Hansard* House of Lords vol. 532, 25 November 1991, col. 1171).

Language, as we can see, is a key concept in this context. In Eurosceptic discourse, one of the ways in which the 'foreignness' of Europe is emphasised is its linguistic diversity, just as closeness to the US, Canada, Australia and New Zealand is stressed by referring to the comforting familiarity associated with the English language. Distance from the one and proximity to the other are two sides of the same argumentative coin. In the following letter, both sides are present, with the author explicitly contrasting what he sees as 'a world-wide confederation of fairly prosperous, English-speaking states' with 'the polyglot federation that Europe apparently insists on becoming'. Note also that to refer to economic relations he uses the positively loaded metaphor of *home*, its emotional appeal further enhanced by the modifying adjective *natural*:

> Sir: As the difficulties of the UK with the EU continue, I am led once again to wonder why it seems never to have occurred to anyone else that a natural economic home for this nation would be in a world-wide confederation of fairly prosperous, English-speaking states: the UK, Ireland, the US, Canada, Australia and New Zealand. It has seemed to me ever since 1956 that such an economic union would best serve as counterweight to the polyglot federation that Europe apparently insists upon becoming [...]. (Letter to the editor by Anatole Beck, *Department of Mathematics* of the *London School of Economics and Political Science*, *The Independent*, 11 April 1995, p. 14)

Both Margaret Thatcher and John Major went even further by identifying multilingualism as a threat to democratic values and national independence. In Volume II of her autobiography, for example, Thatcher maintains that 'democracy cannot function in a federal superstate where the multiplicity of languages makes democratic debate and democratic accountability mere slogans' (Thatcher, 1995b, pp. 470-471). By the same token, she argued in a speech in Washington, also quoted in her autobiography, that '[a] Community lacking a common language can have no public opinion to which the bureaucrats are accountable' (Thatcher, 1995b, p. 477). John Major made an implicit link between multilingualism and national identity when he said in a speech that 'they [i.e. our peoples] do not feel that a huge, remote, multilingual, multicultural, multinational amalgam would be responsive to them or could properly reflect their national identities' (quoted in *The Daily Telegraph*, 8 September 1994, p. 9). What we find in these quotes is the interweaving of three anti-European motifs: the language problem, federalism, and bureaucracy. We will return to the implications conveyed by *federal superstate* in the next section. Suffice to say here that it is a highly emotive watchword which has considerable persuasive force for the Eurosceptic cause in the British context, but clearly would not have the same impact in continental Europe in general, and Germany in particular.

Sovereignty and Anti-Federalism

Sovereignty is not only 'the cornerstone of the British constitution' (Norton, 1994, p. 281), but also a well-established ingredient of the national myth and a powerful symbol of national identity. Conservative Eurosceptics see it as an all-or-nothing affair, rejecting the idea that in a united Europe, individual nations' sovereignty would not be lost but 'pooled'. In fact, acceptance or rejection of the concept of 'pooling' is a clear indicator of people's pro or anti-European inclinations: those in favour of further integration use it, whereas those against do not, preferring instead expressions such as *loss* or *surrender* (cf. Barker, 1993, p. 41). Margaret Thatcher, for one, left no doubt as to her misgivings about the pooling of sovereignty and realised too late that she had signed away part of it herself in the Single European Act (Thatcher, 1995a, pp. 556-557):[1]

> Our choice is clear. Either we exercise democratic control of Europe through co-operation between national governments and parliaments which have legitimacy, experience and closeness to the people.
> Or, we transfer decisions to a remote multi-lingual parliament, accountable to no real European public opinion and thus increasingly subordinate to a powerful bureaucracy. No amount of misleading language about pooling sovereignty can change that. (Thatcher, 1993, p. 27)

In this extract, stark black-and-white contrasts are used as an argumentative pattern: nation-states are associated with exclusively positive terms (*legitimacy, experience, closeness to the people*), whereas Europe is identified only with negatively loaded expressions (*remote multilingual parliament, accountable to no real European public opinion, powerful bureaucracy*), including, once again, *multilingualism* and *bureaucracy*.

One of the arguments that Conservative Eurosceptics use in defence of sovereignty is that Britain has more to lose than other European nations because its institutions are older, more revered and altogether more worth protecting than their counterparts on the continent. Margaret Thatcher made this point repeatedly, and with varying degrees of subtlety. In a Lords debate on the Maastricht Treaty, she lamented that 'by extending majority voting' the Treaty 'will undermine our age-old parliamentary and legal institutions, both far older than those in the Community. We have so much more to lose by this Maastricht Treaty than any other state in the European Community' (Hansard / House of Lords, vol. 546, 7 June 1993, col. 565). In a more polemical vein, she argues in her autobiography, 'if I were an Italian, I might prefer rule from Brussels too' (Thatcher, 1995a, p. 742). Underlying these and many similar statements from other sources are two argumentative strategies that are effectively twinned: positive evaluation of the 'self' and negative evaluation of the 'other'. Britain is talked up by talking Europe and Europeans down. In pro-EU discourse, incidentally, such a pair of twinned strategies occurs, too, though the other way round, so that Europe is talked up and Britain down by expressing approval of European institutions and political traditions – such as federalism – while criticising Britain's apparent lack of integrationist effort as evidence of a 'little Englander' mentality. Witness, for example, the following statement made in the Commons by the Labour MP Brian Sedgemore:

> In Britain we have nothing to lose and much to gain from federalism. It is time that we preferred success to failure and stopped sneering at the material wealth and culture of the French, Germans and Italians. It is time that we spurned small-minded and shrivelled isolationist views and on this side of the House at least co-operated with our Euro-socialist friends on the continent to inspire our nation. (*Hansard / House of Commons,* vol. 193, 26 June 1991, col. 1075)

Federalism is indeed an important keyword in the debate on sovereignty. Though the political élite and many commentators are aware that English *federalism* and German *Föderalismus* conjure up quite different associations and are thus to all extents and purposes *faux amis*,[2] misunderstandings persist and are exploited to suit the rhetorical ploys of those with an axe to grind. In Britain, *federalism* is commonly associated with centralisation, whereas its German counterpart implies the devolution of power and decision-making away from the centre and to smaller regional units. So, while in mainland Europe *federalism* has positive connotations likely to further the pro-integrationist cause, the British interpretation of what the popular media have often referred to as the *f-word*[3] is overwhelmingly negative and thus ideally suited to being used as an anti-European motif (Musolff, 1996, pp. 16-19). The adjective + noun combination *federal superstate* is a case in point. In Britain, both parts are negative and thus mutually reinforcing. In Germany, by contrast, *federal superstate* is almost a contradiction in terms because one of the things that the German brand of *Föderalismus* is supposed to prevent is precisely the emergence of an over-powerful 'superstate'.

Though it is quite clear that educating the public about the cross-cultural difference in meaning would help shed light on the problem, it is equally clear that it is simply not in the interests of Eurosceptics for the misunderstanding to be cleared up. Both politicians and the media exploit the rhetorical potential of *federalism* and indeed increase it further by linking it to the emotive concept of national identity. At a Conservative

Party Conference, John Major once proclaimed, 'I will never – come hell or high water – let our distinctive British identity be lost in a federal Europe' (quoted in *The Daily Telegraph,* 10 October 1992, p. 11).

Because anti-federalism is very much tied to the use of the actual words *federal, federalist* and *federalism*, it makes sense to investigate both their frequency of occurrence and collocational profile by looking at the concordances generated from the machine-readable part of the corpus, that is, the 350 leading articles. Comparing the evidence from the *The Daily Telegraph* and *The Guardian*, what one discovers, first of all, is that the whole family of keywords is considerably more frequent in the *Telegraph* than in *The Guardian*.[4] The conservative paper with a rather sceptical attitude towards the EU uses the negative keyword much more often than the left-wing pro-European paper. This is quite consistent with other findings from the corpus: again and again we find that the Eurosceptic side is very adept at mobilising anti-European sentiment by addressing key political and cultural sensibilities, whereas the Europhile camp seems to have nothing to offer in reply and does not even enter the fray. In essence, one of the reasons why anti-federalism can carry the day is that those in favour show nowhere near as strong a commitment to tackling the issue.

The qualitative analysis of collocational patterns also reveals interesting results. We find that not only does *federalist/s* and *federalism* occur more often in the *Telegraph* than the *Guardian*, but the conservative paper also uses it as a distinctly negative keyword in the way in which the Eurosceptic camp is wont to do. This becomes apparent when we look at a wider collocational span of 25 words to the left and right of the searchword in question and discover that there is indeed what Louw (1993, p. 157) would call 'a consistent aura of meaning', or 'semantic prosody'. The negatively loaded forms around *federalis** include *misgivings, objections, fanciful notions, potentially embarrassing, threat, doubts, mistrust, deep unease, fanaticism, bitter hostility* and, last but not least, though entirely predictably, *superstate* and *highly centralised.*

Pragmatism

The debate about sovereignty and federalism, though grounded in 'hard' political and institutional traditions, is also connected with 'soft' issues in the realm of mentality and the nation's self-image. The following extract from *The Telegraph* shows what this link is like:

Mr Major should not be ashamed of having no towering 'vision' to match those of his partners. It may be argued that, had Britain kept less aloof from the innermost councils of the European Community in the Eighties, our task in strapping the visionaries into their seats might be much easier today. [...] we are not merely engaged in protecting our independence, but limiting the injury that could be suffered by others if the Europe of the philosophers runs so far ahead of itself down the federalist road that it falls over its own peoples. [...] Britain's diplomatic difficulty today is that, while we believe that our limited view of the EC's future is more practical than the grand schemes of some of our partners, their own convictions are just as strong as ours. [...]
[...] if a reasonable agreement can be achieved that enables us to remain in the long negotiating game that lies ahead, to check the extremists and put the EC on a sane and realistic path for the future, then that will be the best outcome both for the Government and for this country. (*The Daily Telegraph*, 9 December 1991)

In these paragraphs from an editorial, a contrast is established between Britain's 'practical', 'sane' and 'realistic' approach to Europe, whereas its European partners are criticised as 'philosophers', 'extremists' and 'visionaries' that need to be 'strapped into their seats'. There are similar, though of course rather cruder, examples from *The Sun*, such as the headlines 'European superstate dream' (21 September 1992, p. 1) and 'Euro idiots and dreamers' (22 September 1992, p. 24).

From a discourse analytic point of view, what is interesting is first, how lexemes like *vision, philosophers*, and *dream*, which in other contexts have very positive connotations, come to be 'prosodically loaded' (Louw, 1993, p. 172) in a negative way, and second, how this negative prosody is embedded in and draws upon the wider social and historical framework. The negative loading of otherwise neutral or positive terms is achieved by clustering expressions around them whose referential and associative meanings are clearly negative, like *injury, extremists*, and *idiots*. The effect is further reinforced by extended metaphors using vehicles referring to unfortunate aspects of the human condition. Fervent pro-Europeanism is not simply rejected as a political position that one may or may not agree with, but is instead, through the metaphor, equated with insanity. By contrast, the British position is described as the 'sane' counterbalance.

The second question goes beyond the text in hand and is concerned with identifying the overall significance of 'pragmatism' as an element of national identity. The roots are manifold and hard to trace, yet the evidence is consistent and points to what Tom Nairn (1988, p. 92) calls 'an indispensable national aversion to theory', leading, among other things, to words like *intellectual* and *academic* having largely negative connotations. Whether anti-intellectualism is a British phenomenon or confined specifically to the English, whether it is a general national trait or mostly at home in Tory circles is difficult to determine empirically, not least because a diffuse issue like this is unlikely to be reflected reliably in any one corpus of text. There are indications, it is true, that the enthusiastic defence of pragmatism as a political creed is indeed mainly associated with English Conservatives (rather than with the British as a whole, or with conservatives with a small 'c'). 'The English', the editor of the *The Sunday Telegraph* once declared, 'are lazy-minded, stolid, moderate and anti-theoretical' (quoted in *New Statesman and Society*, 24 February 1995, p. 37), and then Foreign Minister Douglas Hurd announced proudly, though with unintentional irony, that 'Tories believe in taking decisions at the lowest practical level' (*The Daily Telegraph*, 27 June 1991, p. 16). In her famous Bruges speech, which was to become 'the sacred text of Euro-scepticism' and 'a charter for the Tory sceptics' (*The Daily Telegraph*, 8 September 1991, pp. 2, 9), Margaret Thatcher (1988) also made an impassioned plea for taking 'practical steps' and attending to 'the immediate and practical requirements' with respect to Community policies, for listening to 'plain commonsense' and against being 'distracted by Utopian goals', because, after all, '[u]topia never comes, because we know we should not like it if it did'. Nonetheless it would be too restrictive to localise pragmatism only in Conservative (in the sense of Tory) ideology. Perhaps the most famous counterexample, of a representative of the left expressing similar views, is George Orwell's dictum that 'the English are not intellectual' and have 'a horror of abstract thought' (Orwell, 1970 [1941], p. 77). Not surprisingly, Conservatives have repeatedly appropriated Orwell, quoting selectively from his works to support their own arguments.[5]

Material Symbols

In addition to the intangible components of national identity discussed above, there is also a host of material symbols which play a key role in establishing, asserting and maintaining national identity. Those particularly relevant in the EU context include the currency (Pound Sterling vs. Euro), the flag (the Union Jack vs. the European flag with a circle of stars on a blue background), food (traditional British cuisine vs. allegedly standardised European fare), as well as weights and measures (imperial vs. metric systems). Common to all of these topics is the general argument that the EU is a threat to the British way of life, imposing bland uniformity on much cherished diversity.

Take the debate on monetary union, for example. In a single week in 1990 (30 October until 7 November) *The Sun* ran several articles on the introduction of what was then still called the Ecu, and it systematically disparaged the European currency by giving it negative attributes such as *meaningless hybrid, oddly named, faceless, boring* and *dreary*. The pound, by contrast, was extolled as *cherished, dear,* and *great,* and was frequently referred to as *our pound* and *our quid,* the *our* as well as the colloquial *quid* heightening the emotional quality of the expressions. What the ongoing discussion on the common currency shows very clearly is that the economic realities and technical practicalities of monetary union, including the vexed question of Britain's opt-out, are not the whole story, and that policy-makers would be well advised to take heed of the emotional, and indeed often irrational, reactions on the part of non-expert citizens.

The flag, too, is a powerful national symbol, and also one where the European Union appears to be encroaching on national territory by introducing its own variety. On some occasions, these can be seen to be in direct opposition. When during the *Last Night of the Proms* European flags were once waved alongside Union Jacks, a commentator in the *The Sun* sneered about 'the ludicrous European symbol' and gloomily surmised that 'next year we'll probably have the orchestra playing Deutschland Uber [sic] Alles' (*The Sun*, 12 September 1994, p. 6). The heavily symbolic status of the flag makes the Union Jack generally available as an anti-European motif which is not confined to the populist chauvinism of tabloids. At a Party Conference, John Major used the flag as a metaphor supporting his Eurosceptic position:

> Let no one in this conference be in any doubt: this Government will not accept a centralised Europe. If there are those who have in mind to haul down the Union Jack and fly high the star-spangled banner of a United States of Europe, I say to them: you misjudge the temper of the British people; and you do not begin to understand the determination of this Prime Minister to put the interests of this country first - now and always. (quoted in *The Daily Telegraph*, 10 October 1992, p. 11)

Finally, there are two elements of everyday life that are also given symbolic value in the context of European integration, namely foods as well as weights and measures. Because both are areas that anyone can relate to, they are particularly well suited to being used as anti-European motifs in political and media discourse. The foods supposedly affected by the standardising efforts of 'Brussels bureaucrats' have, over the years, included a wide variety ranging from cucumbers to prawn crisps. To name but one example often quoted in the 70s and the early 90s, it was traditional British sausages that were assumed to be under threat from EU regulations, immediately causing an outrage focussing on what Andrew Marr (1995, p. 216) ironically calls '[t]he survival of the Briton's historic right to consume inedible sausages'. Not unlike British beef during the BSE crisis, the sausages were used as a vehicle to assert national independence and, in some cases, to express fear of foreign domination, as in a columnist's defiant outcry, put into the mouth of Corporal Jones from the TV serial Dad's Army, 'I did not fight two wars to have some foreigner tell me what kind of sausages I can sell' (*The Sun*, 14 September 1992). Again, it would be wrong to assume, though, that this kind of argumentation is restricted to tabloids. It can be present equally strongly in élites' primary political discourse such as parliamentary debates. Compare, for example, Baroness Platt of Writtle's comments below, from which it emerges very clearly how the food issue forms an integral part of a whole cluster of Eurosceptic motifs which are all linked to the fundamental question of identity:

> I count myself as British first but also a European. [...] However, I agree with my right honourable friend the Foreign Secretary that Europe is interfering more and more in every nook and cranny of national life. We do not need nannying about planning from Brussels. When I travel in Europe I am pleased to meet variety; to enjoy the idiosyncrasies and variety of national habits. French *saucisson*, German *wurst* and Italian *salami* are all delicious. But I am still pleased to come back to British 'bangers and beans'. And we certainly do not need a European sausage. (Baroness Platt of Writtle [Conservative], *Hansard / House of Lords*, vol. 532, col. 1196f.; italics in the original.)

A problem closely related to food is weights and measures. The imperial units, though being phased out officially, are still far more common in everyday usage than the metric system. *Inches*, *ounces* and *pints* are firmly embedded in the national consciousness in a way that *centimetres*, *grams* and *litres* are not, and the lack of general familiarity with the latter is exploited by Eurosceptics to highlight Britain's uniqueness, assert its independence, and to foster a sense of alienation vis-à-vis Europe. In the following extract from *The Mail on Sunday*, we find the food motif coupled with several others, including Magna Carta, democracy, traditions, and anti-French polemics:

> *Fathoms, inches, feet, yards, miles, acres, ounces, gallons, pounds, therms —*
> *all will be banished by a diktat of the European Commission.*
> After January 1, 2000, the local greengrocer will no longer be allowed to sell you a pound of apples. He could be prosecuted and fined for such licentiousness. Instead of quoting '50p per pound', he will have to say '50p per 0.454 of a kilogram'.
> Here in Britain, the land of Magna Carta, the birthplace of modern democracy, we are allowing meddling Brussels regulations to wash over most of our national life and destroy many of our long-cherished traditions and practices.
> Future generations will grow up unable to understand most of the statistics or literature that form part of our history.
> Yet, astonishingly, we are consciously submitting to the imposition of this Napoleonic totalitarianism. Napoleon may have lost the Battle of Waterloo but we are losing the Battle of Brussels day by day. [...]
> Perhaps we can in this case make a symbolic gesture of defiance. Stand out against the Euro-nanny and preserve a small but historic piece of our national heritage.
> *For who can forget the adage — give an inch and they'll take a mile...*
> (*DO WE REALLY WANT 0.454KG OF APPLES AND NOT 1LB?* by Neil Hamilton, THE MAIL ON SUNDAY, 26 February 1995, p. 28; italics in the original.)

What is particularly striking, perhaps, given that the UK has been an equal partner in the EC/EU since 1973, is the choice of vocabulary associated with dictatorship and war: *diktat, totalitarianism* and *battle*. The same is true for a similar article in *The Sun* (22 August 1995), the headline of which reads 'Beaten by the Euro Dictators', and which goes on to berate 'the faceless dictators in Brussels', complaining that British politicians 'have surrendered another facet of our Britishness'.

What most articles in this vein also have in common is the strategic use of figures. They invariably give examples of imperial-to-metric conversion in such a way that the metric version is a figure with several digits behind the decimal point. So, instead of talking about 'half a kilo of potatoes, 250 grams of bacon and 100 grams of Cheddar', as one would on the continent of Europe, it says, for example, '[a] pound of spuds will become 453 grams, eight ounces of bacon will be 227 grams and a quarter of Cheddar will be 113 grams' (*The Sun*, 22 August 1995, p. 6). The environment into which the fictitious shopping scenarios are placed is fairly standardised, too: the retailers mentioned are 'the local greengrocer' (*The Mail on Sunday*, 26 February 1995) or 'butchers, grocers and fishmongers' (*The Sun*, 22 August 1995, p. 6), and never modern hypermarkets of the Tesco type. Another rhetorical device applied in connection with the food motif is the use of common colloquialisms, such as *spuds* and *toms*, which reinforce the contrast between the unfamiliar sounding units of measurement and the produce they measure. It is not a coincidence either, but clearly a matter of systematic lexical choice, that the foods given as examples in such instances are always staple and traditional ones, such as potatoes, bacon and Cheddar cheese, which, unlike fancier imports, carry pleasant nostalgic associations.

Conclusion

National identity in Europe is currently in a state of flux, with old allegiances to nation-states being challenged by the emergence of an increasingly united Europe. Although this is bound to affect all member states in some way, Britain's position in the Community appears to be rather more precarious than that of most: at best a matter of economic and political expediency rather than the result of genuine commitment.

The aim of this chapter was to identify the traces left in discourse by the changes that national identity is currently undergoing. The emphasis was on motifs, argumentative patterns, and linguistic detail on various levels, including lexis and collocational patterns. Evidence from various corpora, gathered partly with the help of concordancing programs, supports the hypothesis that among Conservatives, in particular, assertions of national identity invariably imply distancing from Europe. In politics and the economy, tackling the distance in people's minds ought to be appreciated as a prerequisite for further integrationist activities. As a matter of fact, opinion leaders aiming to promote cohesion among European nations will eventually have to come round to the idea that economically defined convergence criteria are bound to remain ineffective unless attitudes and identities follow suit.

Notes

1   Note also her comment in the House of Lords, when she referred to the signing of the Single European Act as an occasion 'when we got our fingers burnt' (*Hansard / House of Lords*, vol 546, 7 June 1993, col. 563).

2   Compare, for example, the following statement made by Lord Cledwyn of Penrhos, in a debate on Maastricht: 'The use of the word "federal" has confused matters. When we use it, we in this country think of the United States. When our partners use it, they think of a looser form of association. We must try to find a definition on which all can agree' (*Hansard / House of Lords*, 25 November 1999, vol. 82, col. 1155). Note also how the speaker makes his point by setting up an 'us versus them' contrast.

3   Cf., the following headlines from *The Sun*: *Major won't horse trade over f-word* (5 December 1991, p. 2), *Delors blasts PM's 'shame' over f-word* (9 December 1991, p. 2) and *'F' Off. Major wins fight on 'federal' but £ is ambushed* (10 December 1991, p. 1).

4   *Federal*: 12 (*Telegraph*) vs 8 (*Guardian*); *federalist/s*: 13 (*Telegraph*) vs 2 (*Guardian*); *federalism*: 13 (*Telegraph*) vs 3 (*Guardian*).

5   Cf., for example, an article by John Major in the Conservative newspaper *Conservative Newsline* (June 1993, p. 4), in which he quotes part of a sentence from Orwell's essay *The Lion and the Unicorn* – the description of 'old maids bicycling to Holy Communion through the morning mist' – without mentioning that in the very same sentence, Orwell also mentions 'Lancashire mill towns, the to-and-fro of the lorries on the Great North Road, the queues outside the Labour Exchanges [and] the rattle of pin-tables in the Soho pubs' (Orwell 1970 [1941]: 75), none of which would, obviously, be particularly conducive to the image of blissful rural England that Major is trying to conjure up.

It is interesting to note, too, that in the same essay, Orwell maintains that:

[i]n intention, at any rate, the English intelligentsia are Europeanised. They take their cookery from Paris and their opinions from Moscow. In the general patriotism of the country they form a sort of island of dissident thought. England is perhaps the only great country whose intellectuals are ashamed of their own nationality. In left-wing circles it is always felt that there is something slightly disgraceful in being an Englishman and that it is a duty to snigger at every English institution, from horse racing to suet puddings. It is a strange fact, but it is unquestionably true that almost any English intellectual would feel more ashamed of standing to attention during 'God save the King' than of stealing from a poor box. (Orwell 1970 [1941]: 95)

Though nearly 60 years old, this assessment still rings true, reminding us also that the concept of national identity is not a monolithic block but needs to be seen in relation to other social variables such as political affiliation, education and social class.

References

Barker, G (1993), 'A Nation at Risk', in S. Hill (ed.), *Visions of Europe. Summing up the Political Choices,* Duckworth, London, pp. 36-45.

Billig, M. (1995), *Banal Nationalism*, Sage, London, Thousand Oaks and New Delhi.
Cohen, R. (1994), *Frontiers of Identity. The British and Others*, Longman, London and New York.
García, S. (1993), 'Europe's Fragmented Identities and the Frontiers of Citizenship', in S. García (ed.), *European Identity and the Search for Legitimacy*, Pinter, London and New York, pp. 1-29.
George, S. (1994), *An Awkward Partner. Britain in the European Community*, 2nd ed., Oxford University Press, Oxford.
Leggewie, C. (1994), 'Ethnizität, Nationalismus und multikulturelle Gesellschaft', in H. Berding (ed.), *Nationales Bewußtsein und kollektive Identität. Studien zur Entwicklung des kollektiven Bewußtseins in der Neuzeit 2*. (= Suhrkamp Taschenbuch Wissenschaft 1154.), Suhrkamp, Frankfurt/Main, pp. 46-65.
Louw, B. (1993), 'Irony in the Text or Insincerity in the Writer? The Diagnostic Potential of Semantic Prosodies', in M. Baker, G. Francis, E. Tognini-Bonelli (eds.), *Text and Technology. In Honour of John Sinclair*, John Benjamins, Philadelphia and Amsterdam, pp. 157-176.
Marr, A. (1995), *Ruling Britannia. The Failure and Future of British Democracy*, Michael Joseph, London.
Mautner, G. (1997), *Der britische Europa-Diskurs. Reflexion und Gestaltung in der Tagespresse* (*Habilitationsschrift, Wirtschaftsuniversität Wien*, to be published by Passagen-Verlag, Wien).
Mercer, K. (1990), 'Welcome to the Jungle: Identity and Diversity in Postmodern Politics', in R. Rutherford (ed.), *Identity. Community, Culture, Difference*, Lawrence & Wishart, London, pp. 43-71.
Morley, D. and Robins, K. (1995), *Spaces of Identity. Global Media, Electronic Landscapes and Cultural Boundaries*, Routledge, London and New York.
Musolff, A. (1996), 'False Friends Borrowing the Right Words? Common Terms and Metaphors in European Communication', in A. Musolff, C. Schäffner and M. Townson (eds.), *Conceiving of Europe – Unity in Diversity*, Dartmouth, Aldershot, pp. 15-29.
Nairn, Tom (1988), *The Enchanted Glass. Britain and Its Monarchy*, Century Hutchinson, London.
Norton, P. (1994), 'The Changing Constitution', in B. Jones, et al., *Politics UK,* 2nd ed., Harvester Wheatsheaf, New York, pp. 279-294.
Odermatt, P. (1991), 'The Use of Symbols in the Drive for European Integration', in J.Th. Leerssen, and M. Spiering (eds), *National Identity — Symbol and Representation* (= Yearbook of European Studies 4), Editions Rodopi, Amsterdam and Atlanta, GA, pp. 217-238.
Orwell, G. (1970 [1941]), 'The Lion and the Unicorn. Socialism and the English Genius', in S. Orwell, and I. Angus (eds), *The·Collected Essays, Journalism and Letters of George Orwell*, Vol. 2, Penguin Books, London, pp. 74-134.
Picht, R. (1993), 'Disturbed Identities: Social and Cultural Mutations in Contemporary Europe', in S. García (ed.), *European Identity and the Search for Legitimacy,* Pinter, London and New York, pp. 81-94.
Schlesinger, P. (1992), 'Europeanness: A New Cultural Battlefield?', in J. Hutchinson and A. D. Smith (eds), *Nationalism*, Oxford University Press, Oxford, pp. 316-325. [= Reprint of extracts from *Innovation* 5 (1) (1992), pp. 12-18; 22.]
Smith, A. D. (1991), *National Identity,* Penguin, London.

Thatcher, M. (1988), *Text of the Prime Minister's Speech at Bruges on 20th September 1988*, London, Conservative Political Centre.

Thatcher, M. (1993), 'Europe's Present Political Architecture', in S. Hill (ed.), *Visions of Europe. Summing up the Political Choices*, Duckworth, London, pp. 17-30.

Thatcher, M. (1995a), *The Downing Street Years*, HarperCollins, London [Original hardback edition published in 1993.]

Thatcher, M. (1995b), *The Path to Power*, HarperCollins, London.

Wallace, H. (1993), 'Deepening and Widening: Problems of Legitimacy for the EC', in S. García (ed.), *European Identity and the Search for Legitimacy*, Pinter, London and New York, pp. 95-105.

Wallace, H. (1995), 'Britain out on a Limb?', in *The Political Quarterly*, vol. 66, no. 1, pp. 46-58.

2 Representations of Germany in the Context of European Integration in Margaret Thatcher's Autobiographies

RUTH WITTLINGER

Introduction

During the 1980s, Margaret Thatcher left her imprint on many policy areas but it was in the context of European integration that she expressed her attitude towards Europe or rather against Europe most forcefully and vocally.[1] Helmut Kohl's 'two sides of the same coin' – European unity and German reunification – were both part of Thatcher's personal and political nightmare scenario and she tried to fight both unification processes vehemently as well as unsuccessfully. Apart from losing both battles, her attitude to Europe also contributed considerably to her own political downfall within the Conservative Party. This correlation between her fight against the two unification processes and her personal political fate, makes her autobiographies, *The Downing Street Years* and *The Path To Power* particularly interesting and revealing sources from which to gain insight into the reasons behind her aversion to a reunited Germany within the context of European integration.[2]

After some introductory comments about autobiographies/memoirs as historical and political literature,[3] this paper will look at the main features of Margaret Thatcher's approach to Europe, namely her political style, her belief in the importance of the nation-state, the impact of the Cold War on her attitude towards Europe and finally, the connection she made between socialism and Europe. This will provide the background for the final part which looks at the way Germany and the Germans are portrayed in her memoirs. Rather than adopting the commonly held view that her attitude and policy towards Germany was based on stereotypes and driven by prejudice, I will argue that her memoirs reveal several rational considerations which suggest that her antagonistic attitude towards Germany within the European context was guided by power politics and that she employed stereotypical representations of Germany in this context to justify her political strategies.

Reconstructing the Past

The Downing Street Years which was published in 1993 covers Margaret Thatcher's years as Prime Minister from 1979 until 1990. *The Path to Power,* published two years later, consists of two parts. The first part leads the reader from her childhood to the 1979 general election which brought her to power and supplies those stages of Margaret Thatcher's early life not covered in the previous volume. Indicating that her sense of mission has not come to an end with her leaving office, the second part of this volume consists of various chapters in which she deals with major policy areas, in order 'to give encouragement to those who thought and felt as I did, the next generation of political leaders and perhaps even the ones after that, to keep their gaze fixed on the right stars' (Thatcher, 1995b, pp. 466-67).

Considering how Margaret Thatcher's fall as leader of the Conservative Party was closely linked to her policy on Europe, the following point made by Egerton is particularly relevant in our context because it reminds us of the retrospective element inherent in political memoirs, i.e. the reconstruction of the past to fit in neatly with subsequent events:

> No doubt, as studies of specific memoirs regularly show, political memoir invites retrojection of personal and political interests held by the memoirist at the time of writing into the narration of the past, in the attempt to persuade contemporary and future readers. (Egerton, 1992, p. 232)

Accordingly, Hugo Young (1999, p. 308) has pointed out that in the case of Margaret Thatcher's memoirs, '[I]t is hard to decipher, as one reads this work, how much of it is a genuine recollection of the time, and how much the pasted-on hindsight of a retired politician'. However, rather than dismissing memoirs as a source unworthy of study because of these alleged 'flaws', Egerton (1992, p. 233) has pointed out that 'modern historians are not only prepared to control narrative sources for this factor but also to exploit the evidence of personal interest as a vital datum itself'.

Interestingly, on one occasion, Margaret Thatcher herself actually does point out the shortcomings and restrictions of hindsight: 'As for the international scene, everyone's recollections of the thirties, not least those of a child, are heavily influenced by what came later' (1995b, p. 24). As we will see later, there is no evidence, however, that she is prepared to acknowledge this relationship with regard to German reunification and European integration.

Whereas Churchill seemed to be very aware of the partisan nature of his account by stating '[T]his is not history, this is my case' (quoted in *The Economist*, 9 October 99, p. 41), Margaret Thatcher in the acknowledgements to *The Path to Power*, seems keen to create the opposite impression. Intent on giving it an air of objectivity, she points out that this volume is based on documents and research and that she depended on her 'memoirs team to display even greater resourcefulness and powers of detection than for Volume 1 in the search for letters, diaries, cuttings, conference reports and all the multifarious files where little bits of modern lives are written down and stored away' (1995b, p. xiii).

Thatcher's Approach to Europe

Throughout its history, Britain's membership of the European Union has been characterised by a certain degree of ambivalence at best and outright reluctance to go down the integrationist path at worst. The reasons which are usually suggested for British singularity in the European context include firstly, her late accession to the Community - although as Helen Wallace (1997, p. 677) has pointed out this was not an historical accident but a reflection of a commonly held policy preference and a 'retarded Europeanisation' could have nevertheless been expected to occur, secondly, her insular geographical position, and thirdly, the so-called 'special relationship' with the US.

Within this difficult tradition of Britain's Community membership, Margaret Thatcher's premiership occupies a special place. Not only did she leave her mark on the European stage, the issue of European integration also left its imprint on her political career: 'For it was her stance on Europe and the future shape of the Community that had been not only the pretext but also, it seemed, the profound and ultimate cause of the party's removing its support from her' (Young, 1993, p. xiv).

What is of particular interest is the discrepancy between what she did while in office, i.e. take Britain further and further into Europe and her rhetoric at the time. It is the latter which also sets the tone when she is reconstructing this particular part of her past in her memoirs which she wrote in what Young (1999, p. 329) called 'the phobic years of her retirement'. Referring to this discrepancy, Douglas Hurd suggested that her policy on Europe during her first few years as Prime Minister was 'No. No. Yes' (quoted in Young, 1999, p. 351).

The prospect of giving the free market theme a European dimension made her a keen supporter of the Single Market project. Geoffrey Howe referred to the Single Market as Thatcherism on a European scale (quoted in Sowemimo, 1996, p. 91).

Her preoccupation with firstly, getting 'her money back', and secondly, with the Single Market project arguably had the effect that she did not notice the creeping in of further integration. Hence, it has been suggested that she did not know what she was signing up for. There are several remarks in her memoirs which support this point. For example, her reference to the Declaration issued at the Stuttgart Council in 1983, which she dismissed at the time as having no legal force and which she therefore felt able to go along with. In retrospect she claims that 'the linguistic skeleton on which so much institutional flesh would grow was already visible' (Thatcher, 1995a, p. 314). Further on she comments: 'We had to learn the hard way that by agreement to what were apparently empty generalisations or vague aspirations we were later held to have committed ourselves to political structures which were contrary to our interests' (Thatcher, 1995a, p. 319).

An open admission of her lack of foresight is best illustrated by the following quote: 'The Single European Act (SEA), contrary to my intentions and my understanding of formal undertakings given at the time, had provided new scope for the European Commission and the European Court to press forward in the direction of centralisation' (Thatcher, 1995b, p. 473). And further: 'But I still believe it was right to sign the Single European Act, because we wanted a Single European Market' (Thatcher, 1995a, p. 557). These last two comments taken together give rise to the suspicion that in retrospect she preferred to admit ignorance rather than acknowledge that she knowingly led Britain further into Europe because she thought it was a price worth paying for achieving the Single Market. Her reputation of usually being well briefed and informed would support this.[4]

On the whole, this first phase of her relationship with the Community was characterised by her battle for a better budget deal for Britain and her support for the Single Market. She either did not see or chose to ignore the writing on the wall which pointed to closer integration to uphold the momentum created by the SEA. Whilst she described the first three European Councils of her second term as having been very much of the traditional mould and their outcome to have been equally traditionally 'a British victory on points' (Thatcher, 1995a, p. 727), from 1987 onwards she herself perceived a change:

> But from then on the Community environment in which I had to operate became increasingly alien and frequently poisonous. The disputes were no longer about tactical or temporary issues but about the whole future direction of the Community and its relations with the wider world changing so fast outside it. (Thatcher, 1995a, p. 727)

By 1988, following a speech made by Jacques Delors in which he outlined his vision of a social and political Europe, Margaret Thatcher felt it necessary to counterbalance his views and did so in her famous Bruges speech. This second phase was marked by open hostility and determined opposition to further moves towards integration, namely monetary union and the establishment of a European central bank.

Before dealing with another development which occupied her intensely at the end of the 1980s, i.e. the collapse of communism and its implications for Germany in particular, it is necessary to look at some general factors which decisively shaped her approach to Europe, these being her political style, the importance she attached to the role of the nation-state, the impact of the Cold War on her European policy and the link she construed between socialism and European integration.

Political Style

When referring to the impact of Margaret Thatcher's premiership at home and abroad, it is customary to examine not only the content and direction of her policies but also the distinctive style which accompanied them. This is of particular significance in the European context since her confrontational style, which might have been appropriate in the British context of one party government, was in stark contrast to the style of most continental European politicians who traditionally rely on team-playing skills for coalition building and who are by and large used to negotiating and then governing by compromise and consensus. To criticisms made by Sir Edward Heath who accused her of having abandoned consensus politics, she replied: 'For me, consensus seems to be the process of abandoning all beliefs, principles, values and policies' (Kavanagh, 1987, p. 7). Her different approach soon became obvious in her unrelenting perseverance regarding a budget settlement beneficial to Britain - gaining prominence with the phrase 'I want my money back' - which she pursued from first getting to power in 1979 until she reached a permanent settlement in 1984.

Her uncompromising style and stubbornness as a politician found expression in phrases like 'The lady is not for turning' and 'TINA' (There is no alternative). In her memoirs, she recalls that her father, one of the most important single influences on her life and who she devotedly admired said to her once: 'Never do things just because other people do them' (Thatcher, 1995b, p. 6). She goes on: 'Whatever I felt at the time, the sentiment stood me in good stead, ...' (Thatcher, 1995b, p. 6). Unsurprisingly, this theme crops up again and again: 'These upright qualities, which entailed a refusal to alter your convictions just because others disagreed or because you became unpopular, were instilled into me from the earliest days' (Thatcher, 1995b, p. 7).

In her memoirs, she attempts to justify the relentless pursuit of her own, nationally determined goals in the European context as follows: 'Finally, our partners should not assume that we will always want to sign an agreement in the end. Although we prefer cooperation, we should be quite prepared to be very un-cooperative indeed' (Thatcher, 1995b p. 499). Showing stamina and not surrendering in the face of strong opposition, she regarded as an accomplishment. Apart from being out of line with most of her continental counterparts, her adversarial style and her unwillingness or, maybe even, inability to employ diplomacy in the relationships with her European partners also went against most of what the British Foreign Office stood for. Accordingly, she dismisses her then Foreign Secretary Geoffrey Howe's willingness to compromise partly as a reflection of his temperament and partly as 'the Foreign Office's *déformation professionnelle*' (Thatcher, 1995a, p. 550).

The Importance of the Nation-State

Much of Margaret Thatcher's policy on Europe was based on her strong belief in the nation-state in general and more importantly, in Britain as a strong and independent nation-state. She made her intergovernmental approach with its emphasis on the nation-state and rejection of supranational bodies quite clear in the Bruges speech:

> My first guiding principle is this: willing and active co-operation between independent sovereign states is the best way to build a successful European Community. To try to suppress nationhood and concentrate power at the centre of a European conglomerate would be highly damaging and would jeopardize the objectives we seek to achieve. (Thatcher, 1997, p. 319)

Referring to her time as leader of the opposition, she explains that already then she had reached the conclusion that artificial Europe-wide institutions are undesirable when people don't share the same language and traditions (Thatcher, 1995b, p. 337).

In a linguistic analysis of the Bruges speech, Hans-Jürgen Diller points out that she strongly opposed Europe as an agent, i.e. she was not anti-European but anti-EC (Diller, 1994, p. 105). In the Bruges speech, she made it quite clear that her idea of Europe was not restricted to the EC: 'The European Community is *one* manifestation of that European identity. But it is not the only one' (Thatcher, 1997, p. 318).

In her relations with the Community, she repeatedly polarised Britain and Europe, for example when she asserted that she could not play 'Sister Bountiful' to the Community while asking her electorate to forego improvements in domestic affairs (George, 1990, p.162). In this context, Stephen George has identified the following motive: '[I]n the face of criticism from within as well as outside her own party that she was dividing the nation, she attempted to unify it by wrapping herself in the Union flag and going into battle for the national interest' (George, 1990, p. 163).

The Impact of the Cold War

Another significant factor which contributed to Margaret Thatcher's policy on Europe is that her attitude towards Europe was predominantly shaped by the Cold War rather than the European idea. She considered the development of the European Community as having as one of its main functions the task of acting as a counterbalance to the 'evil empire' of the Soviet Union and its satellite states rather than having any merit in its own right (with the possible exception of the Single Market project). In her memoirs, she says that she 'did not regard the EEC as merely an economic entity: it had a wider strategic purpose' (Thatcher, 1995b, p. 347).

Young has suggested that this attitude is due to Margaret Thatcher being Britain's first Prime Minister who did not experience or see the destruction of war at first hand to the extent other British politicians had who then under the influence of these images came to believe in the importance of an ever closer union among European states in order to maintain peace (Young, 1999, p. 307).

Socialism and European Integration

One last feature that influenced Margaret Thatcher's assessment of initiatives within the Community greatly was a concern she expressed clearly in her Bruges speech: 'We have not successfully rolled back the frontiers of the state in Britain only to see them re-imposed at a European level, with a European super-state exercising a new dominance from Brussels' (Thatcher, 1997, pp. 319-20). Her strong feelings about a free market devoid of any intervention also put her in opposition to other European leaders, even conservative ones, who believed in a more corporatist model. Having by and large neutralised socialism in the form of the Labour Party in Britain as well as the moderate wing of her own party who wanted to emphasise the 'social dimension' of Conservatism, Margaret Thatcher clearly did not want imports from 'foreign wets'[5] to dilute her project in 1980s Britain. In her autobiographies, for example, she speaks of her fear of imposing the high social costs of Germany and France on Britain through the back door (Thatcher, 1995b, p. 484). Accordingly, Jacques Delors, then President of the European Commission committed what in her assessment must have been a cardinal sin when he spoke at the annual conference of the British Trades Union Congress and claimed that it was an impossibility to build Europe only on deregulation and that there was a need to add a social dimension in terms of workers' right to the Single Market project.

Margaret Thatcher's distinctive style of politics and the key tenets which shaped her attitude towards Europe in general, as identified in this section, provide the framework for the next part which takes a closer look at Germany.

Representations of Germany

There is no question that Germany and the Germans occupied a central role in Margaret Thatcher's thoughts on Europe. Accordingly, Hugo Young in his book *This Blessed Plot* subtitled his chapter on Margaret Thatcher's European policy 'Deutschland über alles' stating: 'In the complex of prejudices, whether rational or, just as often, visceral, that Margaret Thatcher brought to "Europe", none was more potent than her attitude to Germany' (Young, 1999, p. 357). Lord Watson, chairman of the British-German association commented that Margaret Thatcher's memoirs make it quite clear which role Germany occupies in the discourse on Europe: 'If you want to say that European unification is a threat to Britain, the easiest way to say it is to say that it's all about the power of Germany' (*The Guardian,* 28 January 2000, p. 4).

Germany and the Germans

Margaret Thatcher's remarks about Germany and the Germans in general seem to fall into two categories. Firstly, she regularly evokes images of Germany's pre-45 history. In *The Path To Power* she recalls an incident during her first visit to Germany in 1975 after she had won the party leadership. Reacting to the news of a by-election victory for the Conservative Party at home, she attempted to make the victory sign, adding that the victory sign was 'all the more appropriate since I was in Germany' (Thatcher, 1995b, p. 343). Incidentally and to the delight of the cameramen she raised her two fingers the wrong way round.

Another incident which illustrates her attitude towards Germany and the omnipresence of its past, which she does not mention in her memoirs, took place at a dinner held at the Königswinter Conference in Cambridge in 1990 to mark 40 years of Anglo-German friendship. Sitting next to the German Ambassador, she said that it would take another 40 years 'before we can forget what you have done' (Marsh, 1994, p. 146).

The second category of remarks is characterised by a tendency to lapse into cliché - presumably based on a lack of knowledge - when she talks about Germany. Recalling her visit to Deidesheim, Margaret Thatcher remembers Germany in a very stereotypical fashion:

> And indeed the atmosphere at Deidesheim was otherwise [referring to the SNF negotiations] amicable. It was jolly, quaint, sentimental and slightly overdone - *gemütlich* is, I think, the German word. Lunch consisted of potato

soup, pig's stomach (which the German Chancellor clearly enjoyed), sausage, liver dumplings and sauerkraut. (Thatcher, 1995a, pp. 747-48)

Referring to this passage, David Marsh (1994, p. 145) has pointed out that it was particularly 'quaint' that in her opening remarks to Kohl, Margaret Thatcher spoke of her pleasure at being in France. With this comment she was presumably alluding to the period when this region was in the French occupational zone.

Again, resorting to stereotypes, she describes Franz-Josef Strauss and Helmut Kohl whom she met for the first time at the launch of the European Democratic Union in 1978 in Salzburg as 'very large and very German' (Thatcher, 1995b, p. 347). She does not elaborate on this, obviously assuming that describing somebody as 'very German' says it all.

With regard to her interaction with other people, it has been suggested that Margaret Thatcher 'almost chemically' was able to make instant judgements about being able to do business with someone or not (Young, 1999, p. 314). This also seemed to apply to German politicians. As her relationships with the social democrat Schmidt and the conservative Kohl showed, party affiliation only played a secondary role. Helmut Schmidt was the first head of a foreign government to visit her as Prime Minister and in her memoirs, in spite of being a social democrat, he features positively: 'I had met Herr Schmidt in Opposition [sic!] and had soon developed the highest regard for him. He had a profound understanding of the international economy on which - although he considered himself a socialist - we were to find ourselves in close agreement' (Thatcher, 1995a, p. 34). And later on, she says that she always had 'the highest regard for Helmut Schmidt's wisdom, straightforwardness and grasp of international economics. Sadly, I never developed quite the same relationship with Chancellor Kohl, though it was some time before the implications of this became important' (Thatcher, 1995a, p. 257). This latter comment should be seen in the context of German reunification. As I will discuss in more detail later, Margaret Thatcher tried her best to stop it from happening and has never quite forgiven Kohl for negotiating reunification 'behind her back' and against her expressed wishes.

However, there are also positive comments to be found about Kohl, particularly in the context of situations when she considered Germany an ally against perceived third party aggressors. Regarding his conduct concerning the deployment of cruise and pershing missiles and the invasion of Grenada at the beginning of his chancellorship she writes: 'Helmut Kohl was showing a good deal of courage as well as political cunning in handling West German public opinion at this crucial time, and I admired him for it' (Thatcher, 1995a, p. 335). When Kohl shortly before her resignation as party leader demonstrated his support, she thought it was big-hearted of him, especially since - by her own admission - her removal from office would make things easier for him on the European stage (Thatcher, 1995a, pp. 842-43).

The German Economy

When comparing Britain's to other European countries' post-war economies, Margaret Thatcher felt that Britain at least in comparison, had not done very well: 'But if we never had it so good, others - like Germany, France, Italy, Denmark - increasingly had it better' (Thatcher, 1995a, p. 7). In the case of Germany, this must have seemed particularly unfair as a fairly wide-spread perception in Britain, summed up in the phrase that 'Britain had won the war but lost the peace', expresses (*Die Zeit*, 22 July 1999, p. 9).

Although she made favourable comments about Germany's economy, she dismissed the German model, the 'social market economy', a more corporatist order of capitalism as being unsuitable as a model for the British context because it 'only works as well as it does because of the remarkable qualities of the Germans' (Thatcher, 1995b, p. 596). In *The Downing Street Years* she had already hinted at another difference, coming to the same conclusion: 'German trade unions were also far more responsible than ours, and of course the German character is different, less individualistic and more regimented. So the "German model" was inappropriate for Britain' (Thatcher, 1995a, p. 94).

'*Sozialmarktwirtschaft*' [sic!], she explains in a more critical tone to be 'a kind of corporatist, highly collectivised, "consensus"-based economic system, which pushed up costs, suffered increasingly from market rigidities and relied on qualities of teutonic self-discipline to work at all' (Thatcher, 1995a, p. 751). This last quote illustrates particularly well how Margaret Thatcher resorted to clichés in order to dismiss the German model which entailed many features which she rejected on ideological grounds.[6]

The 'German Problem'

In the context of its divided history, West Germany was portrayed as an ally and a co-defender of freedom and democracy in the face of communism. With the fall of the wall and German reunification entering the agenda, this picture changed dramatically and Margaret Thatcher was quite obviously not prepared to extend her belief in the nation-state and the right to self-determination to the German case.[7] Her use of emphatic metaphors also increases drastically: she is now referring to the 'German giant' (Thatcher, 1995a, p. 798), 'Gulliver' (Thatcher, 1995b, p. 491 and p. 613; Thatcher, 1995a, p. 814) and the 'German juggernaut' (Thatcher, 1995a, p. 797). Here is her assessment of the new situation:

> There was and still is - a tendency to regard the 'German problem' as something too delicate for well-brought-up politicians to discuss. This always seemed to me a mistake. The problem had several elements which could only be addressed if non-Germans considered them openly and constructively. I do not believe in collective guilt: it is individuals who are morally accountable for their actions. But I do believe in national character, which is moulded by a range of complex factors [...]. Since the unification of Germany under Bismarck [...] Germany has veered unpredictably between aggression and self-doubt. [...] But perhaps the first people to recognize the 'German problem' are the modern Germans, the vast majority of whom are determined that Germany should not be a great power able to exert itself at others' expense. The true origins of German *angst* is the agony of self-knowledge. (Thatcher, 1994a, pp. 790-91)

In order to explore the German 'national character', Margaret Thatcher together with her then Foreign Secretary Douglas Hurd called a seminar at Chequers in March 1990 to which she invited various British and American historians of Germany.[8] The guiding questions of the seminar were related to the nature of the 'German national character' (there was no discussion as to the validity of such a generalisation), its impact on a reunited Germany, and its potential consequences for the European balance of power. Furthermore, it focussed on the question of what the guiding principles of the British policy towards a reunited Germany should be. The whole event caused considerable embarrassment to the government when a highly confidential memorandum of the meeting, written by Margaret Thatcher's foreign affairs private secretary Charles Powell, was leaked to *The Independent on Sunday* and *Der Spiegel.* Timothy Garton Ash, one of the participants, felt the need to comment on this document which one British minister called 'Ver-bloody-batim':

> But ver-bloody-batim is precisely what it was not. Rather it was a report, with no views attributed specifically to anyone, but some by implication to all.

And like all good Whitehall *rapporteurs,* Mr. Powell managed to flavor this rich cream soup with a little of his own particular spice. (Garton Ash, 1990, p. 65)

One particular sentence which, Timothy Garton Ash claims, did not represent a collective view of the participants but contained some attributes which were mentioned in the meeting at one point or other along with many more positive ones, went as follows:

> Some even less flattering attributes were also mentioned [at the meeting] as an abiding part of the German character: in alphabetical order, angst, aggressiveness, assertiveness, bullying, egotism, inferiority complex, sentimentality. [sic] (quoted in *Garton Ash,* 1990, p. 65)

The infamous memorandum was published only a day after the resignation of Nicholas Ridley from his post as Trade and Industry Secretary over what has been termed the Ridley affair.[9] In an interview with *The Spectator,* entitled 'Saying the Unsayable about the Germans', Nicholas Ridley, among other things, claimed that if you give sovereignty to the European Commission, you might as well give it to Adolf Hitler (quoted in Garton Ash, 1990, p. 65).

Apart from creating waves on the domestic as well as the European level, these incidents along with evidence from Margaret Thatcher's memoirs illustrate that the Thatcher government was intensely pre-occupied with the issue of German reunification and its consequences for Europe, even if the outcome of its efforts was far from constructive.

In contrast to the French, who, once they realised that they could do little to stop reunification from happening, resorted to tying Germany more closely into Europe in order to control it, Margaret Thatcher came to the opposite conclusion. The following quote illustrates clearly how the two threads, Germany and Europe, come together in her thinking:

> This desire among modern German politicians to merge their national identity in a wider European one is understandable enough, but it presents great difficulties to self-conscious nation-states in Europe. In effect, the Germans, because they are nervous of governing themselves, want to establish a European system in which no nation will govern itself. Such a system could only be unstable in the long term and, because of Germany's size and preponderance, is bound to be lop-sided. Obsession with a European Germany risks producing a German Europe. (Thatcher, 1995a, p. 748)

Reasons for Thatcher's Anti-German Course

As the last section has illustrated, Margaret Thatcher's perceptions and representations of Germany are largely based on Germany's pre-45 history on the one hand, and stereotypes regarding the post-45 era on the other. It would therefore be easy as well as tempting to dismiss her attitude towards Germany as part of what, in the context of her policy on Europe, has been termed her 'personal obsessions' (Young, 1999, p. 307).

Margaret Thatcher's provincial background is likely to have exerted considerable influence on her attitude towards foreign affairs as a national politician. Young has pointed out that a certain parochialism was instilled into her by her home. Her father once told the Grantham Rotary Club that he would rather be a bootblack in England than a leading citizen in one of the other leading countries of the world. (Young, 1999, p. 307). The first chapter of *The Path To Power* is therefore aptly called 'a provincial childhood'.

Margaret Thatcher's life as a child in inter-war Grantham revolved around the grocery shop of her parents, Methodism and the Rotary Club, an atmosphere which Andrew Sullivan has described as 'oppressively English' (1996, p. 39). Leaving Grantham for Oxford, she describes as 'leaving home [...] for a totally different world' (Thatcher, 1995b, p. 34).

In this context, the aforementioned Charles Powell, has pointed out that for a small girl growing up in Grantham, 'the Germans were about as evil as anything you could think of' (quoted in Young, 1999, p. 320).

Her simplistic attitude towards 'otherness' even as an elder stateswoman writing her memoirs becomes obvious when she comments on her first trip to London: 'For the first time in my life I saw people from foreign countries, some in the traditional native dress of India and Africa' (Thatcher, 1995b, p. 10). Even in retrospect, it seems to have escaped the political memoirist Thatcher that she might have met people from foreign countries (e.g. other Europeans) before but that their 'native dress' resembled her own to such an extent that she could not have told whether they were foreign or not.

The restrictive and small-minded environment in which Margaret Thatcher spent the formative part of her life indisputably left a mark regarding her attitude to international politics in later years. In his diaries, Alan Clark, one of her most enthusiastic admirers, relates an anecdote according to which Margaret Thatcher, then leader of the opposition, at a conference asked Frank Cooper, a civil servant, whether she must do all this 'international stuff'. After his affirmative answer she is said to have pulled a face (Clark, 1994, p.219).

Although the personal background of Margaret Thatcher might to some extent explain her anti-German course as part of a larger tendency which could be described as a general dislike of anything non-British, her memoirs - bearing in mind that they represent *her story* - reveal a range of reasons which serve to explain her attitude towards Germany in terms of her power politics.

Hierarchical Relationships: Britain as the Dominant Partner

In relation to other states, with the exception of the US whose lead she usually was quite happy to accept, Margaret Thatcher made no secret of the hierarchical relationship she envisaged between Britain and other countries: 'Later, I seriously considered going into the Indian Civil Service, for to me the Indian Empire represented one of Britain's greatest achievements' (Thatcher, 1995b, p. 24).

Combining her perception of Britain's superiority with her own sense of mission, she contemplates in her memoirs: 'I had a romantic fascination for out-of-the-way countries and continents and what benefits we British could bring to them'(Thatcher, 1995b, p. 24).

Consequently, she found the European stage too restrictive for the role she had in mind for Britain. Talking about the approaching G7 summit in Houston in July 1990, for example, she makes it quite clear where her preferences were: 'To get away from the often parochial atmosphere of the over-frequent European Councils to a meeting of the G7 was always a relief' (Thatcher, 1995a, p. 763). The place she envisaged for Germany becomes particularly obvious when, referring to the 'two-plus-four' talks between the two Germanies and the Allied Powers, she commented that she preferred to call them 'four-plus-two' talks (Thatcher, 1995a, p. 799).

From a Divided Germany to a United Germany

Whilst Germany was divided, Margaret Thatcher acknowledged West Germany's important strategic position in the context of NATO defence. Literally faced with communism, she even puts Germany on an equal footing:

> After talks with Chancellor Helmut Kohl in Bonn, I flew to Berlin and gained
> my first sight of the Berlin Wall and of the grey, bleak and devastated land
> beyond it in which dogs prowled under the gaze of armed Russian guards

[sic!]. Chancellor Kohl accompanied me on this visit and, whatever difficulties would arise in the future, on matters like the evils of communism and commitment to our American allies we were as one. (Thatcher, 1995a, p. 263)

The tone changed fundamentally, however, when German reunification entered the agenda. As becomes apparent in the following quote, in her opinion, closer European integration did not offer a solution to Germany's potential dominance:

> In fact, Germany is more rather than less likely to dominate within that framework; for a reunited Germany is simply too big and powerful to be just another player within Europe. [...] Germany is thus by its very nature a destabilizing rather than a stabilizing force in Europe. (Thatcher, 1995a, p. 791)

There is one key sentence in which she brings together three strands, all of which she disapproved of, with the responsibility for their emergence resting firmly with Germany because of its pursuit of reunification:

> Arriving prematurely as it did, a united Germany has tended to encourage three unwelcome developments: the rush to European federalism as a way of tying down Gulliver; the maintenance of a Franco-German bloc for the same purpose; and the gradual withdrawal of the US from Europe on the assumption that a German-led Europe will be both stable and capable of looking after its own defence. (Thatcher, 1995a, p. 814)

This quote makes it quite clear that far from being based on irrational thoughts and prejudices, Margaret Thatcher, at least in retrospect, had some kind of rationale, however justified, for her fierce opposition to German reunification. In her view, German reunification resulted in closer European integration, a strengthening of the French-German axis which she feared would isolate Britain, and the withdrawal of the United States. She considered all three developments to be detrimental to the balance of power in Europe and the position of Britain.

Britain's Relationship with America

During Reagan's presidency, the Anglo-American relationship had flourished. When Bush took over, however, this special relationship nearly turned sour, because Bush seemed to favour Germany at the expense of Britain:

> I had breathed a sigh of relief when George Bush defeated his Democrat opponent in the US presidential election, for I felt that it ensured continuity. But with the new team's arrival in the White House I found myself dealing with an Administration which saw Germany as its main European partner in leadership, which encouraged the integration of Europe without seeming to understand fully what it meant and which sometimes seemed to underestimate the need for a strong nuclear defence. I felt I could not always rely as before on American co-operation. This was of great importance at such a time. (Thatcher, 1995a, p. 768)

Again, using Germany's pre-45 past as an argument, Margaret Thatcher dismisses the status the Americans have given to Germany as inappropriate as well as undeserved:

> The main results of this approach as far as I was concerned were to put the relationship with Germany - rather than the 'special relationship' with Britain - at the centre. I would be the first to argue that if one chose to ignore history and the loyalties it engenders such an approach might appear quite rational. (Thatcher, 1995a, p. 783)

After Bush's remarks in 1989 about the Germans as 'partners in leadership' in his speech in Mainz on 31 May, he came to London to appease the British ally. However, in Margaret Thatcher's view, it was to no avail:

> When the President came to London he sought to deal with the problems those remarks had caused by saying that we too were partners in leadership. But the damage had been done. Now, as 1989 wore on, the march of events in eastern Europe and the prospect of German reunification added a new element, inclining the United States to take German issues still more seriously. (Thatcher, 1995a, p. 789)

These quotes make it quite clear that Margaret Thatcher feared that the loss of the highly valued 'special relationship' with America would occur as a consequence of German reunification. The loss itself must have seemed regrettable enough but losing it to Germany, of all countries, must have made Bush's comments about the possibility of a 'special relationship' between America and Germany, especially as 'partners in leadership' sound particularly distressing to the British leader. The only argument left against these developments was her appeal to history and its loyalties.

The Franco-German Axis

Just as Margaret Thatcher was deeply concerned about losing Britain's special place in her relationship with the US, she was equally apprehensive about what she called the 'French-German axis' which would potentially marginalise Britain. Talking about foreign affairs in her first few months in office, she explains:

> I was also very much aware of another feature of the EC, which had been apparent from its earliest days, continued to shape its development and diminished Britain's capacity to influence events - namely, the close relationship between France and Germany. Although this relationship may have seemed to depend on personal rapport - between President Giscard and Chancellor Schmidt or President Mitterand and Chancellor Kohl - the truth is that it was explicable more in terms of history and perceptions of long-term interest. France has long feared the power of Germany and has hoped that by superior Gallic intelligence power can be directed in ways favourable to French interests. Germany, for her part, knows that although she has contributed considerably more to the EC financially and economically than any other state, she has received an enormous return in the form of international respectability and influence. The Franco-German axis would remain a factor to be reckoned with [...]. (Thatcher, 1995a, p. 61)

There are numerous comments in her memoirs which provide evidence of Margaret Thatcher's deep distrust of the relationship between France and Germany. Her suspicions were confirmed when Mitterand, who shared her apprehension about a reunited Germany decided that if it could not be stopped, it should at least happen within a framework that would tie Germany closely into Europe.[10]

Conclusion

Margaret Thatcher's approach to Europe was by and large driven by the opportunities it opened in terms of markets and its strategic importance before the collapse of communism rather than by, what has been loosely termed, the 'European idea'. Together with her strong belief in the nation-state, especially the British one, and her concern that other European leaders envisaged the inclusion of a 'social dimension' to the European project, which - from this point of view - would be detrimental in terms of her free market project in Britain as well as Britain's sovereignty, this resulted in an antagonistic attitude. The end of the Cold War and German reunification intensified these hostile attitudes, as these developments went completely against her convictions, i.e. closer European integration, a strengthening of the French-German axis and the withdrawal of the US from Europe. Linked to that, she saw the danger of Britain being isolated.

Rather than claiming that her antagonistic attitude towards Germany was determined by stereotypes and clichés, I would therefore suggest that the evidence from her memoirs shows, that these attitudes have their roots, firstly, in power politics, especially, of course, the power and status of Britain, and secondly, in the key tenets of her political agenda (e.g. the free market and deregulation). She merely instrumentalised existing prejudices and references to the past to support her argument, being well aware that in Britain she could rely on common preconceptions to appeal to with regard to Germany and the Germans. On a wider scale it can be argued that she instrumentalised the whole German issue in her fight against further European integration.

Bearing in mind that these observations regarding her attitude towards Germany are predominantly based on Margaret Thatcher's memoirs, however, the question will have to remain open as to whether, with hindsight, she simply reconstructed this part of the past in her memoirs in order to mask her own personal prejudices. Recalling Egerton's remark about memoirs inviting the retrojection of views held by the memoirist at the time of writing, we have to remember that the main sources for this paper, i.e. her memoirs, are 'Margaret Thatcher's case'.

Apart from that, many of the concerns she expressed were shared by most, if not all of Germany's neighbours, and indeed many Germans themselves. Germany's past is still an important factor influencing Germany's domestic as well as foreign affairs. What made it easy to dismiss them as prejudices which turned into an obsession in Thatcher's case, was the adversarial style that knew no diplomacy with which she voiced them. The most recent example was offered nine years after she left office: 'In my lifetime all the problems have come from mainland Europe, and all the solutions have come from the English-speaking nations across the world' (quoted in *The Guardian*, 6 October 1999, p.11).

It is ironic that because of her political style, some of the negative characteristics which have been used to describe the 'German national character' at the Chequers seminar are the very same attributes which have been assigned to Margaret Thatcher herself.

Notes

1   Although to some extent imprecise, I have adopted the conventional usage of the term 'Europe' when quite often referring to the EC (and later EU). Equally, when referring to Britain within the EU context, strictly speaking, 'The United Kingdom of Britain and Northern Ireland' might have been more precise.

2   Autobiographical writing tends to concentrate on the subject (i.e. *who* is remembering) and incorporates the environment only as far as it is necessary to understand the life story. Memoirs , esp. political memoirs, on the other hand, concentrate on *what* is being remembered, i.e. it has at its core people and events which accompanied the subject in a particular period of his/her life. In the case of Margaret Thatcher's two volumes, *The Path to Power* and *The Downing Street Years*, we would therefore normally speak of memoirs. However, since her strong personality in the form of her *authorial* voice is felt in nearly every sentence therefore not allowing us to forget *who* is remembering, in the following I will use these terms interchangeably, as indeed do most of the reviewers.

3   There is an argument (see Mary Evans, 1999) which suggests that autobiographies and memoirs should be treated as fictional rather than political/historical literature but as will become apparent in the course of the paper, I will include them in the latter without ignoring their potentially fictional qualities.

4   Hugo Young (1999, p. 336) quotes two officials who confirmed that Margaret Thatcher knew what she was doing when she signed the SEA: David Williamson said: 'I was present in 10 Downing Street on one occasion when Mrs Thatcher came down the stairs and said to me, "I have read every word of the Single European Act"'. In more general terms, Michael Butler recalls: 'I never remember an occasion in the six years when I worked for her, when she negotiated something without knowing what she was talking about'.

5   Margaret Thatcher introduced the term 'wets' to dismissively refer to the more moderate wing of the Conservative Party under her leadership, for the origins and development of the term see also Hugo Young (1993), page 198-99.

6   Regarding 'corporatist': she did not want a role for the trade unions as 'social partners', regarding 'collectivised economic system': she favoured privatisation, and regarding 'consensus': that was a swear word in Margaret Thatcher's vocabulary of political style.

7   Ironically, with this view she had some soulmates on the German left, some of them not believing in fast reunification either, whereas others felt that Germany had lost the right to self-determination and unification because of Auschwitz.

8   The American historians were Gordon Craig and Fritz Stern, the British experts on Germany were Lord Dacre (Hugh Trevor-Roper) Timothy Garton Ash, Norman Stone, and George Urban.

9   For a detailed account of these two affairs, see Lachlan R. Moyle (1994), 'The Ridley-Chequers Affair and German Character. A Journalistic Event'.
10   This view has been confirmed by the publication of *Verbatim*, written by Mitterand's special adviser Jacques Attali in which he claims that Mitterand only then decided to support German reunification when he could not see a possibility anymore of either blocking or delaying it. See Martin Mantzke (1996), ' ... nicht auf der Tagesordnung. Der Westen und die deutsche Einheit', p. 60

References

Clark, A. (1994), *Diaries*, Phoenix, London.
Diller, H. (1994), 'Thatcher in Bruges: A Study in Euro-rhetoric', *Journal for the Study of British Cultures*, vol. 1, no. 2, pp. 93-109.
Egerton, G. (1992), 'Politics and Autobiography: Political Memoir as Polygenre', *Biography: An Interdisciplinary Quarterly*, vol. 15, no.3, pp. 221-242.
Evans, M. (1999), *Missing Persons*, Routledge, London.
Garton Ash, T. (1990), 'The Chequers Affair', *The New York Review of Books*, vol. 37. No. 14, 27 September 1990, p. 65.
George, S. (1990), *An Awkward Partner. Britain in the European Community*, Oxford University Press, Oxford.
Husemann, H. (1994), *As Others See us. Anglo-German Perceptions*, Peter Lang, Frankfurt/Main.
Kavanagh, D. (1987), *Thatcherism and British Politics*, Oxford University Press, Oxford.
Mantzke, M. (1996), ' [...] nicht auf der Tagesordnung. Der Westen und die deutsche Einheit', *Internationale Politik*, vol. 51, no.3, pp. 59-62.
Marsh, D. (1994), 'Margaret Thatcher's The Downing Street Years', *German Politics*, vol. 3, no.1, pp. 144-147.
Moyle, L. R. (1994), 'The Ridley-Chequers Affair and German Character. A Journalistic Event', in H. Husemann (ed.), *As Others See us. Anglo-German Perceptions*, Peter Lang, Frankfurt/Main, pp. 107-120.
Sowemimo, M. (1996), 'The Conservative Party and European Integration', *Party Politics*, vol. 2, no. 1, pp. 77-97.
Steedman, C. (1992), *Past Tenses. Essays on Writing, Autobiography and History*, Rivers Oram Press, London.
Sullivan, A. (1996), 'The Path to Power by Margaret Thatcher', *New Republic*, vol. 214, no. 7, pp. 36-43.
Thatcher, M. (1995a), *The Downing Street Years*, HarperCollins, London. [Original hardback edition published in 1993]
Thatcher, M. (1995b), *The Path To Power*, HarperCollins, London.
Thatcher, M. (1997), 'Bruges Speech, 20 September 1988', in R. Harris (ed.), *The Collected Speeches of Margaret Thatcher*, HarperCollins, London, pp. 315-325.
Wallace, H. (1997), 'At Odds with Europe', *Political Studies*, vol. 45, no. 4, pp. 677-688.
Young, H. (1993), *One of Us*, Pan Books, London.
Young, H. (1999), *This Blessed Plot*, Macmillan, London. [Original hardback edition published in 1998].

3 A Province of a Federal Superstate, Ruled by an Unelected Bureaucracy - Keywords of the Euro-Sceptic Discourse in Britain

WOLFGANG TEUBERT

1. The Free Britain Corpus

A special discourse such as the contemporary British Euro-sceptic discourse is a segment of the general discourse in Britain. The general discourse in Britain consists of all the spoken and written texts that have been communicated within the British discourse community. Most of these texts have been lost over time. But even what remains, in the form of texts which have been written or, more recently, stored on acoustic memories, is so gigantic that it could never be analysed as a whole. All discourse analysis can ever hope for is to look at sub-discourses, small selections of texts, defined by parameters such as time span, authorship, audience, region, domain or medium. It is the discourse analysts who determine the parameters of the special discourse they want to study. Within this framework the present chapter looks at the topic of Euro-scepticism as it is being discussed in Britain today.

The British Euro-sceptic discourse consists of the totality of oral and written texts expressing a sceptical attitude towards the establishment of a supranational structure in post-war (Western) Europe and British membership within this structure. The discourse community includes British politicians, business people, academics, journalists and the public at large. Whether a text belongs to the British Euro-sceptic discourse can, in principle, be determined by the density of occurrence of pre-selected keywords. However, most texts of this discourse will not be easily accessible to analysis. Very few parliamentary speeches survive only in the

Hansards and will never be referred to again; most newspaper articles are tucked away in remote archives; and generally, most texts are only redundant reduplications of what has been said before. Only a few texts are really relevant in the sense that they will influence what is being said in subsequent texts. Very few texts become key texts in the sense that new texts refer to them even after years or decades. Most texts of a discourse, therefore, will not be remembered. They are transient phenomena.

Therefore, it makes sense to analyse the British Euro-sceptic discourse not as a whole, but in the form of a cross-section of those texts that can be accessed electronically. Such a principled collection of electronic texts is called a corpus. The relatively new discipline of corpus linguistics can tell us what texts are about by extracting semantic data from corpora, by using statistical methods in processing this output, and by the interpretation of the results. Thus, corpus linguistics is a method that can help us with the analysis of a discourse.

Analysing a discourse means finding out about the relationships between texts, about features of intertextuality. Everyone contributing to a discourse will be aware of some of what has been said before, and they will try to make clear what they accept and where they may differ. Relevant texts are those to which many subsequent texts refer; irrelevant texts are those that are never referred to again. There are different ways to refer to a text. Text segments can be explicitly quoted, but they can also be repeated verbatim or just paraphrased, that is, rephrased with a similar meaning. References are strictly unidirectional. It is only possible to refer to previous texts. Discourses always have a diachronic, a historical dimension.

Discourse analysis tells us what a discourse is about and what is common to all texts of a discourse or to particular subsets. Discourse analysis is primarily interested in meaning. If discourse analysis is based on a corpus whose contributions are chronologically dated, it becomes possible to analyse semantic change. We could then see how new topics can be introduced (e.g., the human rights issue) and how old ones can disappear (e.g., the Communist Bloc issue). Issues can change their deontological status: metrification was, decades ago, something even Euro-sceptics did not oppose in principle (Celsius has successfully replaced Fahrenheit); today it is seen as a dictat from Brussels. We would like to find out which texts are referred to more frequently than others, and it would be interesting to know if politicians take up issues that have been introduced in newspaper editorials or if it is the other way around.

The corpus used in this analysis is the Free Britain Corpus. It consists of roughly 1000 texts taken from British Euro-sceptic websites during mid-February and early March 2000. Its size amounts to ca. 1.8 million words. In the corpus composition phase, our team started with the *Home Page for FREE BRITAIN* and extended their search from there to other websites linked to *FREE BRITAIN* or to the links we found at these websites. As there was not enough time, it has not yet been possible to standardise the bibliographic references. Thus, in this analysis, it is not possible to trace back corpus citations to a particular text, author, source or a precise publication date. The Free Britain Corpus consists of relevant texts only in as far as the website providers decided to put them on their servers. This still makes our corpus a principled collection of texts. But the principles are extra-linguistic: they are the principles of professional (or at least highly organised) British Euro-sceptics. Since a number of these websites have a broader focus than just Euro-scepticism, it was necessary to add, as another filter, the requirement that the selected texts deal with one of the issues of British Euro-sceptic discourse. Here is a list of the websites from which texts were collected for the Free Britain Corpus:

1. The Home Page for FREE BRITAIN! http://www.freebrit.demon.co.uk/
2. HM Treasury. http://www. eurocritic.demon.co.uk
3. HM Treasury. http://www. connect.co.uk/nott_commission
4. HM Treasury. http://www.hm-treasury.gov.uk/pub/html/panel95/euro.html
5. BUSINESS FOR STERLING. 'The leading anti-euro campaign'.
   http://www.bfors.com/
6. Jersey Bean Crock! http://www.beancrock.com/
7. University of Exeter, Roy Davies' web page.
   http://www.ex.ac.uk/~RDavies/arian/emu.html
8. 70% are against the Single Currency. http://www.sjgwp.co.uk/noemu/message.htm
9. UK Independence Party. http://www.independenceuk.org.uk/cgi/
10. UK Independence Party Parliamentary Group Website. This Euro-sceptic Web Ring site owned by Peter North. http://www.eukip.org.uk/
11. UK Independence Party. http://nav.webring.org/
12. EUROKNOW - Library of speeches. http://www.euro-know.org/lib.html
13. EUROKNOW - Economists wire. http://www.euro-know.org/econ_write.html
14. In For a Penny... In For a Pound (a link from Euro-sceptic Web Ring).
    http://www.aber.ac.uk/~eww9
15. First, Holland. Always Holland. A website for the preservation of Dutch culture.
    http://www.geocities.com/eerstnl/
16. The European Union and the Euro. http://www.maughan.clara.net/europe.htm
17. CRITICAL EUROPEAN GROUP. http://www.keele.ac.uk/socs/ks40/ceghome.html
18. THE TRUTH ABOUT EUROPE. http://members.tripod.com/~eurotruth/index.htm
19. Welcome to Redoak. http://www.redoak.co.uk/hpeuro.html
20. EUROPEAN UNION FOLLIES AND MYTHS. http://www.kc3.co.uk/~dt/

21. Campaign for an Independent Guernsey. http://www.cig.cc/
22. WELCOME TO MARKS PAGE OF OPINIONS.
    http://www.netcomuk.co.uk/~cmdixon/emu.html
23. EmuNet / Politics and economics / Soapbox. http://www.euro-
    mu.co.uk/pubs/bergsten1.shtml
24. *The Times*. http://www.the-
    times.co.uk/news/pages/tim/96/10/07/timnwsnws03011.html
25. NARPSG - The National Association of Referendum Party Supporters
    Groups.http://www.damak.freeserve.co.uk/narpsg.htm
26. *EuroFAQ* - Questions and Answers about Britain and the European Union.
    http://memberrs.aol.com/eurofaq/
27. Eurocritic Web Magazine. http://www.eurocritic.demon.co.uk/
28. Wells Conservative Association. http://www.wells.tory.org.uk/
29. Campaign for an Independent Britain. http://www.bullen.demon.co.uk/index.htm
30. Friends of the Earth. http://www.foe.co.uk/camps/susdev/
31. New Europe. http://www.new-europe.co.uk/news/index.html
32. European Economic and Monetary Union. http://www.sysmod.com/maneuris.htm
33. Free Nations - The Enemy Within.
    http://www.freenations.freeuk.com/content/enemy1.htm
34. ICC - The Independent Computer Contractors. A Specialist Group of the British
    Computer Society. http://www.bcs.org.uk/siggroup/icc/6point.htm
35. New alliance. http://www.users.dircon.co.uk/~iits/newalliance/

The Free Britain Corpus is freely accessible at these two websites:
www.dur.ac.uk/SMEL/depts/german/euro-arc.htm and www.tractor.de.
Anyone interested can look up the citations presented here and identify
author, title and publication date. It is also possible to search for other key
words not covered in this analysis. The Free Britain Corpus is unique in
that a relatively large number of texts is contained in more than one
version. This is a consequence of our collection principles. The remaining
text are texts found on more than one website. Sometimes versions are
identical: sometimes there are major or minor differences. According to an
initial estimate, discounting repetitions, the corpus probably contains 1.2
million running words. I hope that by the end of the year 2000 a detailed
documentation of the Free Britain Corpus will be available. It is obvious
that the Free Britain Corpus contains many quite recent texts and relatively
few, but relevant older texts. For a diachronic analysis, it would be
necessary to regularly add new texts, taken from the same websites.

This analysis of the Free Britain Corpus focuses on 25 keywords. The
original set of keywords was selected on the basis of a small pilot corpus of
Euro-sceptic texts. Additional keywords were only chosen in the course of
analysing the corpus citations of the first set of keywords. These additional
keywords were added as significantly frequent collocates of the original

keywords; they were frequently found in the context of the original keywords.

There are two kinds of keywords: stigma words and banner words, a distinction introduced by Fritz Hermanns (Hermanns, 1994). Stigma words are words used by a discourse community to implicate the adversaries, what they stand for and what distinguishes them from the members of the discourse community. Stigma words have a negative deontological value: they signify something one should not be or have. *Corruption* is unethical, and nobody wants to be called *corrupt*. It is a typical stigma word. Somewhat similar is *bureaucratic*. It may not be immoral to be a *bureaucrat*, but it is always the others and not ourselves that we call *bureaucrats*. Banner words are words that positively identify a discourse community and the ideas it stands for. Banner words must always bear positive connotations; they must have a positive deontological value, signifying people or ideas one would like to be sympathetic with. *Independence* and *prosperity* are typical banner words. No one would like to trade *independence* for *dependence*, and no one prefers poverty to *prosperity*. The problem with banner words is that they must not be too general. Everybody is in favour of peace and against war, so *peace* as a banner word does not help to advertise a discourse community, and at the same time, give it a unique identity. Banner words must also have a certain amount of specificity. A good example is the adjective *transatlantic*. Not many people are really opposed to a *transatlantic* relationship. Most people would agree that it is something positive, but not everyone would be willing to fight for it.

In some instances, words having the same stem or belonging to the same semantic field were counted as one keyword, for example, *federal*, *federalist*, *federalism*, are all summed up under *federal-*.

In chapters 2 and 3, corpus citations of all 25 keywords are presented. Chapter 2 brings together 15 keywords focussing on Britain's relationship with Europe. Chapter 3 contains 10 keywords emphasising Britain as a nation state and her role within the wider world. The maximum number of citations per keyword is 17, the minimum is 14. The difference reflects different frequency as well as the richness of variation. The keyword in question is presented in bold face; other keywords occurring in a citation are given in italics.

The selection of citations cannot but mirror my bias. My goal is to present what I take to be outstanding examples of the essence of the Euro-sceptic discourse. Nothing is included that does not contribute to this goal.

The keyword 'independence', for example, is used in a large number of contexts that have nothing to do with the independence of Britain as a nation state. Generally, usages not specific to Euro-scepticism are ignored. This selection of citations is intended to illustrate how collocation patterns arise, how the same idea or argument is repeated in a sheer endless number of minute permutations of one single phrase. But the selection is also intended to show the tight semantic network of our keywords evidenced in their co-occurrence within one citation. This is why, in a few instances, the same citations are repeated in connection with another keyword. As a result, the picture presented here makes Euro-sceptic discourse appear much more homogeneous than it is in reality. It is, I hope, a fairly reliable glimpse of the core of Euro-scepticism. By making the Free Britain Corpus accessible, the readers can check for themselves how relevant and focused this selection is.

2. Britain and Europe

2.1 federal-

Total frequency: 1112

1. The single European *superstate*, also known as a **federal** Europe
2. a **federal** tax system across the EU
3. the appalling 'f' word, **Federalism**, is in the public domain
4. to say no to **federalism** and *bureaucratic dictatorship* from Brussels
5. to say no to the **federalism** and *bureaucratic dictatorship* from Brussels
6. the **federalist** babblings of Europe's oleaginous political servants
7. a *province* of a European **federal** *superstate*, ruled by an *unelected immovable bureaucracy*
8. their desire to see the UK as a *province* of a **Federal** Europe
9. those who *worship* at the *altar* of European **federalism**
10. those who wish her to be a *province* of a **federal** state, governed by *bureaucratic dictat*
11. those who see [Britain] as a number of *provinces* of a **federal** Europe
12. politicians conspiring together to create a **federal** *monster*
13. to see this country *subsumed* in a **federal** state
14. to see her *subsumed* within a **federal** European state

15. seeing this country *submerged* into a **federal** *superstate*
16. to *submerge* the UK in a **federal** European state
17. it will lead to a **federal** Europe which is a fundamental and crucial loss of *sovereignty*

The *'f' word* (3) denotes the core issue of British Euro-scepticism, and it has often been pointed out that it is based on a misunderstanding (cf. Musolff 1996). In the usage of most continental languages, *federal* has a positive connotation, and it implies the devolution of political power from the central government to smaller geographical units, regions, provinces, or districts, to maintain a balance between the central and the regional administrations. But there is also another usage on the continent. A *federal tax system* (2) would mean a central tax system, just as a *federal police* can only be understood as a central police. In British English, this is generally the case; *federal* and *central* are largely synonymous, and, in addition, *federal*, unlike central, bears a pejorative connotation. For a nation state like Britain, where people share the same *values* (see 3.2), a central government, controlled by a central parliament, is something positive, but not for the amalgam of Europe. A *federal*, that is, a centralised Europe would be an undesirable *superstate* (1, 5) with *unelected oleaginous political servants* (6) in power; it would be a *bureaucracy* (7), more a *dictatorship* (8) than a democracy. Europe symbolises a primitive, heathen society where *monsters* (12) are worshipped (9). In such a Europe, Britain would become a mere *province* (7, 8, 11), *subsumed* (13, 14) and *submerged* (15, 16) in a federal *superstate* (1, 15), and, worst of all, she would have to give up her *sovereignty* (17).

Our examples illustrate the web of intertextual relations well. Some citations are almost identical clones of others (4, 5). Britain as a *province* or a number of *provinces* (7, 8, 10, 11) of a *federal (super)state* is obviously a nightmare for many authors, and the recurrence of *submerge* and *subsume* (13, 14, 15, 16) gives evidence of the fear of losing one's identity beguiles the minds of British Euro-sceptics.

2.2 superstate

Total frequency: 193

1. the revulsion we feel at the construction of the European *federal* **superstate**

2. find a way out of this *corrupt*, inefficient and autocratic European **Superstate**
3. cannot stop the Euro-*federalists* from creating a European **superstate**
4. the imposition of this forced *federal* **superstate** will eventually provoke civil wars
5. a *province* of a European *federal* **superstate**, ruled by an *unelected* and immovable *bureaucratic* elite
6. *provincial* status within an undemocratic European **superstate**
7. political servitude in a socialist **superstate**
8. the malign influence of the emergent **superstate** which calls itself Europe
9. their dream, and our nightmare of a *federal* European **superstate**
10. no nation could withdraw from this new German **superstate**

Margaret Thatcher, in her Bruges speech, still spelled this stigma word *super-state*. Now that it has boomed, with 193 occurrences, it has (often, but not always) lost its hyphen. The *superstate* Europe is *federal* (1, 4, 5, 9), *corrupt, inefficient and autocratic* (2), *undemocratic* (6), *socialist* (7), and *German* (10). Why would anyone want it?

2.3 bureaucra-

Total frequency: 442

1. the handing of *accountable* democracy to an *unelected* **bureaucratic** *dictatorship*
2. determined to destroy our democracy and replace it with a **bureaucratic** *dictatorship*
3. trick them into surrendering their democracy and freedoms to the **bureaucrats** of Brussels
4. save this country's *sovereignty* and democracy from destruction by the **bureaucratic** *monster* of Brussels
5. regulated by petty **bureaucratic** *dictators*
6. a one way road to a single European state run by a **bureaucratic** *dictatorship*
7. another step on the road to **bureaucratic** *dictatorship*
8. signing away our rights and our *accountable* democracy to the **bureaucratic** *monster*

9. signing away their democratic rights to a **bureaucratic** *monster*, run by self-serving apparatchiks
10. to champion the cause of the European **bureaucrats** and those who loathe their own country

The word family *bureaucracy, bureaucratic* and *bureaucrats* are typical stigma words; they are used to disparage all kinds of adversaries working at desks. As can be seen from its frequency, it has become an imperative in Euro-sceptic polemic to call the enemy in Brussels a *bureaucrat*. While many on the continent might think *bureaucrats* and *dictators* an oxymoron, these two words frequently co-occur in this discourse (1, 2, 5, 6, 7). The continental bureaucrats are worse than their British counterparts; they have the characteristic traits of Slavonic, Bolshevik societies: *self-serving apparatchiks* (9), and in addition, they are *petty* (5).

As these bureaucrats are *unelected* (1) and therefore not *accountable* (8), the European superstate cannot be anything but a *bureaucratic monster* (4, 8, 9). Britain, on the other hand, is not a dictatorship but a *democracy* (1, 2, 3, 4, 8, 9). Therefore, the only way to explain why there are British europhiles is that they must *loathe their own country* (10).

Again, we find fairly stable collocations and set phrases indicating intertextual coherence based on the propensity of Euro-sceptic authors to borrow freely from their colleagues. There are, among our examples, four citations of *bureaucratic dictatorship* (1, 2, 6, 7) and three citations for the *bureaucratic monster* (4, 8, 9). There is *a one way road* and a *step on the road* to Europe (6, 7), and we find *signing away our rights* as well as *signing away their democratic rights* (8, 9). It is this tight network of intertextual references that is indicative of groups basing their identity on an ideological foundation not shared by their environment.

2.4 unelected; faceless

Total frequency: *unelected 170; faceless 8*

1. a centralised European "superstate" run by **unelected** and **faceless** *bureaucrats*
2. ruled by an incompetent, corrupt, **unelected** group of self-seeking shysters and *bureaucrats*
3. **unelected** and out-of-control officials who enjoy expensive lifestyles

4.   an **unelected** and an *unaccountable bureaucracy*
5.   the **unelected** people who run the EU
6.   **unelected** centralised and *unaccountable* institutions
7.   **unelected** *dictators* of the EU
8.   **unelected** bankers, *bureaucrats* and judges
9.   the **unelected** European Court of Justice
10. **unelected** group of bankers
11. **unelected** and *unaccountable* professional bankers
12. policy made by **unelected** foreigners
13. a bunch of **unelected** stooges
14. the **unelected** lunatics
15. a central budget administered by **faceless** *bureaucrats* in Brussels
16. laws passed by **unelected** '**faceless** *bureaucrats*'
17. surrendered *sovereign* powers of the Queen in Parliament to an **unelected** body in Europe

The adjective *unelected* has been promoted to an ubiquitous stigma word; whoever and whatever is *unelected* is evil. As a stigma word, *unelected* loses its proper meaning and can be applied to people and bodies that are not normally elected in Britain. Thus, we find *unelected dictators, bankers, judges* (7, 8, 10, 11), as if *dictators* were in power by public consent and as if *bankers* and *judges* were elected by general franchise in Britain. European *bureaucrats* become *shysters* (2), *stooges* (13) and even *lunatics* (14), or, generally, *unelected foreigners* (12). Here it becomes evident how the Euro-sceptic attitude is related to xenophobia. While *European institutions* are pronounced *unelected* (6), the British monarchy apparently does not invite this attribute; the *sovereign powers of the Queen* do not compare to *unelected bodies* in Europe (17).

The use of quotation marks in (1) and (16) draws our attention to the key text of the Euro-sceptic discourse, Margaret Thatcher's Bruges speech, where she referred to the European civil servants as 'faceless bureaucrats' and to the European administration as the 'super-state' (Thatcher, 1988). A tightly knit discourse like this does not easily permit its participants to introduce new ideas and to coin novel, unfamiliar expressions, if they want to meet with approbation. It is permitted, however, to bolster existing collocations, as this device can draw special attention to a new text. This is why *unelected bureaucrats* became elevated to *shysters, lunatics* and, finally, to *foreigners*.

2.5 accountable; unaccountable

Total frequency: *accountable* 146; *unaccountable* 76

1. a blueprint for the destruction of **accountable** democracy throughout Europe
2. made by people who are not democratically **accountable** at all
3. the handing of **accountable** democracy to an *unelected bureaucratic dictatorship*
4. the real power and administration rests with political and **unaccountable** appointees
5. they are *unelected* and **unaccountable**
6. the Commission is **unaccountable**, ridden with a culture of fraud
7. fraudulent practices of the EU's **unaccountable** institutions
8. this power will instead be exercised by **unaccountable** EU bankers
9. we have developed a far better system of **accountable** government than most continental nations
10. we believe that our Parliament should be directly and solely **accountable** to the British electorate

Unelected bureaucrats are *unaccountable*; these adjectives are used rather synonymously in our corpus, as we can see in (3) and (5). In a true democracy like Britain, it seems that institutions, politicians and apparently even *bankers* (8) are accountable. The antonym in deontological value, but synonym in meaning proper, to the stigma word *unaccountable* ('don't be unaccountable!') is the flag word *independent* ('be independent!'), with largely identical content; thus, *unaccountable bankers* are negative, while an *independent central bank* (see 3.4) is seen positively. Anyway, in Britain, but not on the continent, *democracy* or *democratic* and *accountability* belong together (1, 2, 3). In Europe, we find instead a *bureaucratic dictatorship* (3), a *culture of fraud* (6), *fraudulent practices* (7). The British *system of accountable government* is superior to that of *most continental nations*, because the British voting system is not proportional (see 2.12).

2.6 monster

Total frequency: 29

1. signing away our rights and our *accountable* democracy to the *bureaucratic* **monster** being constructed across the channel
2. to create a *federal* **monster** which will allow the political class to escape from *accountability*
3. to create this new *bureaucratic* **monster**
4. the **monster** striving to be born in Brussels
5. the **monster** slouching towards Brussels to be born
6. horrified by the undemocratic nature of the Brussels **monster**
7. the struggle against the tentacled **monster**
8. the suffocating embrace of this *bureaucratic* **monster**
9. the Liberal Democrats have been seduced by a **monster**
10. [to save] sovereignty and democracy from destruction by the *bureaucratic* **monster** of Brussels

It would be useful to find out in which text Brussels was first referred to by the metaphor *monster*; it could be an influential key text for other set phrases as well. We are not surprised by the epithets *bureaucratic* (1, 3, 8, 10), and *federal* (2), those being standard attributes of Brussels. The *monster* is *tentacled* (7), it *slouches towards Brussels* (5) and *strives to be born* (4, 5); but, on the other side, it is also *constructed* (1) or *created* (2, 3). It can *destroy sovereignty and democracy* (6) and is therefore *undemocratic* (6). The *monster* allows *escape from accountability* (2), and ugly as it may be, it is also *seductive* (9).

2.7 Frankfurt

Total frequency: 188

1. a Committee of *unelected* Central Bankers in **Frankfurt**
2. little reality will come from the *bureaucrats* in **Frankfurt** of Brussels
3. undemocratic institutions in Brussels and **Frankfurt**
4. politicians and *bureaucrats* whose featherbedded posts in Brussels, Frankfurt etc. are the real reason for their enthusiasm
5. a *province* governed from Brussels and **Frankfurt**
6. control over tax and spending to Brussels and **Frankfurt**

7. handing control of our economic affairs to bankers in **Frankfurt**
8. some commentators say that the City would lose out to **Frankfurt**
9. the levers of fiscal control will be operated from **Frankfurt**, not London
10. EU traders would flock to a new banking home in **Frankfurt** and our financial centre would become a ghost town
11. surrender to the European Central Bank in **Frankfurt** much of our £7 billion gold and currency reserves
12. the gold reserves which will be physically transferred to **Frankfurt** and lost forever

The place names *Brussels* and *Frankfurt* symbolise the two faces of the Euro-sceptic coin: in Brussels, the Britons will lose their democracy, and in Frankfurt, their *prosperity*. As we will see below (3.3), *prosperity* and *democracy* go hand in hand in the UK; therefore, we find *Brussels* and *Frankfurt* conjoined quite regularly (2, 3, 4, 5, 6, 7), expressing the apprehension that these values will be lost once power is handed over to these two continental towns. We are not surprised that the *Central Bankers* in Frankfurt are *unelected* (1) (what about the Bank of England?) and that they cling to their *featherbedded posts* (4). *Control* (6, 7, 9) will be handed over to *undemocratic institutions* (3). It is not only the fear that Britain will be a *province governed from Brussels and Frankfurt* (5), it is also the apprehension that the City will lose out (8) and indeed become a *ghost town* (10). Worst of all, the *gold reserves* will be *surrendered* and *physically transferred* to Frankfurt and *lost* forever (11, 12).

2.8 dictat-

Total frequency: 173

1. ruled from Brussels and dominated by a *bureaucratic* **dictatorship**
2. the *unelected* **dictators** of the EU
3. the answer is a **dictatorship** and not a democracy
4. the European Union is imposing a **dictatorship** on the people of Europe
5. the petty **dictators** of the European Commission
6. another step away from democratic *accountability* and towards **dictatorship** by an oligarchy

7. take away our traditional right to trial by jury and replace it with a **dictatorial** European Public Prosecutor with immense powers
8. the plans of a pan-European liberal elite for an *unaccountable* **dictatorship**
9. to force them to use metric measurements in accordance with the **dictates** of Brussels
10. to say no to *federalism* and *bureaucratic* **dictatorship** from Brussels

Dictates is a stigma word we already find in Margaret Thatcher's Bruges speech: 'The Community is not an end in itself. Nor is it an institutional device to be constantly modified according to the *dictates* of some abstract intellectual concept' (Thatcher, 1988, my italics). Now the *dictates* are issued by the *European Union* (4), the *European Commission* (5), the *European Public Prosecutor* (7) or just *Brussels* (9, 10). A *dictate* forces Britain to adopt the *metric system* (9). Of course, these European *dictators* are not only *petty* (5) but also *unaccountable* (6, 7) and *unelected* (2). The result is a *bureaucratic dictatorship* (1, 10).

2.9 submerge-; subsume-

Total frequency: *submerge-* 23; *subsume-* 18

1. those who wish to see our country **submerged** in a European *superstate*
2. seeing this country **submerged** into a *federal superstate*
3. we must not **submerge** our nation into the stagnant economic backwaters
4. to **submerge** our nation completely in the stagnant economic backwaters
5. all should be **submerged** beneath one flag and in one vast political superpower
6. the British people would never support the **submergence** of their country into a European *superstate*
7. to see this country **subsumed** in a *federal* European state
8. those who cannot wait to see her **subsumed** within in *federal* European state
9. not to be **subsumed** into an integrated European state
10. institutions which bind British people to each other are to be **subsumed** into a meaningless European political identity

While British sovereignty is *abandoned, abolished, ceded, destroyed, eroded* and *undermined*, to name just a few verbs (see below 3.5), Britain, British institutions and Britons themselves are, in the eyes of British Euro-sceptics, in danger of being *submerged* and *subsumed*. The uniformity of the collocations denoting the goal of *submergence* is amazing. It is the *federal* (2, 7, 8) *European superstate* (1, 2, 6), *superpower* (5), *state* (7, 8, 9). Originality is displayed by *meaningless political identity* (10; *identity* perhaps should be read as *entity*), and, of course, by the collocation *stagnant economic backwaters* (4, 5), giving evidence of how one author copies from another. This is a good example illustrating how some ideas catch on, how we can find traces of earlier texts, and how some concepts succeed in becoming more established than others. The innocent verbs *submerge* and *subsume* indicate how intertextuality works, how the homogeneity of a special discourse can be established by the recurrence of larger semantic units, units which are lexically not completely stable but which can be identified by family resemblance. The greater the evidence for intertextual features, the more important texts are for the coherence of special discourse communities such as the British Euro-sceptics. Two-thirds of all the occurrences of *submerge* and *subsume* have *Europe* as a goal.

2.10 altar; sacrifice-; worship-

Total frequency: *altar* 23; sacrifice- 101; worship- 21

1. Britain's economy is to be offered up as a **sacrifice** on the **altar** of European political union
2. must not be **sacrificed** on the **altar** of European integration
3. were some kind of ritual blood **sacrifice** on the **altar** of European integration
4. those who **worship** at the **altar** of Euro*federalism* and would **sacrifice** everything
5. British jobs and *prosperity* will be **sacrificed** on the **altar** of the European project
6. a continual **sacrifice** of British jobs to the advantage of Germany
7. who are prepared to **sacrifice** our democracy and *prosperity*
8. who would **sacrifice** everything good about this country
9. these people are prepared to **sacrifice** everything decent about our country

10. in a vain attempt to build a viable *superstate*, to **sacrifice** all that we have built over the centuries
11. our spineless politicians, who will **sacrifice** anything, rather than admit that the EU is a fraud
12. politicians will **sacrifice** anything to pay their dues to the EU club

The keywords *altar, sacrifice-* and *worship-* are evocative of a primitive pagan society, particularly when used metaphorically as in our Euro-sceptic corpus. This is evident in (3): *some kind of ritual blood sacrifice*. For joining the EU, the British have to sacrifice their *economy* (1), *jobs* (5, 6), *prosperity* (5, 7), *democracy* (7), *everything good* (8), *everything decent* (9), *all we have built over the centuries* (10), *everything* (4), *anything* (11, 12). The discourse is tied together by collocations occurring in certain variations: *sacrifice everything good about this country* (8), where *good* can be replaced by *decent* in (9). This illustrates how homogenous this discourse is. Only those texts are admitted that do not deviate from a given main line.

2.11 corrupt-

Total frequency: 326

1. the *Continental* **corrupt** men and their successors are now governing us
2. the **corrupt** model beloved by *Continental politicians*
3. politics and **corruption** in Europe seem two sides of the same coin
4. the European Parliament is itself racked with sleaze and **corruption**
5. political **corruption** is the norm in some of the EU member states
6. as seen in other countries, collectivism always leads to **corruption** and chaos
7. the equally **corrupt** Belgium
8. Helmut Kohl is in reality yet another one of those **corrupt** European politicians
9. which seeks to establish the **corrupt** practices of Italy and France as the norm
10. the only way to escape from this quagmire of **corruption** and incompetence is for the UK to withdraw
11. the only way for the UK to escape this web of **corruption** is to leave the EU

12. *accountable* democracy has the power to hold **corruption** in check

In a straightforward way, *corruption* describes the continental way of doing things, while *sleaze*, with its carnal undertones, seems to be more indicative of the English vice. There are only ten occurrences of *sleaze* in our Euro-sceptic corpus, as compared to 326 occurrences of *corrupt-*. *Corruption* is not only *the norm in some of the EU states* (5), corruption is the *model beloved by Continental politicians* (2), and indeed, on the continent, *politics and corruption seem two sides of the same coin* (3). A brief glance at the corpus singles out *Italy, France, Belgium*, and recently also Germany in the person of *Helmut Kohl* as the centres of *corruption*, together with the *European Parliament*. In Britain, there is no corruption because it is an *accountable democracy*, which Europe is not (see 2.5).

2.12 proportional

Total frequency: 44

1. a closed list system of **proportional** representation, depriving the electorate of the traditional right to vote for a particular candidate
2. proposals for **proportional** representation in General Elections, closed party-list systems, a nominated House of Lords – all these point to the elimination of political *accountability*
3. the effects of **proportional** representation and the anti-democratic nature of such systems
4. different systems of **proportional** voting are used in nearly all European countries

European (in the sense of continental) ideas threaten to infect the British model of *accountability* (2), even if it remains to be seen how *nominated* Lords are less accountable than hereditary ones. *Proportional representation* is found in most continental countries; it is (therefore?) *anti-democratic* (3), depriving *the electorate of the traditional right to vote for a particular candidate* (1).

2.13 continental

Total frequency: 567

1. hand over its own economic affairs to the *superstate* in **continental** Europe
2. a province of a new *superstate* run by **continental** bureaucrats and politicians
3. the financial profligacy of our **continental** 'friends'
4. the *corrupt* model beloved by **Continental** politicians
5. a far better system of *accountable* government than most **continental** nations
6. the closed ranks of implacable **continental** *federalism*
7. the UK's pattern of trade is global, not **continental**
8. **continental** economies are uncompetitive and inflexible
9. our system of justice is fundamentally different from those of the **Continental** countries
10. in **continental** countries 'trial by jury' is unknown
11. judges in **continental** Europe 'follow the rules'
12. the **continental** system of justice teaches subservience to a higher authority
13. **continental** interests and *values* are profoundly different from our own
14. the totally different paradigm of **continental** Europe
15. the **continental** excuse of 'I voss only followink zee orders'

The adjective *continental*, sometimes spelled with a capital *C*, embodies everything that is not British in Europe, that is, *the totally different paradigm of continental Europe* (14). In the Euro-sceptic context, the most important differences are on the political level (1, 2, 5, 6); and then also on the economic level. Perhaps economics generally plays a larger role in public British discourse than in most continental countries; or it is mostly economic issues British Euro-sceptics are concerned with. Continentals, in their eyes, have a tendency towards *financial profligacy* (3), and the *continental economies* are seen as *uncompetitive and inflexible* (8). The underlying sentiment is expressed in (7): *the UK's pattern of trade is global, not continental*, a statement echoed by many citations for *global* (see 3.10). British Euro-sceptics have strong misgivings about the judicial systems found on the continent: *our system of justice is fundamentally different* (9). *The continental system of justice teaches subservience to a higher authority* (12), probably *because judges in continental Europe follow the rules* (10). The notions of *subservience* and of *following the rules* evoke the typical German character trait expressed in (15): '*I voss only followink zee orders*'.

2.14 *fortress*

Total frequency: 18

1.   in effect a **fortress** Europe has been created
2.   the danger from the '**Fortress** Europe' mentality
3.   the resistible appeal of **fortress** Europe
4.   we regard any EU moves towards further protectionism and '**Fortress** Europe' as wholly disadvantageous
5.   it was from our island **fortress** that liberation of Europe itself was mounted

The interesting aspect of the rather infrequent *fortress* citations is that here we can observe a change in the usage of this word. The source for (5) is Thatcher's Bruges speech, and here *fortress* stands for the WWII Britain and has a distinctly positive bellicose connotation. The *Fortress Europe mentality*, on the other hand, implies *protectionism* (4), is *dangerous* (2), has *resistible appeal* (3) and is *wholly disadvantageous* (4).

2.15 *province*

Total frequency: 91

1.   transformed from an *independent* state into a **province** of the United States of Europe
2.   the 'third way' between being an *independent* nation and a **province** of the United Stated of Europe
3.   Britain will be a **province** in a German Europe
4.   if Britain wants to become a **province** governed from Brussels and *Frankfurt*
5.   ancient nation states such as France and Britain will become mere **provinces**

6. whether Britain is to be a democratic nation or a supplicant **province** of a *bureaucratic superstate*
7. to become a peripheral **province** of an economically backward single European state
8. who wish to see her a series of **provinces** within a European *federal* state
9. those whose ambition is to see her a **province** of a European *superstate*
10. to see the UK as a **province** of a *federal* Europe
11. who see it as a number of **provinces** of a *federal* European state
12. this does not imply we must accept our fate as a European **province**
13. ordinary people who are determined to prevent Britain becoming a **province** of a bureaucratic European *superstate*
14. an independent nation and a member of the world *community*, not as a **province** of a European *federal superstate*

Europhiles want to turn Britain into a *province* of a united Europe; an idea expressed 91 times in our Euro-sceptic discourse. *Province* does not occur in Margaret Thatcher's Bruges speech; instead she says: 'Britain does not dream of some cosy, isolated existence on the fringes of the European Community. Our destiny is in Europe, as part of the Community' (Thatcher, 1988). The Euro-sceptic discourse has developed, has become more pronounced and more extreme. Britain does not want to become a *province* [or a *series of provinces* (8) or *a number of provinces* (11)] of *the United States of Europe* (1, 2), of *a bureaucratic superstate* (6), of *an economically backward single European state* (7), of *a European federal state* (8), a *European superstate* (9), *a federal Europe* (10), *a federal European state* (11), a *bureaucratic European superstate* (13), *a European federal superstate* (14). Again we find a single theme being expressed in a collocation pattern united by family resemblance, giving us about as many permutations of a single theme as seems possible.

The counter image to the *European superstate* is the *world community*, not made up of *provinces* but of *independent nations* (14). In a similar vein, Margaret Thatcher evoked an *Atlantic Community*, with *Europe on both sides of the Atlantic* which she sees as a *family of nations* and not as a spiteful *federal superstate*.

3. Britain and the World

3.1 Anglo-Saxon

Total frequency: 53

1.   the United Nations was founded upon an Anglo-American (i.e. **Anglo-Saxon**) agreement. There were no European players
2.   who reject with contempt the ideals of **Anglo-Saxon** democracy
3.   **Anglo-Saxon** is now a term of abuse
4.   a liberalised and decentralised labour market that has characterised the **Anglo-Saxon** economies
5.   **Anglo-Saxon** economies with their greater flexibility
6.   as continentals might put it, our aggressively competitive **Anglo-Saxon** ways
7.   in France and Italy labour flexibility is a dirty word, synonymous with nasty **Anglo-Saxon** capitalist excesses
8.   they cannot afford Britain to succeed and prosper on this detested **Anglo-Saxon** model only twenty miles from their shores
9.   it has paid them to put up with all that dreadful **Anglo-Saxon** inequality
10. it was the **Anglo-Saxon** model which proved to be the inspiration
11. in many parts of the **Anglo-Saxon** world, especially America
12. this **Anglo-Saxon** world

There can hardly be any doubt that *Anglo-Saxon* is the focal banner word of the British Euro-sceptic discourse, a word signifying most straightforwardly what is British and what is not. And yet in many citations, we can sense a curious uneasiness about this word. It almost seems as if *Anglo-Saxon* is felt to be originally a stigma word applied by others to the British way of life and only later on adopted by the British in a defiant attitude. We find *aggressively competitive Anglo-Saxon ways* (6), *nasty Anglo-Saxon capitalist excesses* (7), *this detested Anglo-Saxon model* (8), and *that dreadful Anglo-Saxon inequality* (9). The continentals *reject with contempt the ideals of Anglo-Saxon democracy* (2). *Anglo-Saxon* seems to be a word charged with high emotions, much more than the descriptive adjective *British*. Margaret Thatcher did not use it in her Bruges speech; instead, she spoke of 'our ancestors – Celts, Saxons and Danes' and then of Britain being '"restructured" under Norman and Angevin rule'

(Thatcher, 1988). Perhaps *Anglo-Saxon*, to her ears, sounded too Germanic, and she was afraid it would make her audience oblivious of the roots the British have in common with the French. In our citations, *Anglo-Saxon* is often put into the mouth of people on the continent as *a term of abuse* (this may well be a misconception), while we are told that it is these continentals who profit from this *Anglo-Saxon* model they despise : *it has paid them* (9), and *it proved to be the inspiration* (10).

Another surprising aspect of *Anglo-Saxon* is that it is being used synonymously with 'white English speaking'. The UN is *founded on an Anglo-American (i.e. Anglo-Saxon) agreement*, and there is an *Anglo-Saxon world* apparently including America (10, 11*)*. *Anglo-Saxon* is definitely *global* (see 3.10), while *European* seems confined to Europe.

3.2 value-

Total frequency: 602

1. we believe that in an uncertain, competitive world, the nation state is a rock of stability. A nation's common heritage, culture, **values**, and outlook are a precious source of stability
2. nation states should take the most sensitive policy decisions, because they require democratic control, and democracy can work only with a nation state where people share **values**, history and cultural tradition
3. strong *communities* depend on shared **values** and a recognition of the rights and duties of citizenship
4. the peoples of Europe are too different from one another, their histories, cultures and **values** are too diverse, for them to be brought together in one state
5. British people have some considerable unease about sharing *sovereignty* with other nations whom they may like and admire but who have markedly different histories, traditions, priorities, **values** and ways of doing things
6. unlike Germany, France and Britain experienced the civilising influence of the Roman Empire [...] We share a long history and have influenced each other greatly and at bottom believe in much the same civilised **values** [...] None of the above make it necessary, or desirable, that Britain and France *submerge* their unique identities in a European *superstate*

7. British **values** such as tolerance, fair play, the notion that our home is our castle derive from the mainspring of democracy in this country, namely that government is *accountable*
8. I am born English and proud of it. I **value** the Queen, the Pound, the British Isles, British justice and the British way of life. I do not wish to be *dictated* by the Germans, French or anyone else
9. its foreign policy agreements should ... reinforce our shared **values** with the United States
10. we are inevitably a part of Europe. We are also inevitably a part of a *transatlantic* relationship, a Commonwealth relationship, an English speaking relationship and a *global* set of **values** and outlooks

In order to find out more about British *values*, it was necessary to expand the contexts of these citations. I still found only two instances where these values were listed: (7) mentions *tolerance, fair play, the notion that our home is our castle*, and (8) mentions *the Queen, the Pound, the British Isles, British justice and the British way of life. Strong communities depend on shared values* (3); therefore, a United Europe cannot work: *the peoples of Europe are too different from one another, their histories, cultures and values are too diverse* (4). Sometimes it seems as if it were British *values* against continental *values*: *sharing sovereignty with other nations who have marked different histories, traditions, priorities, values and ways of doing things* (5). We are not told how these *values* (often co-occurring with *culture* and *history*) differ. *Civilisation* seems to be an important feature which puts France and Britain into the same class (but apparently not Italy): *unlike Germany, France and Britain experienced the civilising influence of the Roman Empire ... at bottom [we] believe in much the same civilised values* (6). This citation resonates Margaret Thatcher's Bruges speech: 'We British are as much heirs to the legacy of European culture as any other nation ... For three hundred years we were part of the Roman Empire' (Thatcher, 1988) Subtle historic considerations apart, the divide seems to be between British and continental values: *I do not wish to be dictated to by the Germans, French or anyone else* (8). On the other hand, *Britain shares values with the United States* (9), giving rise to a *transatlantic community* (see 3.7, 2).

The alternative to Britain's membership in the European community is, in the Euro-sceptic discourse, her membership in the *world community* (see 3.9). Thus, we find juxtaposed those *continental values* (differing from British values) and *a global set of values* which Britain is *part of* (10).

3.3 prosperity

Total frequency: 165

1. British jobs and **prosperity** will be *sacrificed* on the *altar* of the European project
2. continued membership of the European Union will spell disaster for the **prosperity** and democracy of the United Kingdom
3. a European *superstate* which will destroy their democracy, their **prosperity** and their whole way of life
4. motivated by a genuine desire to save British democracy and **prosperity** from destruction
5. the threat this would pose to Britain's economic **prosperity** and political democracy
6. those who are prepared to *sacrifice* our democracy and **prosperity**
7. those who suffer most if their freedom and **prosperity** is surrendered to *unelected* officials in Brussels
8. the case for Britain's increased **prosperity** as a *global* trading nation is compelling

Prosperity is, in continental eyes, a somehow unexpected banner word of the British Euro-sceptic discourse: it seems to imply that the continental member states of the EU are less prosperous than Britain. However, this message is never explicit in the corpus. Instead the corpus tells us what will happen to Britain's *prosperity*: it will be *sacrificed* (1, 6), *destroyed* (3, 4), *threatened* (5), *surrendered* (7); *it spells disaster for prosperity* (2). However, an intriguing feature of these citations (1 to 7) is that *prosperity* is always conjoined with another noun: *jobs* in (1), *freedom* in (7) and *democracy* in (2 to 6). This can be an indication that the case of *prosperity* alone is not sufficiently convincing and needs augmentation. *Prosperity* is primarily used in conjunction with an invocation of the EU. But there are also citations when *prosperity* is a promise in connection with Britain's *global* role as in (8) (see also 3.10).

3.4 independen-

Total frequency: 1639

1. our **independence** is something Britain has fought many wars over

2. a vigorous defence of Britain's **independence** in matters of culture, the welfare state and taxation
3. the British **independence** of mind is one of the things we are seeking to preserve
4. we should not be afraid to stand up for our country and our right to be **independent**
5. I make no apology for believing in an **independent** Britain
6. a democratic parliamentary democracy, **independent** of the *monster* striving to be born in Brussels
7. the first thing that any country does, on gaining **independence**, is to establish its own currency
8. to give away the heart of national **independence**, our currency
9. we would merely be rejoining the family of **independent** nations
10. monetary policy must be conducted by a politically **independent** central bank

Ever since the days of Margaret Thatcher's famous Bruges speech, *independence* (like *sovereignty*, see 3.5) has been one of the focal banner words of the Euro-sceptic discourse. In the speech she said: 'My first guiding principle is this: willing and active co-operation between *independent sovereign* states. (Thatcher, 1988, my italics). The importance of the concept of independence is illustrated by its high rate of frequency: 1639 occurrences. About one-half of these citations refers to the independence of the nation state, mainly that of Britain. It is perhaps no coincidence that this figure matches the frequency of *sovereign-*: 886 occurrences.

The loss of *independence*, on the other hand, had been, a long time ago, the fate of all the other countries which are now members of the Commonwealth (see 3.6) a fate Britain fears it might suffer if the Maastricht treaty is fully implemented. Besides national *independence*, there is also the *independence of mind* (3) and the *independence in matters of culture, the welfare state and taxation* (2). Citation (6) is overdoing it a bit: a *democratic parliamentary democracy* is one of those tautologies frequently occurring in tightly knit discourses. Whoever wants to have a voice in such a discourse must keep closely to the received argumentation and can catch attention only by seeking refuge in hyperbole.

Surprising at first sight are the citations (7) and (8) which place *currency* at the core of *national independence*. But if we view them in connection with the keyword *global* (see 3.10), it becomes evident that the subtext refers to the role of the City as a global financial centre.

Citation (10) presents one of the other usages of *independent*. Here it is the Bank of England which is hailed as politically *independent*. In the case of the European Central Bank, the same concept is stigmatised as *unaccountable EU bankers* (2.5) or *unelected group of bankers* (2.4).

3.5 sovereign-

Total frequency: 886

1. in Europe the **sovereignty** of the people was being undermined
2. their desire to undermine national parliamentary **sovereignty**
3. the **sovereign** rights of the British people have been undermined
4. the illegal transfer of our independent **sovereignty**
5. in a free democratic nation, **sovereignty** is never given away
6. by law the **Sovereignty** is in the Crown and cannot be delegated
7. under our Common Law Constitution the kings were **sovereign** under God and the Law
8. **sovereignty** is about the power to choose
9. basically, **'sovereignty'** means retaining the right to govern ourselves
10. Parliament is **sovereign**; it can make any laws
11. **sovereignty** belongs to the people, not to their Government
12. What do we mean by **sovereignty**?
13. isn't **'sovereignty'** just an abstract term?
14. my forefathers fought to preserve Britain's **sovereignty** and died for it
15. our historic path as a **sovereign**, world trading nation
16. incidentally, the establishment of NATO did not infringe the **sovereignty** of its members

Sovereignty is a more elusive concept than *independence* (3.4). This becomes visible in citations (12) and (13) inviting semantic speculation. *Independent sovereignty* (4) is, in its effect, somewhat similar to *democratic parliamentary democracy* (3.4, 6). These citations show that it is not quite clear who or what is *sovereign*: in (6) and (7), it is the Crown and the kings. In (10), *Parliament* is *sovereign,* and (11) tells us that *sovereignty belongs to the people, not their government.* In Europe, we learn, *the sovereignty of the people was being undermined* (1), and the desire of those in Brussels is *to undermine national parliamentary sovereignty* (2); we also find: *the sovereign rights of the British people have been undermined* (3). The verb *undermine* evokes an image of darkness and clandestineness. *Undermining sovereignty* is one of those recurrent collocations specific to the Euro-sceptic discourse. Here is an incomplete list of other verbs co-occurring with *sovereignty* in our corpus: *abandon, abolish, cede, destroy, erode, give away, infringe, legislate away, surrender, illegally transfer*. In (15), *sovereign* precedes *world trading nation*, reminding us that Britain must preserve her *sovereignty* in order to live up to its destiny as a *truly global nation* (see 3.10, 9). In (16), *NATO* is rendered as the positive counter image to negative Europe (see also 3.8).

3.6 Commonwealth

Total frequency: 96

1. we must choose the **Commonwealth**
2. we British have our own **Commonwealth**
3. we should seek to reinforce ties of friendship and culture with all the **Commonwealth** and American peoples
4. central to this network are the **Commonwealth** and the United States of America
5. we are also inevitably a part of a transatlantic relationship, a **Commonwealth** relationship, an English speaking relationship
6. we can go on being also Atlanticist, **Commonwealth**, an English speaking nation and all the other things
7. the arguments in favour of the USA and the **Commonwealth** are much stronger than those for Continental Europe
8. we do indeed have more in common with the people of the **Commonwealth** and the USA than we have with the continental Europeans

At a time when the *continental* nations were still warring, the British already had their Empire and their *own Commonwealth* (2) and were not troubled by the European Community which they were only allowed to join after two unsuccessful applications. The *Commonwealth* is, unlike Europe, a real community tied together by *friendship* and *culture* (3), where people *have more in common than the British with the continental Europeans* (8). The *Commonwealth*, it seems, includes Australia, New Zealand and Canada, but does it also include Zimbabwe, India and Pakistan? In many citations the *Commonwealth* is conjoined with the *USA* (3 to 8), also indicating that the common bond is Western civilisation rather than multiculturalism. Margaret Thatcher in her Bruges speech equated *colonisation* with *civilising* 'much of the world', 'a tale of talent, skill and courage' (Thatcher, 1988). We are somewhat perplexed by the *American peoples* (3), which probably should not be read to include the Latin American nations. Part of the *common culture* seems to be the *English* language (5, 6), and this may well be one of *the arguments in favour of the USA and the Commonwealth* (7) (see also 3.10).

3.7 transatlantic

Total frequency: 47

1. de Gaulle famously vetoed Britain's application to be a member of the EEC on the grounds that Britain's interests were **transatlantic** rather than Eurocentric. The president was right
2. we already belong to the **transatlantic** *community*
3. the importance of the **transatlantic** relationship is unquestioned in our country
4. we are inevitably a part of Europe. We are also inevitably a part of a **transatlantic** relationship
5. but we need a **transatlantic** relationship for other reasons as well
6. the fabric of the **transatlantic** security bond
7. the danger of a **transatlantic** trade war generated by European intransigence

The obvious fact that Britons in general feel more akin to their American cousins than to the peoples on the European continent is expressed in the *transatlantic relationship* (3, 4, 5), the relationship between Britain and the USA which excludes continental Europe. Of course, Britain is *a part of Europe* (4). But the European destiny is confined by its borders: Europe is *Eurocentric* (1). Britain is, unlike the other European countries, a *global* nation (see 3.10); her *interests* are *transatlantic*. The *transatlantic community* (2) is older and more important than the *European Community*. Britain's safety rests on the *transatlantic security bond* (6) more than on the EU. As a member of the EU, Britain could easily become the victim of a *transatlantic trade war* set off by the folly of *intransigent* (7) bureaucrats in Brussels.

Just like *NATO* (see 3.8), *transatlantic* invokes a very special and undisputed partnership with the USA, the world's leading power. As a partner in the *transatlantic relationship*, Britain proves her claim that she is truly part of the *world community* (3.9).

3.8 NATO

Total frequency: 339

1. **NATO** has no *federalist* destiny
2. incidentally, the establishment of **NATO** did not infringe the *sovereignty* of its members
3. **NATO** is a good example of how nations can co-operate
4. the principal guarantor of peace in Europe has been **NATO**
5. Europe must continue to maintain a sure defence through **NATO**
6. the European Union's own defence forces undermining **NATO**
7. **NATO**, the most successful alliance the world has known
8. Britain is a member of the *Commonwealth*, **NATO**, the World Trade Organisation and G8

The citations show how NATO is juxtaposed to the EU. Where the EU fails, NATO has been successful: the most successful alliance the world has known (7), the guarantor of peace in Europe (4), and a good example of how nations can co-operate (3). Unlike the EU, it is not federalist (1), and it does not infringe the sovereignty of its members (2). This, indeed, seems to be the common British view of NATO, owing perhaps to the special transatlantic relationship between Britain and the USA (see 3.7). Euro-sceptics are afraid that this special transatlantic relationship could be in jeopardy. European defence forces would undermine NATO (6) and implicitly weaken also Britain's position based on its membership of the Commonwealth, the World Trade Organisation, G8 and NATO (8). The source for citation (5) is Margaret Thatcher's Bruges speech.

3.9 community

Total frequency: 900

1. an *independent* nation and a member of the world **community**, not a *province* of a European *federal superstate*

2. the European Union, instead of being a **community** of nation states, became a 'legal personality'
3. a sense of political **community** extending across the whole of the EU simply does not exist
4. their status as *sovereign* nations in the international **community**
5. they will instead become fully part of the world **community** of *sovereign* nation states
6. acting together in the interests of the greater world **community**
7. we already belong to the *transatlantic* **community**, ... we are an integral part of it
8. Britain's ability to defend its interests in the international **community**

We are interested only in those citations where *community* evokes the vision of a global community, while the EU is explicitly stripped of this epithet. Instead of being a *political community*, the EU is seen as a *legal personality*, nothing more than a euphemism for *bureaucratic monster*. In the Euro-sceptic discourse, the counter image of the netherworldly European Community is the paradise of the *world community* (1, 5, 6) also called the *international community* (4, 8) with the *transatlantic community* at its centre. This global *community* does not consist of *provinces* but of *sovereign* (4, 5) or *independent* (1) *nations* (1, 4) or nation state*s* (2, 5). The aim is to be a *member* (1) or *fully part* (5) or an *integral part* (7) of this *community* and to *act together* (6). The keyword *world community* is closely related to the equally positively connoted *global* (4, 10).

3.10 global

Total frequency: 581

1. however, the EU is not **global**, it is regional
2. Europe will become the marginalized victim in this competitive **global** struggle
3. we are a **global** trading and investing nation – not simply a European one
4. the UK's pattern of trade is **global**, not *continental*, and that pattern is set to continue
5. our huge trading links are truly **global**
6. the City of London is the international **global** financial centre

7.   London is Europe's leading financial centre and one of the top three **global** centres, alongside New York and Tokyo
8.   London's pre-eminence as a **global** financial centre
9.   we are truly a **global** nation
10   .our language has **global** reach

Britain's manifest destiny is her *global* role, while Europe's will never be more than merely European. This is the consummate argument brought forth by British Euro-sceptics. Britain will always be more than just a *province* of the *bureaucratic monster* in Brussels. Britain is and will remain an *independent* and *sovereign* nation state, with *transatlantic* ties, hub of the *Commonwealth* and part of the world *community*. *We are truly a global nation*, we are told in (9).

More than *international*, global *refers* to the economy. All our citations from (2) to (8) deal with trade and money. *London* is asserted as the *global financial centre* (6, 7, 8). Membership in the EU, even more so membership in Euroland, would pose a threat to this position.

Citation (10) deserves special attention. Scattered all over our corpus we find *English* being mentioned. In 3.6 (5), we read *we are part of ... an English speaking relationship*, and (6) reads *we can go on being ... an English speaking nation*. Is the EU so unattractive because it is outspokenly multilingual, because there *English* is, at least in theory, just one of many languages with equal status? Indeed, here we find one fundamental difference between the EU and the *Commonwealth*, the *transatlantic relationship* and the world community. Outside of Europe, *English* is the unrivalled *global* interlingua. This gives the *English* speaking nations an advantage which they, British Euro-sceptics may fear, would not enjoy in Europe.

4. Evaluation

4.1 The Euro-sceptics' Vision

All 25 keywords on which this analysis of the British Euro-sceptic discourse is based are indicative of long-term dispositions and attitudes: they are not connected to specific events (in the sense that the word *beef* would refer to the BSE controversy). This is why these keywords (with the exception of *superstate*) do not appear in the report *Addressing the Bias* in

Presswatch, Number 9, April 2000, issued by the European Commission's London representation and focussing on British newspaper articles dealing with specific Europe-related news items. Our keywords have been selected to convey the background on which particular news events are anchored.

At the heart of the Euro-sceptic picture, we find three entities: *Britain* as it is today torn by the choice between two options, namely, to become part either of the dystopian *Europe* or of the utopian *World community*. This Britain is, in spite of the Scottish, Welsh and Northern Irish questions, seen as a clearly defined nation state. Unpatriotic Britons, politicians not committed to British heritage, culture and values, have allowed themselves to be persuaded to renounce British independence and sovereignty and to turn the United Kingdom into a province of a European superstate.

There are certain aspects under which Britain can be seen as a part of Europe. Like some other European countries (notably France), she was civilised by the Romans; and to some extent, these countries share a common cultural heritage and, to a lesser extent, a common set of ideas. But there are other aspects where Britain differs from continental Europe. Some countries (such as Germany) have never been properly civilised, and others, like Italy and France, have disregarded important civil achievements and values that used to be shared. Corruption, fraud, bureaucracy and undemocratic decision-making is the norm not only in Brussels but also in many member states of the EU. Because the European bureaucrats are neither properly elected nor accountable to a real parliament or to an electorate, they are transforming European institutions into a dictatorship. Continental Europeans allow this to happen because they do not know better. Their political systems are not true democracies, rather they are based on proportional representation which results in unaccountable governments. This is why the continental countries are less reluctant to give up their sovereignty to the Brussels monster: the people on the continent have never enjoyed full democratic rights.

If Britain were to join Europe fully, she would have to give up her independence as a sovereign nation state, and thus, she would become just a province (or perhaps three) within the European superstate. The British would have to give up their values, their democratic system and their way of doing things. And they would have to give up their prosperity. Instead of running the City of London, the world's leading financial centre, the British would have to live a life of drudgery, while their gold reserves would be handed over to Frankfurt. The Bank of England would be surrendered to a Committee of unelected Central Bankers. Europe is a bleak place where people are taught subservience to some higher authority; unlike the British, they never enjoyed the status as sovereign citizens.

Why, then, should Britain join Europe? She has always been part of the world community of independent nation states. The British Empire colonised the undeveloped world in order to civilise it. Is the civilised world today not Anglo-Saxon; and is it not English speaking? Europe is, in comparison, a rather strange entity, neither part of the underdeveloped world nor of the English speaking or Anglo-Saxon one. What would be the point of joining such an entity? Britain is the heart of the Anglo-Saxon Commonwealth, and she enjoys a special relationship, a strong bond with her transatlantic *alter ego*, the United States. British values are shared by the world community of independent nation states. The United Nations, properly viewed, is, or at least should be Anglo-American, that is, Anglo-Saxon. In short, Britain's manifest destiny is global; together with the USA, , she is a major player in the global arena. She owes her prosperity to her global outlook.

By contrast, Europe is protectionist and confined to itself; it is self-contained, without the Anglo-Saxon entrepreneurial spirit and it lacks Britain's global aspirations. Therefore, withdrawing from Europe and rejoining the world community is the only option that makes sense for Britain. The British Euro-sceptic discourse draws a picture of an idyllic Britain, shut off from and unperturbed by continental bleakness, yet open to the global community at large, a place where tradition and modernity are reconciled by British values. This Britain is evoked in this consummate portrayal by John Redwood:

> On the Isles of Scilly [...] there is no visible police presence, yet people leave the money for the milkman by their gate and no one steals it [...] Many leave their doors unlocked and unbolted when they are out [...] Locals are at one with their past and their environment [...] The Scilly community [...] shows in a microcosm how, even in a global market place with access to the best in the world, it is possible to keep something unique, distinctive, special which everyone there values [...] The endless search for greater prosperity through the market place needs to be supplemented by some act of piety, an act of beauty, a belief in tradition, an understanding of what makes a community greater than a market place [...].
> The United Kingdom has been a most successful country [...] British armies and navies [...] have been a force for good in the world, intervening in favour of democracy and the freedom of peoples [...] It is a crowning irony that this Government and this European Union should now be uniting to destroy much

of what is the best of the Mother of Parliaments. (Redwood, 1999, pp. 187, 193)

4.2 The Historical Dimension

The media could not have been so successful in disseminating a general Euro-sceptic bias spreading beyond the Euro-sceptic community proper if it had not hit a long-established pattern of British self-awareness. That Albion's mission is to give the world a model of common sense, civilisation and a decent way of life has been the tacit understanding of the men who built the Empire. This must not necessarily be expressed at surface level. There are times when polite rhetorical embellishments are appropriate, for example, when Margaret Thatcher, in her Bruges speech, paid tribute to a common European heritage: 'But we know that without the European legacy of political ideas we could not have achieved as much as we did. From classical and medieval thought we have borrowed that concept of the rule of law which marks out a civilised society from barbarism' (Thatcher, 1988). But even here, she does not forget to address Britain's unique position in Europe. Britain succeeded where the continent failed: 'Over the centuries we have fought to prevent Europe from falling under the dominance of a single power. We have fought and we have died for her freedom' (Thatcher, 1988).

We can assume that Margaret Thatcher would subscribe to John Buchan's understanding of Britain's world role, which sets her apart from the rest of the world, at least the world that is not Anglo-Saxon. One of Buchan's protagonists, the elusive Sandy, says in *The Three Hostages*: 'Lord, how I loathe our new manners in foreign policy. The old English way was to regard all foreigners as slightly childish and rather idiotic and ourselves as the only grown-ups in a kindergarten world. That meant we had a cool detached view and did even-handed unsympathetic justice' (Buchan 1992 [1924], p. 712).

This understanding is not restricted to those who built the Empire. Britain today may not be the global power she used to be, but she maintains her influence by playing Greece to America's impersonation of Rome in a new global alliance. This is the basic message of Robert Conquest's new *Reflections on a Ravaged Century* (1999). In his critical review of this book, Michael Ignatieff, well known for his Atlanticist view, sums up Conquest's views: 'America and Britain belong together at the heart of an alliance of English-speaking democracies. Only in "English-speaking countries", he argues, has a genuinely democratic culture taken root.

Elsewhere, in Europe, democracy was a frail plant: "It took hold, flickered, faded, failed ... " Liberty, he [Conquest] believes, is an "Anglo-Celtic invention [...]". Britain and the United States, he argues, have more in common with each other than either have with continental Europe [...]. In Conquest's view, South Africa, India and democratic Nigeria share more with Canada, the US and Britain than they do with African and American neighbours with political cultures of non-English origin [...]. Conquest is vague about what form this "association" should take. It should, he says, be "weaker than a federation, but stronger than an alliance." [...] All this sounds like the Commonwealth plus the United States, and seems harmless enough' (Ignatieff, 2000, p. 36).

Conquest's reply to this review reads like the very essence of British Euro-scepticism. He views the EU not only as anti-American but also as 'divisive of European civilisation', 'an (immensely corrupt) bureaucratic and regulationist nightmare; as contrary to the law-and-liberty tradition; and fatally, as missing any real sense of how the feeling of citizenship arises [...]' (Conquest, 2000, p. 61). It is perhaps not irrelevant that Conquest has spent a substantial part of his academic life at the Princeton Institute of Advanced Studies and has his own close ties to the U.S. But views like his are deeply rooted in the last two hundred years of British attempts to define their identity in relation to the continent. While until the late 18th century it had been the enlightened rationality of the Church of England versus the authoritarian papacy in Catholic Europe, it then became the tyranny of the French Revolution and Napoleon's despotism set against the British rule of law, against the acknowledgement of private property and against freedom from state intervention. As Michael Ignatieff sums up this widespread view: 'In Britain – and in America – society created and controlled the state. In continental Europe, the state created and controlled both society and nation'.

The British ideal of property, freedom and democracy is mirrored in the British conception of the ideal landscape, as it was formulated in 1810 by Uvedale Price, who explored the relationship between society and the picturesque: 'A good landscape is that in which all the parts are free and unconstrained, but in which, though some are prominent and highly illuminated, and others in shade and retirement, some rough, and others more smooth and polished, yet they are all necessary to the beauty, energy, effect, and harmony of the whole. I do not see how good government can be more exactly defined'. Ann Bermingham comments: 'Against the levelling tendencies of the French Revolution, individual variety in the landscape came to stand for British liberty, a freedom presumably for the rich to be rich and the poor to be poor' (Both quotes: Bermingham, 1994, p. 85).

This, then, is the real divide between the continental countries and Britain: On the continent but not in Britain, we find, ever since the French Revolution emancipation of the underprivileged and the principle of equality were, generally accepted moral objectives of state intervention. A strong state was considered necessary to achieve these goals. People may have dissented on the best ways leading there. But they agreed that a just society was one where there was at least an equality of opportunities and that the state had the responsibility to promote this ideal. In Britain, on the other side, the primary *raison d'être* of government was seen in the protection of private property, or, in the words of John Locke: 'The great and *chief end*, therefore, of men's uniting into Commonwealths, and putting themselves under government, *is the preservation of their Property* [...]' (Locke 1689/1982, p. 75 [§124]). The British concept of freedom first of all means freedom from state interference. Thus, the British and the continental models of the state are irreconcilable.

In this historical perspective, the reality construed in the British Euro-sceptic discourse is far from implausible; rather it appears backed by factual evidence. Until the Second World War, Britain was a world empire, and ever since she has been the closest ally of the strongest remaining global power. There are still British territories in many parts of the world, and Britain has demonstrated that she is still powerful enough in the remotest parts of the globe. Without Britain, the First World War might easily have been won by the axis powers, and the Second World War might have ended with the subjugation of continental Europe under Nazi rule. Only an independent Britain, outside of the EU, can work towards an equilibrium of political forces on the continent and, thus, prevent Europe from falling under German domination. Only an independent Britain can keep Britain from drifting away from NATO, the singularly successful transatlantic bulwark of Western civilisation.

This Western civilisation has become overwhelmingly Anglo-American, and it is, today, largely synonymous with global culture. The world reads English books, watches English movies and TV productions, browses the predominantly English internet and uses English as global interlingua, in politics, in sports, in the arts and in science. Other languages have their place in folklore and in academia, while English is the language everyone wants to learn. Only on the continent there are still pockets of resistance. The EU has taken on the old role of the Eurocentric Catholic Church and, to some extent, even that of the Socialist Internationale, continuing a tradition of dogmatism, ideology and secretive bureaucracy irreconcilable with the British way of life. It is this historical dimension that makes British Euro-sceptic discourse so convincing.

4.3 Media and Politics

A large part of the Free Britain Corpus consists of texts first published in newspapers. Indeed, the British Euro-sceptic discourse can best be observed in newspaper texts. They are easily accessible, and unlike radio and TV contributions, they do not have to be transcribed. Books, like John Redwood's *The Death of Britain* (1999), are momentary events; their impact on the discourse can only be studied in the textual traces they leave in later texts. It is the steady flow of newspaper texts that give continuity to a discourse. Collecting the texts of the Free Britain Corpus corpus from Euro-sceptic websites was the most economical way of accessing these texts in electronic form. Relying solely on these websites, the Free Britain corpus is not representative of the British press. In this investigation it is not possible to determine how Euro-sceptic the British press in general is.

In their analysis of *The British Press and European Integration: 1948 to 1996* (1998), George Wilkes and Dominic Wring show that the present Euro-sceptic discourse is associated more with *The Times*, *The Daily Telegraph*, *The Sun* and *The Daily Mail* than with *The Guardian*, *The Independent* or *The Daily Mirror*. Still it seems that nowhere in the British press can we find a pro-European discourse of similar weight and continuity. At the same time, the Euro-sceptic tendencies seem to be growing. In the April 2000 issue of *Presswatch*, we read in the editorial: 'Seldom has [British] press coverage been so distorted [...] Much of the British press, fuelled by the claims and counter claims of embryonic domestic political campaigns, continues to obscure the substantive issues by sensationalising the trivial and presenting ill-informed opinion as a fact'. This has not always been the case. For the sixties and seventies George Wilkes and Dominique Wring even detected a 'pro-Community bias in the press' (1998, p. 195). What made things change?

Besides many other reasons, one of the determining factors may well be that the British newspapers which are now more outspokenly Euro-sceptic have changed ownership. They are now owned by Rupert Murdoch, an Australian turned American, and by Conrad Black, a Canadian with interests in the US media. Both are known for their Atlanticist agenda and their misgivings about a fully integrated Europe with its own agenda. Indeed, there is evidence that the radical stance of the Euro-sceptic discourse was never fully shared by British politicians, not even by a large majority in the Conservative Party. In 1996, only 32% of Tory MPs did not believe that the 'disadvantages of EC membership have been outweighed by the benefits' (Ludlum, 1998, p. 39).

But even though neither politicians nor industry share the sentiments of the Euro-sceptic agenda fully, they may still find it advantageous if the discourse audience puts the blame for negative developments in Britain on Europe. This would explain why there is no support for any kind of pro-European counter-discourse. But it is also perhaps the case that in our age the power of the media has become so strong that it has taken over the design space that, in former times, was the realm of politicians. A pro-European discourse balancing the impact of the British Euro-sceptic discourse could only exist if there were a similar density and continuity of widely accessible texts and if there were media publishing them.

4.4 The Impact of Homogeneous Discourses

The Free Britain Corpus is not representative of British attitudes towards Europe. It is representative of the Euro-sceptic discourse (of which it is a segment) only in as far as the texts were selected for inclusion by those who are responsible for the Euro-sceptic websites that we searched. Texts do not have attitudes. Attitudes are a human trait. We cannot even be sure that the writers of these texts believe in what they write. The attitudes of a text audience are even more difficult to determine.

What ties this corpus together? It is the small set of constantly repeated arguments, the relative small number of topics recurring in subtle thematic variations, the homogeneity and closedness of this discourse which strike us as something specific. Why does this discourse give us this impression?

One reason, of course, is that only those citations were selected that seem to epitomise (my understanding of) British Euro-scepticism. Randomly selected citations could have presented a greater diversity, not so much of arguments perhaps, but certainly of topics. The keywords we analysed display quite different senses and usages. More than 95% of occurrences of *community* in our corpus deal with the European Community, the financial, local and many other kinds of communities, while I was interested only in the small remainder where *community* collocates with *transatlantic, world* or *global*. In this keyword-based analysis, I tried to capture not the individual topics addressed by the texts but the background noise common to all of them.

This background noise consists of the verbal traces earlier texts leave in later ones. A discourse is ideologically homogeneous if it contains a common set of explicit and implicit references which can be traced to the same set of more or less canonical texts (exemplified by Margaret Thatcher's famous Bruges speech). Authors wanting their own texts to be relevant and referred to in subsequent texts will make sure that they use the same arguments, the same metaphors, the same epithets so that they will be accepted as contributions to the discourse.

The problem with tightly defined ideological discourses is that they easily become sterile. The texts cease to transmit ideas: their function is to be a part of a reassuring ritual, like a prayer in a church service. John Redwood's *The Death of Britain* contains no ideas that have not been expressed time and again before. Its purpose is to unite the community of Euro-sceptics and to qualify him as one of its speakers. He succeeds if his text resonates the background noise Euro-sceptics expect and if the thematic variations he comes up with are more radical than those of his predecessors. But for those who do not define themselves primarily as Euro-sceptics, such texts are not interesting. Even within the small Euro-sceptic community, it becomes harder to catch the audience's attention once the design space for what can be said diminishes. Success rests in finding a new variation, a new radicalisation of the familiar. Thus, in an article in *The Sun* of January 10, 2000, entitled *Never mind the Euro, the problem is Europe*, we find the hybrid *federasts* instead of the familiar *federalists*. This is a smart pun. But constant hyperbole, as well, can make people grow wary.

The less pluralistic, the less polyphonic, the more homogeneous the British Euro-sceptic discourse evolves, the less seriously it will be taken. An argument repeated a hundred times has lost its strength. In the long run, the distorted reality construed in these texts will be rendered implausible by contravening evidence, that is, by texts not belonging to the Euro-sceptic discourse. The better informed an audience is, the less they will take Euro-sceptic exaggerations at face value.

However, there is one other aspect. In our age of media domination, it seems that our views are less based on personal experience and autonomous thinking than increasingly on reports and comments in newspapers, on the radio and TV. This is particularly the case if no alternative views are presented that offer a choice to the audience. In view of the stunning absence of positive reports on the issue of European integration in newspapers formerly Euro-friendly, such as *The Guardian* and *The Independent*, Euro-scepticism can become the only attitude sanctioned by public consensus. The media's influence on our attitudes can only be contained as long as the media contribute to a pluralism of views. Once this pluralism vanishes, the public will increasingly be exposed to mind control.

4.5 Euro-scepticism: a British Phenomenon?

Discourse analysis cannot show how deeply rooted Euro-scepticism is in the British public. How shocked are people by reports of corruption in European institutions if they are, at the same time, inundated by daily disclosures of sleaze in their own government? How convinced are the British by stories about the impenetrable strangeness of continental ways of life if they are well acquainted with them by personal experience? How do they themselves measure their prosperity? How do they feel unfairly coerced by metrification? How does British membership in an Anglo-Saxon world community affect their personal lives?

What makes the British situation unique compared with other EU countries is that in Britain Euro-scepticism has become a ritual. This makes it easier to identify a Euro-sceptic discourse in Britain than in the other member states. In Germany, for instance, we find almost a reverse situation. In all appropriate situations, official speakers will express full German commitment to European integration while in reality the German administration is often slower and more hesitant to adopt European regulations than the British. The German media incessantly tell their audiences that people must prepare themselves to work more for less money and not to rely on welfare any more, otherwise the German economy will lose out against its European competitors. Statements to this effect do not foster a positive attitude towards Europe.

At the same time, the German media criticise European institutions heavily for their growth of bureaucracy and for the absence of democratic control in the decision-making process. Indeed, all pledges to European integration are complemented by complaints that Brussels increasingly violates German interests. The German discourse on Europe is ambivalent. It is in favour of European integration on the terms dictated by the German economy. It is highly critical of the European Commission if they interfere with subsidising German industry or German agribusiness. The discourse we find in the German media does not advocate the growth of democracy, freedom and equality in a united Europe.

Perhaps we should read the reticence in the German discourse on beneficial aspects of European integration in conjunction with the Euroscepticism of the larger part of the British media as the writing on the wall that something has gone wrong over the last two or perhaps even three decades. Was there not a time when there was a common dream of a Europe where the confinements of the old nation states would give way to an enlightened compact of free citizens? Many shared a view of Europe as the cradle of civil liberties and human rights, first defined prominently in the long struggle in which the British Parliament emancipated itself from the crown, then appropriated by the European peoples in a long sequence of revolutionary conflicts and civil wars and finally victorious with the defeat of Nazism and the collapse of socialist despotism. In the sixties and seventies, a vision emerged of a Europe free of nationalism, where national governments are protecting the rights of free citizens rather than building up increasingly sophisticated surveillance systems. It was a vision of a Europe where all citizens were encouraged to engage in a polyphonic, pluralistic and multicultural dialogue, across language barriers, to propagate the best of their traditions, values and ideas. This vision has disappeared. Fear has done away with openness. Today the Fortress Europe is frightened by the onslaught of the rest of the world. The Europe envisaged many years ago was open to share its ways of life with the rest of the world and to learn from other cultures and civilisations. It fought against the Iron Curtain and for the free traffic not only of goods but also of people and ideas. It was the vision of a multicultural and multilingual Europe, where administrative borderlines had become untimely. This vision was expressed in progressive rhetoric, in a discourse perhaps almost as vigorous as the Euro-sceptic discourse today. This discourse has not vanished altogether. It still manifests itself in many encounters of intellectuals all over Europe, in the growing European dimension of academic life and in a few low circulation publications such as *Le Monde diplomatique*, *Lettre Internationale* and *The Times Literary Supplement*. Today, it is only the discourse of a small privileged elite. Perhaps it is time again to make it more democratic.

References

Bermingham, A. (1994), 'System, Order and Abstraction: The Politics of English Landscape Drawing around 1795', in W.J.T. Mitchell (ed.), *Landscape and Power*, University of Chicago Press, Chicago and London:, pp. 77–102.

Buchan, J. (1992[1924]), 'The Three Hostages', in J. Buchan, *The Complete Richard Hannay*, Penguin, London, pp. 657–928.

Conquest, R. (1999), *Reflections on a Ravaged Century*, W.W. Norton and Company, Inc., New York and London.

Conquest, R. (2000), 'Letter to the Editor', *The New York Review 8*, p. 61.

Hermanns, F. (1994), 'Schlüssel-, Schlag- und Fahnenwörter. Zur Begrifflichkeit und Theorie der lexikalischen Semantik', *Arbeiten aus dem Sonderforschungsbereich 245: Sprache und Situation*, Heidelberg/Mannheim. Bericht Nr. 81.

Ignatieff, M. (2000), 'The Man Who Was Right', *The New York Review 5*, pp. 35–37.

Ignatieff, M. (2000), 'Reply', *The New York Review 8*, p. 61.

Locke, J. (1982[1689]), *Second Treatise of Government*, (ed. by Richard Cox), Harlan Davidson, Arlington Heights, Ill.

Ludlum, S. (1998), 'The Cauldron: Conservative Parliamentarians and European Integration', in D. Baker and D. Seawright (eds), *Britain For and Against Europe. British Politics and the Question of European Integration*, Clarendon Press, Oxford, pp. 31-56.

Musolff, A. (1996), 'False Friends Borrowing the Right Words?', in A. Musolff, Ch. Schäffner and M. Townson, (eds), *Conceiving of Europe. Diversity in Unity*, Dartmouth, Aldershot.

PressWatch 9 (2000), European Commission, London (www.cec.org.uk).

Redwood, J. (1999), *The Death of Britain? The UK's Constitutional Crisis*, Macmillan Press, London.

Thatcher, M. (1988), *Britain and Europe*. Text of the speech delivered in Bruges by the Rt. Hon. Mrs. Margaret Thatcher, OM, FRS, on the 20th September 1988 (www.eurocritic.demon.co.uk/mtbruges).

Wilkes, G./Wring, D. (1998), 'The British Press and European Integration: 1948 – 1996', in D. Baker and D. Seawright (eds), *Britain For and Against Europe. British Politics and the Question of European Integration*, Clarendon Press, Oxford, pp. 185–206.

PART II: GERMAN DISCOURSE ON EUROPE

4　Words, Phrases and Argumentational Structures in the German Debate on Europe in the Early Post-War Period

HEIDRUN KÄMPER

Introduction

'Habt ihr Sehnsucht nach Europen? Vor euch liegt es in den Tropen; denn Europa ist Begriff'. [Do you long for Europe? It is all around you in the tropics; for Europe is of the mind.] (Klemperer, 1987, p. 169).[1] These are the words with which Victor Klemperer attempted to comfort those of his friends who, having emigrated, found themselves filled with nostalgia for the Europe they had left behind them. By 'Europe is of the mind' he meant to say Europe is more than just the name of a particular geographical area, it is an idea. An idea we could also call the occident or the West. For the distinction is no longer made between the originally more religious concept of the occident and the more secular one of Europe. Europe and the occident, European and occidental are almost always used as synonyms of one another, although it should be noted that unlike occident, Europe is also the name of a set of political ideas with a long tradition.

The idea of community has underpinned these ideas since the seventeenth century finding expression, for instance, in the phrase '*europäisches Gleichgewicht*' ['European balance of power']. The notion of a balance is entirely compatible with the idea of a leading power and in German eyes, Germany has played precisely this role of leader since the late seventeenth century - a role legitimised by the incontrovertible argument that Germany is at the geographical heart of Europe. In 1670 Leibniz reasoned that 'the Roman Empire is a country sufficient unto itself, which has only to desire its happiness for it to come about. Europe is the body, Germany the heart of Europe'.[2] In this sense, Germany determined the condition of Europe as a whole. If it were to regain its status as a 'civil entity, clearly delineated', then 'Europe as a whole would return to peaceful ways, its internal discourse would cease' (Brunner, vol. V, 1984, p. 473).[3] In this way, 'Germany would blossom again and equilibrium return to Europe' (Brunner, vol. II, 1975, p. 969).[4]

Novalis took up Leibniz's ideas again in the sense that they involve the cultural dominance of Germany:

> Deutschland geht einen langsamen aber sicheren Gang vor den übrigen europäischen Ländern voraus [...] der Deutsche [bildet sich] mit allem Fleiß zum Genossen einer höheren Epoche der Cultur, und dieser Vorschritt muß ihm ein großes Uebergewicht über die Andere[n] im Lauf der Zeit geben. (Novalis, 1983, p. 519)
> [Slowly but surely Germany proceeds ahead of the other European countries. The sheer application of the German enables him to achieve a higher level of civilisation and through this greater elevation generally to gain dominance over the others.]

In 1801 an unknown author opined that 'peace and security in Germany served at the same time to ensure these conditions in a large part of Europe' (Brunner, vol. V, 1984, p. 481).[5]

The idea of a German leadership sees its apotheosis after the wars of liberation when the argument appeared concerning God's chosen people:

> [...] dieses Volk [ist] von Gott dazu ausersehen [...], der Führer und Vorkämpfer Europas auf der Bahn echt christlicher Bildung zu werden und die Geschichte des ganzen Erdteils in sich selbst vorzubilden. (Brunner, vol. I, 1972, p. 793)
> [[...]this people is predestined by God to be the leaders, to be the vanguard of Europe in its progress towards a truly Christian education and to prefigure in itself the history of the whole hemisphere.]

The legacy of these radical nationalistic ideas was embraced as we now know by the ideology of National Socialism. One phrase will serve to illustrate this in the 1942 edition of what has become known as the 'brown' Meyer, Meyer being a popular German encyclopaedia and the epithet 'brown' referring to the National Socialist bias in the work. The entry under '*Reich*' informs the reader of the 'schicksalhafte Sendungsaufgabe der Deutschen in Europa' ['divine destiny of the Germans in Europe'].

As well as informing the concept of a European balance under German leadership, the idea of community appears from the early years of the eighteenth century onwards in various federalist constructs. A few fixed expressions will serve to illustrate the phases in this process. In 1732,

Johann Jacob Moser laid 'the foundation for the study of the current constitution in Europe' (Brunner, vol. VII, 1992, pp. 119, 120).[6] In 1800 Gentz spoke of the 'natural federal constitution of Europe' (Brunner, vol. I, 1972, p. 639).[7] In 1814 K. C. Krause presented the draft for a European Federation of States. In his 1821 piece entitled *Der Europäische Bund* [The European Federation] Conrad Friedrich von Schmidt-Phiseldeck used alongside of one another expressions such as the *Federal Association of European Peoples, European Federation, European Federal State, European Confederation, European Bund, European Union* (Schumacher, 1976, p. 187).[8] In 1832 Wirth exhorted those taking part in the Hambacher festival with the words: 'Dreimal hoch das konföderierte republikanische Europa!'.['Three cheers for the Republican European Confederation'] (Brunner, vol. V, 1984, p. 628). Friedrich Nietzsche prophesied that: 'Die wirtschaftliche Einigung Europas kommt mit Notwendigkeit'. ['the economic unification of Europe is bound to come about'] (Schlechta, vol. 3, 1960, p. 660) and in his *Jenseits von Gut und Böse* [Beyond Good and Evil] of 1885 he discerned 'signs of Europe's desire to become one' (ibid, vol. 2, p. 724).[9] Finally in 1923 Coudenhove-Kalergi developed the idea of the 'Vereinigten Staaten von Europa' ['United States of Europe'].

No changes in the developments we are describing seem to have been brought about by the hiatus between 1933 and 1945. 'European unity' continued to be the common aim behind many political projects, however differently the concept may have been elaborated. Party political allegiance appeared to be irrelevant in this respect. Europe developed:

> zu einem zentralen politischen Programm und schließlich zu einer Realität, die zunehmend die internationale Politik und den Alltag des einzelnen bestimmt. (Jung/Wengeler, 1995, p. 93)
> [a central political platform and in due course a reality which increasingly determines both international politics and the everyday life of the individual]

Integration of Europe, a phrase already in use in 1943 for instance by Alfred Weber, before Schumacher used it in 1948, became a key political principle. It was variously represented in expressions which had been established usage since the eighteenth century, such as *federation*[10], *bund*[11], *unity*[12], *unification*[13], *United States of Europe*[14] and finally '*community*'[15] which Jung and Wengeler (ibid, p.105) described as a 'willkommene Kompromißbegriff' ['useful compromise expression'] and the aim of the community was to promote economic activity, the 'economic unity of Europe' (Adenauer speech 21/09/1949).[16] Here we get a sense of the

German self-confidence that resulted, at least in part, from the permanent stereotype of Germany as lying at the heart of Europe, in the middle of Europe, as being the heart of Europe. From the German point of view, the logic of the economic reintegration of Europe necessarily involved the proposition 'without Germany, no Europe'. This idea had been expounded by Alfred Weber already in 1943, less forcefully perhaps, but nevertheless quite clearly:

> [für] die produktionswirtschaftliche Integration Europas, das Abhängen der Prosperität des einen Teils vom anderen [...] [ist] das in der Mitte liegende Deutschland, seine große Bevölkerung und Produktivkraft ein unentbehrlicher Teil. [...]Ohne deutsche Lieferkraft und Kaufkraft keine gesunde volle Lieferfähigkeit und Kaufkraft der anderen Teile von Europa, der rings umliegenden, aus ökonomischen und klimatischen Notwendigkeiten wirtschaftlich mit ihm integrierten Gebiete und Bevölkerungen. (Weber, 1946, p. 246)
>
> [[for] the economic integration of Europe and the interdependence of the prosperity of its parts, the central position of Germany in Europe, its huge population and the level of its productive output, are indispensable. Without Germany and without German output and without its buying power, there can be no strong supply or buying power in the other parts of Europe, of those peoples and regions which surround Germany and which are closely integrated with her economically by virtue of climatic conditions and modes of production.]

Kurt Schumacher used the economic potential of the industrial Ruhr area of Germany to put forward the argument for Europe as follows:

> Das Ruhrgebiet ist [...] das stärkste industrielle Kraftzentrum Europas. Und mit und durch das Ruhrgebiet hat ja auch in früheren besseren Zeiten Europa allein leben können. Wir Sozialdemokraten erkennen ausdrücklich an, daß die wirtschaftlichen Kräfte des Ruhrgebietes zur Wiedergutmachung der Zerstörung Europas herangezogen werden müssen [...]. So wie Europa das Ruhrgebiet braucht, so braucht Deutschland als ein Teil Europas die Mitbeteiligung an diesem Ruhrgebiet. (Schumacher, 9.5.1946)
>
> [The Ruhr is the strongest industrial centre in Europe and it was by and through the Ruhr that Europe could remain autonomous in the past. As Social Democrats we state unequivocally that the economic strength of the Ruhr must be harnessed in the task in making good the destruction wrought in Europe. Just as Europe needs the Ruhr, so Germany as a part of Europe, needs to be closely involved in the development of this area.]

In the pan-European perspective, we may instance the 1948 essay by the economist Ernst Brödner, entitled 'Europe and the German Future' the argument was made that Germany was best kept in check by integration. Brödner writes:

> Sicherheit gibt es nur, wenn Deutschlands Industrie ein Teil der europäischen ist. Nur die engste wirtschaftliche Verflechtung durch Arbeitsteilung ist eine wirksame Kontrolle gegen heimliche Wiederaufrüstung und eine Sicherheit, daß europäische Bruderkriege in Zukunft ausgeschlossen sind. (Brödner, S. 429).
>
> [There will only be security if German industry is part of European industry. Only close economic co-operation in the form of shared production will be an efficient brake on secret rearmament and will ensure that in future there will be no more civil wars in Europe.]

So far we have shown that the political, pragmatic, idea of Europe was taken up again after 1945 in the context of the desired restructuring of Europe.

Expressions in European Discourse and their Political Contexts

Most of the concepts of Europe of the early post-war years are deeply rooted in the history of European thought. Thus in texts from this period there is a plethora of references to a European cultural community and a community of values. Political ideas are elaborated which urgently invoke Germany's western tradition, often in a more or less formulaic form. We encounter 'the spiritual and moral values and principles of European culture' (Das demokratische Deutschland, 1945, p. 9):[17] 'the central Christian western values' (Programmentwurf der CDU, 17/06/1945);[18] 'European consciousness [...] western culture [...] preservation of western culture' (Mayer, 1947, p. 232);[19] 'the spirit of the West' (Weber, 1946, p. 221);[20] 'for the sake of the spiritual values and the culture of the West' (Adenauer speech, 24/03/1946);[21] 'the mind of western man' (Künneth, 1947, p. 66);[22] 'the western culture of Christianity' (ibid, p. 254);[23] 'all western values and societal structures which came down to us from the Greeks, the Romans and the Jews, were refashioned by the Germanic tribes' (Niekisch, 1953, p. 266).[24]

Germany and the Germans were given clear prominence as a part of this western history as inheritors of the occidental values and the appearance, for instance, of the possessive pronoun in extracts such as the following:

[das] Grundgesetz unseres Werdens .. heißt: Abendland, Einheit der Romanen, Germanen und Slawen, vor allem aber der Romanen und Germanen im Zeichen von Antike und Christentum. (Dirks, 1990, pp. 192)
[The underlying factors shaping our development are the occident and the unity of the Germanic, Gallic and Slav tribes. Above all of the Gallic and Germanic peoples in the context of the classical period on the one hand, and Christianity on the other.]

Ursprung unserer abendländischen Kultur [sind] die jonischen Griechen, die Männer der Stoa, Cicero. (Röpke, 1947, p. 12)
[The origins of our western culture lie with the Ionian Greeks, the Stoics, Cicero.]

Quellen unserer europäischen Kultur, die aus dem Christentum entspringen. (Adenauer speech, 21/9/1949).
[The wellsprings of our European culture which are fed by Christianity.]

These concepts were clearly influenced by the political conditions of the early post-war period. Post-war Germany was rooted in the experience of liberation from without, National Socialism defeated by the Allies, a war lost by Germany, the lack of a sovereign state, German guilt. No other society had to examine its immediate past, present and future as intensely as German society after 1945. No other society had the opportunity of choosing a new way forward so clearly based on a critique of the immediate past:

Während alle übrigen europäischen Völker [...] ein festes, bestimmtes Verhältnis zu der Wirklichkeit haben, in die sie gestellt sind [...], sind die Deutschen ein Volk der Möglichkeiten, nicht der Tatsachen. (Kogon, 1946,. p.414)
[Whilst all the other European peoples have a clear unambiguous relationship to the reality surrounding them, Germany is a nation of possibilities, not facts.]

One of the possible reasons adduced by Kogon in 1946 for Germany's lack of direction after the war, was the palpable rejection of National Socialism. This had been ordained by the victors, occupiers and liberators. For the moment, Germany was excluded from Europe, indeed, from the world. The Germans stood accused in the eyes of the world, challenged by the Allies to prove the sincerity of what they were saying. These conditions determined post-war reality in Germany, including the German language and therefore also the way in which such key terms as Europe and the West were used:

'Das Abendland'. Das Wort ist, formal gesehen, eine gute Parole: es ist mit Wert und Sinn gesättigt, zugleich aber anschaulich und konkret, man kann es seelisch, man kann es geistig, man kann es politisch nehmen. [...] Der Begriff entspricht offenbar einem geistigen Bedürfnis, er scheint als Antwort auf eine oft gestellte Frage empfunden zu werden. [...] Wie sind wir dahin gekommen, wo wir jetzt stehen? [...] Und wenn wir das zu wissen glauben: wie kommen wir wieder heraus, zurück zu einer echten Ordnung, zu Sinn und Wert? (Dirks, 1990, pp. 192)

[The West'. From a formal point of view, the word is a useful slogan, profoundly meaningful yet solid: it can be taken spiritually or intellectually or politically [...] The concept clearly meets an intellectual need. It seems to be regarded as the answer to a frequent question: How did we get to where we are now? [...] and if we think that we can answer that: How do we find our way out and back to order, to a set of meaningful values?]

This was Walter Dirks' observation on the European discourse of the early post-war period.

The challenge then to 'show you mean what you say' is the subject of the following discussion. The post-war years were characterised in this sense by the instrumentalisation of ideas of Europe in support of certain lines of argumentation.

Argumentational Structures in European Discourse and their Temporal References

The task then was to adduce plausible arguments and to demonstrate the credibility of stated aims. It is in this context that Europe began to be used differently in the early years in the sense that it was made to function as an argument in favour of reintegration. Europe and the West represented a kind of collective super argument at the time. Both terms are components of what Klein has called 'kollektive Argumentationen' ['collective arguments'] (Klein, 1985, p. 217). Toulmin described the main function of argumentational structures as being to justify assertions (Toulmin, 1975, p. 18). The assertion, or in other words, the claim, of the Germans after 1945 could be summed up as follows: 'The Germans stand in the main tradition of western Humanism'. The claim is a reaction, a response, to the difficulty raised by the rest of the world, the Allies, victors and liberators. The problem briefly is 'All the Germans are Nazis, have become culpable, have foregone any claims to integration in the community of nations'.

The quality of arguments may be judged by their acceptability, which is in turn predicated on what is considered to be true, incontrovertible, at the very least, plausible. So, arguments may be more or less acceptable according to how far they fulfil these three conditions.

The most common collective arguments in the political discourse of the early post-war years were therefore, like any arguments, attempts to establish the plausibility of given aims. What the Germans had to do was to use a given positive component of the collective consciousness, here Germany's place in the European cultural community, to transform the collectively problematical, the accusation of moral deprivation, into another collectively acceptable state of affairs, Germany's reintegration into the family of nations. See Klein (1985, p. 213) for the terminology used here such as the concept of 'collective'.

Two temporal frames of reference both encountered frequently in early post war texts bear upon the basic claim asserted in the idea of integration - they are the past and the future. On the one hand the past is explained and assessed, National Socialism and its causes are repeatedly explicated and evaluated. On the other, a version of the future is projected, social and political reconstruction are called into being through a language which declares that which is desirable to be in existence already. Concepts of Europe are introduced into the argumentational structures in a variety of ways. We need to establish the agents in this process and the identity of the participants in the European debate in early post-war Germany. These include not only politicians but also cultural commentators, intellectuals, philosophers, theologians, an intellectual elite, therefore a heterogeneous group holding very different views as to how the recent past might be explained and with different ideas about the future shape of German society. The reflections of this intellectual elite on past and future, centred on a number of key ideas including Europe, or the West. These two concepts are tokens of the very many expressions for an idea which had informed political discourse since the beginning of the modern period, appearing as an ideal, a structural principle and a guide to possible action. Two factors were common to all of the variants of this basic idea, community and unity. The following discussion aims to describe the process whereby concepts of Europe were instrumentalised in a variety of ways according both to the different philosophical outlooks of those taking part in the discourse and to the relationship of the argument in question to the past or the future. Arguments dealing with the causes of historical phenomena draw on the past, those attempting the task of laying these phenomena to rest are future orientated.

Arguments Concerning Causes

When the aim was to identify the causes of a line of development which culminated in National Socialism, historical processes from European or western history were adduced:

> Wir stehen mit der Katastrophe, die wir durchlebt haben und noch durchleben, für jeden, der etwas Blick hat, deutlich am Ende der bisherigen Art der Geschichte, der Geschichte nämlich, die wesentlich vom Abendland her bestimmt war. (Weber, 1946, p. 10)
> [To those with any insight, it must be clear that the cataclysmic period we have experienced and are still going through heralds the end of history as we have known it up until now. A history in other words which was fundamentally shaped by the West.]

Alfred Weber wrote this during the war in 1943, his End of History - *Abschied von der bisherigen Geschichte* - appeared in 1946. Weber claimed to have identified a caesura brought about primarily by scientific discoveries and technological innovations which interrupted the progress of western history and took control of 'unsere abendländischen Masen' ['the western masses'] (ibid, p. 233). Historically this upheaval was reflected in western thought in the form of nihilism, the final formative stage in the progress toward National Socialism:

> Nie wäre es zu diesem [heutigen] Nullpunkt gekommen, wäre nicht seit etwa 1880 [...] jene dem bisherigen Geist des Abendlandes entgegengesetzte Welle in die Höhe gekommen, jene Absage an die frühere Tiefe des Abendlandes, dessen angeblich den Nihilismus überwindender, in Wahrheit vornehmster nihilistischer Höhepunkt der späte Popular-Nietzsche wurde, - jenes in Wahrheit Antigeistige, das sich neben der vornehmen Libertinage des Geistigen und jener brutalen Libertinage der Macht in den immer höhere Wellen schlagenden Naturalismen, in jenen Imperialismen und Nationalismen austobte. (ibid, p. 221)
> [We would never have arrived at our nadir if we had not been gradually overtaken since 1880 by nihilism. Nihilism is a mode of thought profoundly inimical to the western values that had held sway until then. It involved a rejection of our most profoundly held principles. The movement brought forth the popularised figure of the late Nietzsche allegedly overcoming nihilism but in fact representing its most distinguished nihilistic apostle. Nihilism united those anti-intellectual forces which,

taking their place alongside an intellectual abandonment of values and the exercise of violence in the name of uncontrolled freedom, ran their violent course in various ever more alarming naturalistic artistic representations, or inspired imperialist and nationalistic enterprises.]

Nihilism came to be the dominant force 'in people's conduct of their everyday affairs' (ibid, p. 12).[25] Although it was undoubtedly founded by the German Nietzsche, it came to be regarded as a European, western phenomenon. It was 'the underlying cause of the historical cataclysm which we Westerners and the Europeans in particular brought upon the rest of the world' (ibid).[26]

One conclusion which emerges from this way of thinking, had it that it was not, to quote Karl Jaspers, the Germans 'who were responsible for committing the most dreadful atrocities, but Europeans' (Jaspers, 1986, p. 264).[27]

Theological historians such as Künneth, declared these developments to be occidental and European rather than German. Thus in his 'Theological History of the Encounter Between National Socialism and Christianity' published in 1947 under the title 'The Fall' (*Der grosse Abfall*), Künneth similarly set about reconstructing historical movement whose inner logic had led inevitably to National Socialism. He wrote: 'The disaster and the fall of the Titans suddenly illuminated not only the situation of the West as a whole, but of mankind itself' (Künneth, 1947, p. 91).[28] He argued that the 'National Socialist catastrophe' was a symptom of the deterioration of modern western society:

> Unter diesem notwendigen geschichtstheologischen Aspekt wird der enge Rahmen des deutschen Schicksals im mitteleuropäischen Raum gesprengt und damit klar, daß der katastrophale Sturz nicht bloß eine Angelegenheit des deutschen Menschen, sondern ein Weltereignis darstellt, daß hier an einem Teil der Menschheit prinzipiell die Sache aller Völker zur Debatte steht. (ibid, p. 15)
>
> [From the point of view of theology the limited question of the fate of Germany in Central Europe must be abandoned in view of the fact that the catastrophe concerns not merely the Germans, but the whole world, and that although it may appear that only part of mankind is directly affected, the fate of all peoples is in fact at issue.]

From the theological point of view, the onset of the modern period signified a movement away from Christianity common to the whole of the West. Künneth's description of the pathology of the world ran as follows:

Der abendländische Mensch hatte seit langem die Mitte seines Lebens verloren und seine Seele war darüber krank geworden. Diese geheime moderne Weltkrankheit hatte das geistige Dasein aller Völker mehr oder weniger stark vergiftet, sie ballte sich aber im Herzen Europas zusammen und kam im nationalsozialistischen Denken und Wollen zum gewaltsamen Ausbruch. (ibid, p. 66)

[Western man, having lost the core of his being a long time ago, his soul had become sick. As a result of this hidden but ubiquitous modern affliction, the spiritual well-being of all the peoples had become poisoned. This poison was at its most potent in the heart of Europe and finally found violent expression in National Socialist thought and actions.]

Like Alfred Weber, Künneth set out to reconstruct historical tendencies beyond national - perhaps we should read this as German - boundaries, in an attempt as it were, to internationalise the National Socialist phenomenon: 'There is no doubt that this sickness of the western soul could have broken-out elsewhere, possibly differently. The symptoms of the abnormal conditions were in evidence everywhere' (ibid).[29] By internationalising the National Socialist phenomenon in this way, Künneth was able to reject the charge of an ethnically based collective German guilt: 'Grounding the attempt to establish the guilt of the German people for this disaster on the basis that Germans had been worse or more godless than other peoples, betrays a simplistic understanding of history' (ibid).[30] At the same time as he acknowledged a German guilt, he denied that it was amenable to explanation of itself:

Daß die latente Krankheit sich gerade hier in so furchtbarer Eruption offenbarte, ist geschichtstheologisch beurteilt, nicht in einem 'mehr' an Schuld begründet, sondern trägt die Qualität einer jenseits unserer Kategorien liegenden Schicksalsetzung, vor der die Warumfrage verstummen muß. (ibid)
[From the theological historical point of view, the fact that a latent illness could erupt so dreadfully at this place at this point in history cannot be explained by positing a greater degree of guilt. It was a blow of fate, the reasons for which lie beyond human understanding, closed to the question of why.]

This response amounts to an extraordinary refusal to identify causal relationships between National Socialism and particular - possibly German - conditions. The response offered the theologian a scheme of denial. Equating the empirical question with the question of ultimate causes, removed it from possible explanation.

The construction of historical tendencies in the way we have described above, consisting typically of nihilism combined with the rejection of God, invoked the notion of a European destiny leading necessarily to National Socialism, the inevitable endpoint of European history. Under this interpretation, National Socialism is not a German phenomenon, its causes lie rather in the course of western history. This interpretative scheme runs through texts of the early post-war years. The fundamental idea is one of European destiny. This appears in a host of variations, such as 'Geflecht des europäischen Schicksals' ['the destinies of all the European peoples are interwoven'] (Dirks, 1990, p. 195), 'abendländische Tragödie; abendländische Krise' ['western tragedy; the crisis of the West'] (ibid, p. 198), 'dieser unserer geistigen Krise Europas' ['this material and spiritual crisis of our Europe'] (ibid, p. 194); 'europäische Schicksalsgemeinschaft' ['common European destiny'] (Kaiser speech, 16/06/1946); 'Aus dem Europa der letzten Jahrhunderte ist das Verhängnis der gegenwärtigen Weltlage erwachsen' ['the present plight of the world stems from centuries of European development'.] (Jaspers, 1986, p. 262); 'das katastrophale Schicksal, das über die Mitte Europas hereingebrochen ist' ['the catastrophic fate which befell Central Europe'] (Künneth, 1947, p. 9).

Such stereotyped formulations are not solely German. In his famous 'speech of hope' of 6 September 1946, the American Foreign Minister Byrnes used expressions which were translated as 'Germany and Europe's recovery from illness' (Hohlfeld, p. 132).[31] But in written originals in German these phrases seemed to assume a legitimising function. Europe was used as an argument to relativise Germany's guilt. Germany's desire for integration was anticipated linguistically as the precondition for the emergence of National Socialism. A shift of values and the rejection of God and the intellectual decline of Germany were projected onto the whole of the European continent, a wider community of values and culture. The destiny of Germany was identified with that of Europe, the German crisis was identified as a European crisis and in this way via exculpation, Germany established its right to a place in the family of nations. In this way of thinking, the idea of a collective German guilt - subscribed to above all by the Americans - was rejected as unacceptable as the idea that guilt might relate to one country; a possibility articulated as follows by the American Foreign Minister Byrnes in his Stuttgart speech: 'der deutsche Militarismus und der Nazismus [haben] die Gebiete von Deutschlands Nachbarn verwüstet' ['German militarism and Nazism have laid waste the lands of Germany's neighbours'] (Hohlfeld, p. 132).

Europe, or the West, played a key role in early arguments that took the past as a frame of reference. In the context of attempts to internationalise the National Socialist phenomenon, Europe functioned as a key argument in establishing the German claim to reintegration by facilitating the obfuscation, indeed the denial, of the German origins of Fascism and its particular extreme German form. German guilt was relativised and glossed over by means of its Europeanisation. This strategy, incidentally, was not limited to the immediate post-war years. In 1954, six years after Künneth and Weber, a piece appeared by Joachim Moras entitled 'The Middle of Europe'. In it Moras reflected on 'typically German matters' recommending the use of a 'European lens' for any such consideration:

> [...]damit ein plastisches, ein stereoskopisches Bild des Ganzen entstünde - demgegenüber sich dann plötzlich die Frage aufdrängen würde: was ist an alledem ausschließlich deutsches, was allgemeines Symptom dieser Zeit? (Moras, 1954, p. 445)
> [[...] so that a three-dimensional stereoscopic view of the whole be achieved. In this setting an inevitable question would suddenly present itself: what is exclusively German about all of this? What should be regarded as generally symptomatic of the period?']

Almost ten years after the end of the National Socialist era in other words, a way of thinking persisted which involved the Europeanisation of German history.

The argumentational structures we have described so far were, of course, not the only ones which were current. Those critical of events rejected the internationalisation of recent German or Austrian history, preferring a national version which might be instrumentalised for party political purposes. Interpretative schemes were advanced which supported particular socio-political programmes. The position taken by the KPD (Communist Party of Germany), and Kurt Schumacher may be cited as relevant examples. In such cases, notions of Europe were as irrelevant as ideas of decline.

In the modern version of history, arguments like those of Weber and Künneth according to which western civilisations were in their late dying stages, took the place of the typical nineteenth and twentieth century accounts which had seen in the West the highest level of human development. Oswald Spenglers' 'Decline of the West' with its notion of a 'Faustian culture' exemplified this theory of decline.

Arguments which Lay Problems to Rest

Never before had a nation had the kind of opportunity to determine its future course of development such as that given to German society after 1945. We have observed so far that a historical version of Europe which allowed recent German history to be relativised served to internationalise the intellectual movements which led to National Socialism. In European constructs fashioned to account for future developments, we can discern two techniques of legitimisation, the one intellectual, the other programmatic.

The first of these involved elaborating abstract possibilities by mobilising arguments based on historical legacy, cultural community, and shared values. Depending on the philosophy of those concerned, these arguments were couched in theological, philosophical or - if they served political ends - conservative terms.

Having described the structure of the SS-State in four hundred pages, Eugen Kogon called on the Germans to fulfil their true destiny:

> [...] ist es nicht besser, die größte Niederlage seiner [des deutschen Volkes] Geschichte zum Anlaß zu nehmen, um in die eigenen verschütteten Tiefen hinabzusteigen, wo das Gold der hohen deutschen Qualitäten - jawohl: das Gold! begraben liegt, den geschichtlichen und gesamtseelischen Wurzeln der Schuld nachzuspüren und nach Generationen der Geduld gewandelt zur Erfüllung der wahren deutschen Aufgabe in Europa und der Welt, zur Leistung des Beitrags, der seinem gereinigten Wesen entspricht, hervorzutreten? (Kogon, 1946, p. 408)
> [[...] is it not better to use the greatest defeat ever of our people as a reason to descend again into depths which have too long concealed the gold of true German qualities: there we may uncover the historical and spiritual roots of our guilt and then, in due time, re-emerge cleansed and purified to fulfil the true task allotted to the Germans in Europe and the world and make our fitting contribution?]

The theologian, Walter Künneth, was to continue to apply the logic of this interpretation by demanding - once he had construed National Socialism as a western fall from grace - a European return to belief in God: 'die Wendung zur Heimkehr zu Gott, das heißt aber die Rückkehr zur Offenbarungswirklichkeit Gottes in Jesus Christus' ['the return to God is no less than a return to the God revealed in the real Jesus Christ'.] (Künneth, 1947, p. 308). He received support in this from Romano Guardini: 'Europa wird christlich, oder es wird überhaupt nicht mehr sein'

['Europe will either become Christian, or it will simply cease to exist'] (ibid).

The European tradition ended for Karl Jaspers in the final - entirely depoliticised - consequence of the human condition:

> Auch Europa ist nicht das letzte für uns. Wir werden Europäer unter der Bedingung, daß wir eigentlich Menschen werden - das heißt Menschen aus der Tiefe des Ursprungs und des Zieles, welche beide in Gott liegen. (Jaspers, 1986, p. 274).
>
> [Nor is Europe the end for us. In becoming Europeans we become true human beings whose true origins and ultimate goal are in God.]

In the same way, Alfred Weber construed freedom and democracy as historically grounded goals for a future Europe:

> Europa und insbesondere seine deutsche Mitte hat sich .. auf einer die Menschenwürde und Menschlichkeit vertretenden freien demokratischen Basis zu organisieren, sobald man ihm die freie Bewegung dazu läßt. (Weber, 1946, p. 251).
>
> [Europe especially its German centre, must be built on free democratic foundations which represent true humanity and human dignity as soon as it is given the leeway for this to happen.]

Such utterances suggest that the contention of Jung and Wengeler that historical philosophical ideas ceased to exert influence after 1945, is mistaken. Indeed the arguments embedding German in European history continued to play a key role in the debate about the future of Germany. Such arguments were adduced not only by theologian and philosophers, but also by party politicians of a conservative persuasion.

The philosophical and intellectual tradition was assimilated into the conservative party political programme which used Europe and the Christian West as synonyms of one another. Five weeks after the end of the war, the authors of the draft CDU programme invoked Germany's erstwhile greatness which it further described as 'the Christian western values which once held sway among the German people who therefore were held in high regard by the other European nations'. (Programmentwurf der CDU, 17/06/1945).[32]

Konrad Adenauer was convinced that Europe could only become a reality:

[...] wenn eine Gemeinschaft der europäischen Völker wiederhergestellt wird, in der jedes Volk seinen unersetzlichen, unvertretbaren Beitrag zur europäischen Wirtschaft und Kultur, zum abendländischen Denken, Dichten und Gestalten liefert. (Adenauer speech, 24/03/1946)

[[...]if a community of all the other peoples of Europe were recreated, which would allow each nation to make its essential and unique contribution to European culture and commerce and to bring its influence to bear on western literature, thought and the plastic arts.]

And even Jacob Kaiser, the Christian Democrat's declaration to the delegates attending the 1946 CDU Party Conference that 'true democrats are the best Europeans' (Kaiser speech, 16/06/1946)[33] made the connection with the western tradition through his inclusion of the highly positive but usefully vague term 'democracy'. The aim of conservative policies in the post-war period was absolute separation from the communist eastern bloc, an aim served by the construct of a western, Christian Europe.

The liberal version of Europe also subscribed to the same philosophical tradition which we have described. The idea was developed of a relationship between the liberal and the wider western history, indeed they were seen as one and the same tradition. Liberals sought to remove the implications of National Socialist propaganda by redefining liberalism:

[...] in dem ganz breiten und allgemeinen Sinne einer Idee, die im Grunde das Wesen abendländischer Kultur schlechthin ausmacht.[...] In [diesem] Sinne sind wir alle Liberale, soweit wir die uns unersetzlich scheinenden Werte und Einrichtungen gegen jene zerstörenden Kräfte verteidigen, die wir als Kollektivismus, Totalitarismus oder Nationalsozialismus bezeichnen können. [...] Der Liberalismus ist [...] ein machtvoller Stamm, der ein ehrwürdiges Alter aufweist und unter dessen Laubdach wir uns alle heute in dem sicheren Gefühl zusammenfinden, daß wir etwas Gemeinsames zu verteidigen haben, mögen wir uns sonst auch Konservative oder Sozialisten, Demokraten oder Liberale, Protestanten oder Katholiken nennen. (Röpke, 1947, p. 11)

[Liberalism forms] in its most general sense the very bedrock of western civilisation in so far as we defend what we consider to be crucial values and institutions against the destructive forces known as collectivism, totalitarianism or National Socialism. We are all liberals, liberalism is an ancient and mighty tree in whose shade we come together united by our common feeling that we have something to defend together, whatever we may call ourselves - conservative or socialist, democrat or pacifist, Protestant or catholic.]

The liberal world view - reviled by the Nazis as liberalist - was therefore reinterpreted and inherent from the beginning in European culture. In this way, the non-partisan Wilhelm Röpke who was later to become an adviser to the Adenauer government, prepared the foundation on which liberal ideas could be established across party political lines.

Socialists and social democrats politicised their version of Europe so that it could serve as a legitimating function in their own programmatic designs. Whilst they too had recourse to the western history argument, they used it to argue the necessity for particular, quite concrete political measures. In 1945 a phrase appeared which linked 'western democrats and socialists' (Das demokratische Deutschland, 1945, p. 21)[34] and which clearly indicated the sense of their political programmes. Variants of this formulation appeared constantly in the socialist version of society.

In the first issue of the *Frankfurter Hefte* sharp distinctions were drawn not only between socialist Europe on the one hand and Russian bolshevism and a gargantuan American fascism on the other, but between the former and Germany itself, with talk of 'the creation of a new Europe, united in socialism [...] not Russian bolshevism or American fascism, but Europe, not Germany but Europe' (*Frankfurter Hefte* 1/1946).[35]

Walter Dirks one of the editors of the *Frankfurter Hefte* produced a piece entitled 'Socialism and the West' in which he - having interpreted National Socialism as the result of a departure from the western tradition - urged the necessity of re-engaging with the European western legacy, albeit now with a certain critical caution. He described the results of this rediscovery as follows: 'The West will be socialist or it will cease to be. If Europe divides into 'West' and 'socialism', it will collapse' (Dirks, 1990, p. 201).[36] Dirks saw 'socialism as the enterprise which could bring about the painful recovery of the West, the attempt to breathe new life into the legacy of Europe and thus make it viable once more' (ibid, p. 200).[37]

This version of events was rooted in the concept of a European destiny - a key formula in the discourse we have described as using the past - which reveals clearly the inner logic of the argumentation. Projections for the future involved Europe, not Germany. At the same time the European argument served to render the socialistic view of the desirable society acceptable. There is a clear attempt to give socialism a human face, to make it seem familiar by adding some western traits as it were:

> Abendland und Sozialismus müssen einander durchdringen. In einer sozialistischen Ordnung muß sich die abendländische Grundsubstanz die aktuelle, realistische, faktische, moderne Gestalt geben und zugleich das gute Gewissen im Sinn der sozialen Gerechtigkeit wiedergewinnen, das nicht in der Sehnsucht nach dem intakten Abendland (dem mittelalterlichen 'Ordo'

vor dem bürgerlich-kapitalistischen Sündenfall) zu suchen und zu finden ist, sondern nur durch den opfervollen Umbau der modernen Wirtschaft und Gesellschaft wiedererrungen werden kann. Anderseits muß der Sozialismus in der positiven kritischen Aneignung unseres abendländischen Erbes geistige und menschliche Fülle, Maß und Demut suchen und finden. (ibid, p. 201)
[Socialism and the West must inter-penetrate one another. In a socialist order the basic socialist values must take on a modern realistic form. At the same time socialism must rediscover its true sense of social justice, which lies not in some innocent intact version of the West but will be recreated only through selfless devotion to the reconstruction of the economic and social structure here and now. At the same time however, socialism must espouse moderation and humility, must seek to create conditions which will allow all citizens to achieve human and intellectual fulfilment.]

Finally we may turn to Kurt Schumacher who said the following on the subject of the contemporary European debate: 'The debate on Europe is in reality the search for life's deeper meaning after a period of senseless stasis' (Schumacher speech, 29/06/1947).[38] For Schumacher this 'deeper meaning' was in fact a 'united Germany in a socialist Europe' (Schumacher speech, 'Aufgaben und Ziele der deutschen Sozialdemokratie'):

Wir wissen, worum es in Deutschland geht: das ist der gerechte soziale Ausgleich, der sozialistische Neubau der Wirtschaft, der Aufbau der Demokratie und die Erhaltung des deutschen Reiches in einem internationalen europäischen Rahmen. (Schumacher speech, 27/01/1946)
[We know what is at issue in Germany, social justice through a fairer distribution of resources, the socialist reconstruction of the economy, the creation of true democracy and the preservation of the German Empire in an international European framework.]

Schumacher seeks legitimisation of a socialist Europe in the connection between socialism and the West in the form of a surprising causal relationship: 'The West is not dead because socialism and democracy are alive' (Schumacher speech, 29/06/1947).[39]

This is reminiscent in the way that the European idea was updated through the attribution of Christian and western which amounted to a kind of linguistic appropriation, something vehemently rejected by Kurt Schumacher on the grounds that it constituted an exclusive claim to the Christian past of Europe on the part of the Christian Democratic Union. But Schumacher's projection of the coming shape of Europe actually equated the western tradition with a socialist societal order. Schumacher's invocation of the 'western idea' turned out to be based every bit as much on the preservation of conservative values as the philosophy of his opponent Adenauer.

Conclusion

Our findings may be summarised thus: the connotations we associate with the key terms Europe and the West, spell security and order. They are the linguistic expressions of inestimable qualities in an era when people are typically confused, desperate, haunted by apocalyptic fears. The frequency of such references in the early post-war years documents the mental condition of a whole generation. Political circumstances forced the Germans to establish that their desires for re-integration are legitimate. Herein lies the attempt to recover 'a lost unity and security in the idea of the western tradition' (Dirks, 1990, p. 193). This idea is instrumentalised as a political argument after 1945. Such instrumentalisation is part of the history of German political discourse and the German mentality in the early post-war years. Distinguishing between past and future orientations has enabled us to identify two opposite, indeed contradictory attitudes.

The former are explications, that is they seek to explain the way that recent historical developments led to National Socialism. The arguments which follow logically from this explanatory scheme are supported by the notion of the decline of the West, which necessarily culminated in National Socialism. The version of the West is stigmatised as one of death and decay. Concepts in the language of the future orientated schemes of explanation express wishes rather than actuality, serving to give linguistic expression to, and therefore at the same time, be constitutive of, a desired future form of society. This desired state of affairs is based on an argument containing a highly positive version of Europe. The argumentational strategy is based on the arguments of the cultural unity and the community of values which underpin the western tradition.

Various versions of Europe in the early post-war years are revealed as the linguistic documents of an albeit instrumentalised and selective historical consciousness which attempts to correct people's real experience of what they are actually experiencing. This puts a question mark against the idea of a loss of German identity post-1945. The German identity seems indeed not to be lost, the Germans seem to be in no doubt about who they are.

Notes

1   All translations for this chapter have been produced by the editors of this volume. References given in the text refer to original German sources. Unless indicated otherwise all original German quotations are provided in subsequent endnotes.

2   'Das Römische Reich ist ein Land, so vor sich selbst bestehet und in deßen Macht ist, glückselig zu seyn, wenn es will [...]. Das Reich ist das Haupt-Glied, Teutschland das mittel von Europa'.

3   Erhalte es wieder 'eine civil person und Form', werde 'ganz Europa [...] sich zur Ruhe begeben, in sich selbst zu wüten aufhören'.

4   So werde 'Teutschland in sein flor, Europa in die balance [...] wieder kommen'.

5   '[...] durch Deutschlands Ruhe und Sicherheit wird immer die von einem großen Teil Europens zugleich mitgesichert'.

6   'Anfangsgründe von der Wissenschaft von der heutigen Staatsverfassung von Europa'.

7   'natürliche Föderativverfassung von Europa'.

8   'Föderalvereinigung der europäischen Völkerschaften, Europäische Föderation, Europäischer Bundesstaat, Europäische Konföderation, Europäischer Bund, Europäische Union'.

9   Anzeichen, 'in denen sich ausspricht, daß Europa eins werden will'.

10   'The federation of European states', Das demokratische Deutschland, 1945, p. 5.

11   'The desirable European Federation', (ibid, p. 15); 'our moral contribution to thisfederation should be the fact that there is no longer a German state' (Brödner, 1948, p. 429; 'a really viable European federation' (Adenauer, 21/09/1949).

12   European unity (Frankfurter Hefte 1/1946).

13   'In the process of European unification' (Brödner, 1948, p. 429).

14   'The will to create the United States of Europe ... the willingness to cooperate closely in a European community, born out of a healthy, cleansed self-confidence' (Kaiser, 16/06/1946); 'A new Germany would regard being part of the United States of Europe as its highest responsibility'' (Schumacher, Aufgaben und Ziele der deutschen Sozialdemokratie); 'the United States of Europe' (Adenauer, 21/09/1949).

15   'The community of European nations' (Adenauer, 24/03/1946); 'the will to create a European community' (ibid).

16   'wirtschaftliche Einheit Europas'.

17   'geistige und sittliche Werte und Güter der europäischen Kultur'.

18   'die christlichen und abendländischen Lebenswerte'.

19   'europäische[s] Bewußtsein [...] abendländische Kultur [...] Rettung der abend-ländischen Kultur'.

20   'Geist des Abendlandes'.

21   'um der geistigen Werte, um der Kultur des Abendlandes willen'.

22   'abendländische[s] Seelentum'.

23   'die abendländische Kultur der Christenheit'.

24   'alle abendländischen Werte und menschlichen Grundordnungen[...], welche Hellas, Rom, Judäa überliefert haben und die das Germanentum mitgeschaffen haben'.

25   'für die Alltags- und die allgemeine Aufgabenorientierung weitgehend herrschende[..] Nihilismus'.

26 'die tiefere Ursache [...] für den katastrophalen geschichtlichen Zusammenbruch [...], den wir Abendländer, insbesondere wir Europäer, über die Welt gebracht haben'.

27 'Europäer haben sich der größten Schandtaten schuldig gemacht'.

28 'Die nationalsozialistische Katastrophe und der Titanensturz haben blitzartig die gesamte abendländische Situation, ja zuletzt die Lage der Menschheit beleuchtet'.

29 'Fraglos hätte dieses Durchbrechen der Krankheit des abendländischen Seelentums auch an anderer Stelle und in anderer Weise erfolgen können, denn die Symptome dieses anormalen Zustandes sind überall in Erscheinung getreten'.

30 'Es zeugt daher von großer Oberflächlichkeit und mangelndem geistesgeschichtlichen Verständnis, wenn man die Schuld des deutschen Volkes an dieser Katastrophe mit dem Urteil begründen zu können meint, das deutsche Volk sei schlechter, sei gottloser als andere Völker gewesen'.

31 'Gesundung Deutschlands und Europas'.

32 'die christlichen und abendländischen Lebenswerte, die einst das deutsche Volk beherrschten und es groß und angesehen machten unter den Völkern Europas'.

33 'die echten Demokraten[...]sind [...]die besten Europäer'.

34 'abendländische Demokraten und Sozialisten'.

35 'ein neu zu bildendes Europa in einer sozialistischen Ordnung zusammengefaßt [...] nicht russischen Bolschewismus oder amerikanischen Mammutfaschismus, sondern Europa, nicht Deutschland, sondern Europa'.

36 'Das Abendland wird sozialistisch sein, oder es wird nicht sein. Zerfällt Europa in das "Abendland" und in den "Sozialismus", so zerfällt es in sich selbst'.

37 'Sozialismus [...][ist] die Aufgabe [...] an der das Abendland unter Schmerzen gesunden kann [...] das europäische Erbe in gewandelter Form neu lebensfähig zu machen'.

38 'Die Diskussion über Europa ist doch in Wahrheit das Suchen nach einer Sinngebung des Lebens, nachdem wir jetzt eine Periode sinnlosen Vegetierens durchgemacht haben'.

39 'Das Abendland ist nicht tot. Denn Sozialismus und Demokratie leben'.

References

Adenauer Speech of 24/3/1946 at the University of Cologne, in P. Bucher (ed.), (1990), *Nachkriegsdeutschland 1945-1949*, Wissenschaftliche Buchgesellschaft, Darmstadt. pp. 138-165.

Adenauer Speech of 21/09/1949 (1997), in *Akten zur Auswärtigen Politik der Bundesrepublik Deutschland 1949/50*, R. Oldenbourg, Munich, pp. 3-6.

Brödner, E. (1948), 'Europa und die deutsche Zukunft', in P. Bucher, (1990), *Nachkriegsdeutschland 1945-1949*, Wissenschaftliche Buchgesellschaft, Darmstadt, pp. 427-436.

Brunner, O., Conze, W. und Koselleck, R. (eds) (vol. I: 1972; vol. II: 1975; vol. V: 1984; vol. VII: 1992), *Geschichtliche Grundbegriffe. Historisches Lexikon zur politisch-sozialen Sprache in Deutschland*, Klett-Cotta, Stuttgart.

Das demokratische Deutschland. Grundsätze und Richtlinien für den deutschen Wiederaufbau im demokratischen, republikanischen, föderalistischen und genossenschaftlichen Sinne (1945), Hauptvorstand der Arbeitsgemeinschaft 'Das demokratische Deutschland' (eds), Paul Haupt, Bern/Leipzig.

Dirks, W., 'Das Abendland und der Sozialismus' in P. Bucher (ed.), (1990), *Nachkriegsdeutschland 1945-1949*, Wissenschaftliche Buchgesellschaft, Darmstadt, pp. 192-201.

Frankfurter Hefte 1/1946.

Hohlfeld, K. (ed.), *Deutschland nach dem Zusammenbruch 1945. Urkunden und Aktenstücke zur Neuordnung von Staat und Verwaltung sowie Kultur, Wirtschaft und Recht*, Dokumenten-Verlag Dr. Herbert Wendler and Co., Berlin/Munich.

Jaspers, K. (1986), 'Europa der Gegenwart', in K. Jaspers, *Erneuerung der Universität. Reden und Schriften 1945/46*, Lambert Schneider, Heidelberg, pp. 243-274.

Jung, M. and Wengeler, M. (1995), 'Nation Europa und Europa der Nationen. Sprachliche Kontroversen in der Europapolitik' in G. Stötzel and M. Wengeler, *Kontroverse Begriffe. Geschichte des öffentlichen Sprachgebrauchs in der Bundesrepublik Deutschland*, de Gruyter, Berlin/New York, pp. 93-128

Kaiser Speech of 16/06/1946 at the CDU Party Conference, in P. Bucher (ed.), (1990), *Nachkriegsdeutschland 1945-1949*, Wissenschaftliche Buchgesellschaft, Darmstadt, pp. 179-191.

Klein, W. (1985), 'Argumentationsanalyse. Ein Begriffsrahmen und ein Beispiel' in J. Kopperschmidt and H. Schanze (eds), *Argumente - Argumentation. Interdisziplinäre Problemzugänge*, Fink, Munich.

Klemperer, V. (1987), *LTI. Notizbuch eines Philologen*, Röderberg, Cologne.

Kogon, E. (1995 [1946]), *Der SS-Staat. Das System der deutschen Konzentrationslager*, Wilhelm Heyne, Munich.

Künneth, W. (1947), *Der große Abfall. Eine geschichtstheologische Untersuchung der Begegnung zwischen Nationalsozialismus und Christentum*, Wittig, Hamburg.

Loth, W. (1990), *Der Weg nach Europa. Geschichte der europäischen Integration*, Göttingen.

Mayer, Hans, Speech at the deutsche Schriftstellerkongress, 4-8 October 1947, in U. Reinhold, D. Schlenstedt and H. Tanneberger (eds), (1998), *Erster deutscher Schriftstellerkongreß 4.-8. Oktober 1947*, Aufbau Verlag, Berlin, pp. 230-232.

Moras, J. (1954), 'Die Mitte Europas', in J. Moras and H. Paeschke (eds), *Deutscher Geist zwischen Gestern und Morgen. Bilanz der kulturellen Entwicklung seit 1945*, Deutsche Verlagsanstalt, Stuttgart, pp. 441-449.

Niekisch, E. (1953), *Das Reich der niederen Dämonen*, Rowohlt, Hamburg.

Novalis, 'Christenheit oder Europa' in P. Kluckhorn and R. Samuel (1983), *Novalis Schriften. Die Werke Friedrich von Hardenbergs*, Vol. III, Kohlhammer, Stuttgart/Berlin/Cologne/Mainz.

Programmentwurf der CDU vom 17/06/1945, in P. Bucher (ed.), (1990), *Nachkriegsdeutschland 1945-1949*, Wissenschaftliche Buchgesellschaft, Darmstadt, pp. 27-30.

Röpke, W. (1947), *Das Kulturideal des Liberalismus*. Schulte-Bulmke, Frankfurt/M.

Schlechta, K. (1960), *Friedrich Nietzsche, Werke in drei Bänden*, Hanser, Munich.

Schumacher Speech of 27/1/1946, in P. Bucher (ed.), (1990), *Nachkriegsdeutschland 1945-1949*, Wissenschaftliche Buchgesellschaft, Darmstadt, pp. 96-111.

Schumacher Speech (1985), 'Aufgaben und Ziele der deutschen Sozialdemokratie' (Speech at the first post-war Party Conference, 9 - 11 May 1946), in K. Schumacher, *Reden -*

Schriften - Korrespondenzen 1945-1952, Willy Albrecht (ed.), Dietz Nachf., Berlin, Bonn, pp. 387-418.

Schumacher Speech 'Deutschland und Europa' of 29/06/1947 (1985), delivered at the SPD Party Conference, in K. Schumacher, *Reden - Schriften - Korrespondenzen 1945-1952,* Willy Albrecht (ed.), Dietz Nachf., Berlin/Bonn, pp. 486-517.

Schumacher, N. (1976), *Der Wortschatz der europäischen Integration. Eine onomasiologische Untersuchung des sog. 'europäischen Sprachgebrauchs' im politischen und institutionellen Bereich,* Schwann, Stuttgart.

Toulmin, S. (1975), *Der Gebrauch von Argumenten,* Scriptor, Kronberg.

Vogt, R. (1991), 'Die Karriere Europas. Vom Eigennamen zum politischen Schlagwort' in F. Liedtke, M. Wengeler und K. Böke (eds), *Begriffe besetzen. Strategien des Sprachgebrauchs in der Politik,* Westdeutscher Verlag, Opladen, pp. 276-294.

Weber, A. (1946), *Abschied von der bisherigen Geschichte. Überwindung des Nihilismus?* Claaßen und Goverts, Hamburg (approx. written in 1943).

5 Euro: The Career of a European Neologism in German Press Texts (1995-1999)

DIETER HERBERG

Introduction

As part of the larger topic of 'Attitudes Towards Europe', this chapter deals with the sub-topic of the European monetary union. It will focus on the career of the name for the common currency adopted by the members of the Economic and Monetary Union (EMU) – *Euro* – and its rendition in German press texts from 1995 to 1999.

We have chosen a lexicological approach starting with the competing designations of the expressions based on the currency name *Euro*, analysing the word formations appearing with this neolexeme as well as its collocations in three chronological sections. The aim is to demonstrate the communicative power behind the various linguistic realisations of the theme word *Euro*: Not only is it regarded merely as the name for the common currency of the members of the EMU; instead, on a larger scale it may act as a crystallisation nucleus towards the concept of an integrated Europe.

This aim is reflected in the structure of the chapter: We will first outline the factual background as necessary for the understanding of the subject; secondly, we will explain the methods. Thirdly, we will describe the grammatical and morphological properties of the lexeme *Euro*. The final part contains the analytic and interpretative parts and presents the lexical evidence for each of the chronological sections.

Facts

European Economic and Monetary Union (EMU)

Although a full rendering of the history of European integration in all its aspects would exceed the scope of this chapter, let us take a quick glance at the development of the European Economic and Monetary Union (EMU) and its stages, the introduction of the Euro within the framework of the EMU so far being the biggest event in the history of European integration.

The EMU is being brought about in three stages. The first stage commenced on 1 July 1990, when all restrictions on the movement of capital between EU member states were abolished.

The second stage started on 1 January 1994 and ended 31 December 1998. In this stage, the EU member states were expected to meet the economic convergence criteria in order to be eligible for participation in the monetary union. The convergence criteria were laid out in the Maastricht Treaty of 1992, with the following stability aims: price stability; balanced public finances (absence of an excessive government deficit); low long-term interest rates and exchange rate stability. On the basis of the statistical data for 1997, the European Council – the assembly of the Heads of State or Government of the fifteen member states of the European Union and the President of the European Commission – recommended in early May 1998 that from the beginning of 1999 the following eleven countries should participate in the Economic and Monetary Union: Austria, Belgium, Finland, France, Germany, Ireland, Italy, Luxembourg, The Netherlands, Portugal, Spain. The United Kingdom and Denmark, although meeting the convergence criteria, decided not yet to adopt the new currency from 1999 on, thus exercising their special right to opt out afforded by the Maastricht Treaty.

On 1 January 1999 the third and final stage commenced with the implementation of a single monetary policy under the responsibility of the European System of Central Banks (ESCB) and the gradual changeover to the Euro as the common currency of the member countries. There will be a transitional period (1 January 1999 – 31 December 2001) where banking is possible both in Euro and the national currencies. Circulation of Euro coins and banknotes will start 1 January 2002. From 1 March 2002 national banknotes and coins will cease to be legal tender.

The Euro – its Name and History

It has been a long way to the currency unit 'Euro', its immediate predecessor being the 'European Currency Unit', better known in its short form 'Ecu/ECU'. Unlike the Euro, the ECU, which had been introduced on 13 March 1979, had always been an artificial or 'ledger' currency.

It had been established as a common basket currency to accommodate the fixed, but variable exchange rates of the national currencies within the framework of the European Monetary System.

During the preparation stage for the creation of a common European currency for the members of the Economic and Monetary Union, another debate arose when it came to finding a name for the new common currency. Although the original EU treaty proposed to simply keep the name 'ECU', this turned out to be a highly controversial issue within the discussion, as the German partners in particular opposed ECU as the name for the new currency. This name would not appeal to German citizens, who were said to be mostly sceptical towards the monetary union anyway. Moreover, another argument against the use of 'ECU' was to be found in the official German version of the EU treaty, where 'ECU' was spelt with capital letters, thus being not a name but merely an abbreviation for 'European Currency Unit'. The new currency, however, should have a proper name if it was to be accepted by the citizens. But the controversies slowly died down. After a passing predilection for 'Franc' ('Die Euro-Währung wird wohl Franken heißen' ['The Euro-currency will most probably be named Franc'] *Berliner Zeitung*, 29 May 1995, p. 7), 'Euro', the proposal suggested by the then German Finance Minister Theo Waigel during a meeting of the EU finance ministers in October 1995 in Valencia gained ground. The first occurrence of the word 'Euro' within the IDS corpora refers to this meeting:

> Wie das neue Geld heißen wird, darüber gab es einen aussichtsreichen Vorschlag, der immer wieder auf den Gängen des Sitzungssaales kommentierte "Euro". (*die tageszeitung*, 2 October 1995, p. 6)
> [There has been a promising proposal for the name of the new currency, judged by the comments in the conference room: "Euro".]

Shortly after that date, during the Madrid Summit meeting on 15/16 December 1995, the EU Heads of State or Government agreed upon the name 'Euro' for the future common currency, for it was meeting essential criteria such as being acceptable to the citizens, easy to understand and to pronounce, and not biased towards any particular nation.

This decision also put an end to the - however short-lived - discussion of another proposal, mostly designed to build up trust: to combine the name 'Euro' with the national currency denominators, thus naming it 'Euromark', 'Eurofranc', and so on. Finally, in 1996, a name was also given to the coins to be used for small change – 'Cent' or – more precisely – 'Eurocent'. One Euro equals 100 Cent. Thus, a neutral name had been found also for the smaller denomination. Unlike the neologism *Euro, Cent* – deriving from the Latin word for 'one hundred' *centum* – is already used in various countries as a name for the smaller denomination of their currency.

A final remark about the denominations: there will be seven banknotes (of 5, 10, 20, 50, 100, 200 and 500 Euro) and eight coins (of 1, 2, 5, 10, 20 and 50 cent and of 1 and 2 Euro).

Now and then, the name *Euro* has also been subjected to (linguistic) criticism. For instance, the *Deutsche Akademie für Sprache und Dichtung* (German Academy of Language and Literature) criticised *Euro* as an *Unwort* [nonsense word]:

> weil das Abhacken der letzten Silbe einem historisch verwurzelten Begriff wie "Europa" nicht gerecht werde. (Fachdienst Germanistik 4/1998, p. 7)
> [because to simply chop off the last syllable means to disregard the deeply rooted historical context of a word like "Europe".]

However, such critical comments ceased fairly quickly. For *Euro* can indeed be seen as a successful formation, conferring a tangible term on the currency to be shared by several million European citizens. Moreover, the form ending with the vowel –*o* corresponds to a pattern well established with currency names, cf. *Peso, Escudo, Centesimo.*

Among the linguistic aspects typical for currency names is the use of signets and abbreviations.

Besides one or more abbreviations, there are special symbols (signets or 'logos') for some currencies; among the best known are the dollar sign ($) or the symbol used for the Pound Sterling (£). The new European currency unit Euro also has its own symbol, chosen at the EU summit in December 1996 in Dublin: €.

Closely following a press report of April 1997, in which the European Commission presented the Euro sign to the public, Duden – Der Euro (1998, p. 85) explained the Euro symbol as follows:

Das Zeichen für den Euro (Euro-Logo, Euro-Signet) stellt eine Kombination aus dem griech. Epsilon als Symbol für die Wiege der europ. Zivilisation, dem Buchstaben E für Europa und den Parallelen (doppelter Querstrich) als Symbol für Stabilität dar. Dieses symbol. Zeichen für den Euro wird voraussichtlich einen ähnl. Bekanntheitsgrad erreichen wie das Dollarzeichen $ und auch in die Standardbelegung von Computer- und Schreibmaschinen-tastaturen aufgenommen werden.

[The Euro symbol (Euro logo, Euro sign) is a combination of the Greek epsilon symbolising the cradle of European civilisation and the parallel lines (equals sign) symbolising stability. It is expected that the Euro symbol will become as widely known as the dollar sign $ and will soon appear on the standard keyboard layout for computers and typewriters'.]

As far as the abbreviations for currencies are concerned, one has to distinguish between the common abbreviations used by the different nations - for instance DM for Deutsche Mark, Lit for Lira Italiana, FF for Franc Français - and the official abbreviations designed by the ISO (International Organisation for Standardisation), which always consist of three capital letters, such as DEM for Deutsche Mark, ITL for Lira Italiana, FRF for Franc Français and so on. This so-called ISO code is used throughout the whole commerce system, for instance within the giro system and on the foreign exchange markets. The ISO code EUR for Euro was announced in April 1997. Along with this abbreviation, the Euro signet will also be made an ISO standard as the symbol for the new currency.

Method and Approach

As stated in the introduction to this article, we have chosen a lexicological approach to analyse the dynamic usage of the neolexeme *Euro* as an example for conscious, standardised lexical change (cf. Wurzel 1994, pp. 98). Apart from striking collocations of the lexeme, our main focus will be on compounds with *Euro* as one of their constituents. By applying this analysis – or rather, microanalysis – of recent language change we will describe and interpret the changing usage aspects of a neologism acting as a European theme word during a five-year time span ranging from 1995 to 1999.

Here again, we will use the same methods that we applied for the analysis of key words of the *Wende* era, the German re-unification period (cf. Herberg/Steffens/Tellenbach 1997), i.e. a survey based on a defined text corpus, describing and interpreting the use of the neolexeme *Euro* and its combinations in common language. However, an extensive, source-based documentation of the findings would exceed the scope of this article.

As stated above, this chapter presents details of common language usage in the Federal Republic of Germany ranging from the end of 1995 to the beginning of 1999, i.e. from the formation of the currency name *Euro* to the official introduction of the currency thus designated in the countries of the European Union. In order to describe the details of the changes and special features of language use in relation to certain events in history, it is necessary to structure the investigation period. It will therefore be divided into three chronological sections, each of which is characterised by distinct developments and stages within the framework of the EMU. Each section represents an investigation period of four months, with the sections arranged in order to include also the media coverage of the historical environment of the relevant events, developments and issues:

Period 1:
Decision to assign the name *Euro* to the new common currency of the European Union (November/December 1995, January/February 1996).

Period 2:
Debate on the fulfilment of the convergence criteria and on the eligibility of the participating countries for membership in the EMU (November/December 1997, January/February 1998).

Period 3:
Introduction of the Euro as 'ledger currency' on 1 January 1999 (November/December 1998, January/February 1999).

Assigning texts to different periods is a proven heuristic instrument to detect and verify changes in language use and word formation in relation to one or more previous or subsequent periods.

This analysis is entirely based on common language as represented in newspaper texts. Common language use, here also including official use, is of particular interest, as it reflects,

die Intentionen und Interpretationen gesellschaftlich wirksamer Kräfte [...], unabhängig davon, ob diese Kräfte bewußt den Sprachgebrauch zu beeinflussen versuchen. (Stötzel/Wengeler 1995, p. 1)
[the intentions and interpretations of significant forces in society[...], no matter whether they have the intention to change language use.]

The analysed newspaper articles are taken exclusively from the newspaper corpora held at the IDS Mannheim. The following newspapers were selected: The weekly *Die Zeit* and the daily papers *Berliner Zeitung* (*BZ*) and *die tageszeitung* (*taz*). As some of the IDS corpora do not cover all issues for the last few years, the sources are as follows:

Period 1 - *Die Zeit; die tageszeitung;*
Period 2 - *Die Zeit; die tageszeitung; Berliner Zeitung;*
Period 3 - *Die Zeit; die tageszeitung; Berliner Zeitung.*

Features of the Lexeme *Euro* with Regard to Grammar and Word Formation

Grammar

Euro as the representation of the lexicalised name for the currency unit of the European Economic and Monetary Union may be explained as the unisegmental short form of the initial segment of *Euro*pean Currency Unit.

Like many other currency names, *Euro* is a masculine noun in German, thus *der Euro* just like *der Heller, Taler, Dollar, Schilling, Pfennig, Franken, Gulden, Rubel*; but: *die Mark, die Krone, die Drachme; das Pfund* (cf. Duden-Grammatik 1995, p. 198), although there was initially some uncertainty about the gender of the name: 'Denn, soweit ersichtlich, hat Euro kein Geschlecht. Heißt es der Euro, die Euro oder das Euro?' ['For as far as it is possible to tell, *Euro* has no gender. Is it *der Euro, die Euro* or *das Euro*?'] (*Die Zeit*, 23 February 1996). The sub-unit *Cent* already displayed the male gender.

Even today, several years after the formation of this neolexeme, the use of inflected forms is still somewhat ambiguous. The uncertainty reflected in the representation of the lexeme *Euro* in recent dictionaries is a rather common feature with measurement and currency units. The table below shows a comparison of seven language dictionaries with regard to their forms of the singular and plural genitive forms.

Table 1   Euro - Genitive Forms

Dictionary	Genitive Singular	Plural
1 Duden - Rechtschreibung (1996)	- [s]	- [s]
2 Duden - Deutsches Universalwörterbuch (1996)	- [s]	- [s]
3 Langenscheidt - Internet (1999)	- / -s	- / -s
4 Heyne - Wörterbuch (1997)	-s	-s
5 Bertelsmann - Rechtschreibung (1999)	-s	-s
6 Bertelsmann - Fremdwörterlexikon (1999)	-s	-s; if specifying a certain amount: -
7 Duden - Das große Wörterbuch (1999)	- [s]	-s < but: 10 Euro >

We may observe four clearly distinct patterns between dictionaries 1, 2 and 3 (either no ending or the ending -*s* is possible with both forms), dictionaries 4 and 5 (with both forms, only the ending -*s* is possible), dictionary 6 (similar to 4 and 5 except for the plural restriction 'no ending if specifying a certain amount') and dictionary 7 (genitive singular same as in 1,2 and 3, plural the same as in 6). The rules given in dictionaries 1, 2, 3 and 7 are confirmed by the corpus evidence, i.e. the appearance of variants either having no ending or ending with -*s*.

Word Formation

Along with the establishment of the neolexeme *Euro* around 1995, we can observe a novel aspect in word formations with the element 'euro'.

Until then, there had only been numerous – almost exclusively nominal– compounds with 'euro' acting as prefix or prefixoid element (the distinction is somewhat ambiguous in the current literature), summarised by researchers like Born with regard to similar words in other European languages.

According to Born, '[die] Einschätzung von *euro-* als Präfixoid [trägt] dem internationalistischen Charakter dieses Wortbildungselementes eher Rechnung als die Deutung als ein abgekürztes Substantivkompositionselement ['to regard *euro-* as prefixoid takes into account the internationalistic character of this morpheme better than its interpretation as an abbreviated compound noun element'] (1995, p. 350), as expressed for instance in Duden-Grammatik:

> Um Zusammensetzungen handelt es sich z.B. bei Bioladen, Biorhythmus, Euromarkt, bei denen die attributiven Adjektive (biologisch, europäisch) gekürzt in die Wortbildung eingehen, ohne daß die Kurzform als selbständige Einheiten existieren. (1995, p. 411)
> [There are compounds such as Bioladen, Biorhythmus, Euromarkt etc., where the abbreviated attributive adjectives (biologisch, europäisch) enter the word formation process without being free morphemes themselves.]

The morpheme 'euro' can have different meanings such as 'European', 'concerning Europe', 'made in Europe' etc. Among the areas listed by Born as containing these compounds are EU and EU-related institutions (e.g. *Eurokratie, Europarlament, Eurorichtlinien, Euronormen*), the financial sector (e.g. *Eurowährung, Eurobank, Euroanleihen*), but also research, technology, communication, sport and transport. Although we need not and cannot go into detail here, we should keep this background in mind when examining word formations with the neolexeme *Euro*. *Euro* as currency denominator is a noun and may form compounds with other lexemes – mostly nouns, – which it frequently does. It is not always clear from the semantic construction, whether it is the prefix(oid) *euro-* or the noun *Euro* that makes up the first part. Even the context does not always give clues. Here, a clearly defined graphematic convention would be helpful, for instance with prefix(oid) constructions written as one word (without a hyphen), compounds on the other hand requiring a hyphen, i.e. *Eurobürokratie, Eurokartell, Eurotunnel* etc., but *Euro-Kriterien, Euro-Logo, Euro-Münze, Euro-Start, Euro-Umstellung* and so on. However, corpus evidence is showing a more confused situation, as Born states just for the spelling of the prefix(oid) compounds (1995, p. 356): 'In der Realität läßt sich ein ziemlich unmotiviertes Durcheinander beobachten. Die Faustregel, Ad-hoc-Bildungen mit Bindestrich, Lexikalisierung ohne läßt sich jedenfalls bezüglich *euro-* nicht bestätigen'. ['In reality, we find a state of confusion. The rule of thumb to hyphenate ad-hoc-formations and write lexicalised units as one word obviously does not hold true for *euro-*'.]

The situation becomes even more complicated when looking at compounds with the currency denominator *Euro*. For instance, does

Euroskepsis/Euro-Skepsis mean 'scepticism towards Europe' or 'scepticism towards the currency unit Euro'?

Analyses and Interpretations

In this section we will present the results gained from the examination of language use based on texts from the three different periods. In the following, all stages are assigned to separate sections of a similar structure. Firstly, we will examine the usage of the lexeme *Euro* in the relevant period, with special regard to collocations. We define 'collocation' in a wider sense as combinations between *Euro* and other lexemes, realised within the corpus as syntactic entities showing a distinct usage of *Euro*. We will then summarise and interpret those collocations according to their different semantics and content.

Under the sub-title 'word formation' we will then have a look at word formations with *Euro*. Here too, we will summarise and interpret the occurrences after grouping them.

For reasons of space, only very few of the discussed collocations and compounds could be shown in their larger context and with full reference to the source.

Period 1: Decision to assign the name Euro *to the new common currency of the European Union (November/December 1995, January/February 1996)*

Here, the public discussion is mainly concerned with the decision made by the Heads of State and Government of the European Union during the Madrid summit meeting held 15/16 December – as outlined before – to follow the proposal of the then German Minister of Finances Theo Waigel to assign the name *Euro* to the new common currency. Prior to this official decision, there had been discussions on different levels about a variety of alternatives, still reflected in the texts of this period, as illustrated in the sample given below: Here, the *taz* quoted the results of a survey launched by the British newspaper *The Guardian* in conjunction with eleven other European daily newspapers, the *taz* among them. The survey, carried out centrally by *The Guardian*, led to the following results with regard to the question of how to name the new currency:

> Die Mehrheit, 36 % aller europaweit Befragten, wolle es Ecu nennen, an zweiter Stelle rangiert die Euro-Mark, Euro-Pfund, Euro-Franc usw.

Finanzminister Theo Waigels Vorschlag, die neue Währung Euro zu nennen, erreichte einen respektablen dritten, unter *taz*-LeserInnen sogar den zweiten Platz. Dukat, Florin und Franken konnten nur Achtungserfolge erzielen. Weitere Vorschläge waren Euro-Dollar, Taler (in Anspielung auf die Valuta Entenhausens), Pfifferling, Stein, WaiGeli oder Wolpertinger. (*taz*, 13 December 1995, p. 8)
[The majority, 36 percent of those questioned in the whole of Europe, favoured Ecu, followed by Euro-Mark, Euro-Pound, Euro-Franc etc. The proposal of the Minister of Finance, Theo Waigel, to name the new currency Euro, came a respectable third, among *taz* readers it even ranked second. Ducat, Florin and Franc only gained polite acclaims. Among the other suggestions were Euro-Dollar, Taler (an allusion to the German name for the currency used in Ducksburg), Pfifferling ('chanterelle', a reference to the German idiomatic expression keinen Pfifferling wert, roughly to be translated as 'not worth a bean' in English), Stein ('stone'), WaiGeli or Wolpertinger'. (name of a mythological Bavarian creature)]

After the official decision was taken in favour of *Euro*, there followed a short period where some linguistic aspects – such as its pronunciation or gender in the different languages of the participating countries – and questions concerning the introduction of the new currency were the subject of discussion. Here, we have to distinguish between those collocations that refer to the introduction of the Euro in a neutral way and others expressing the collocation partners' approval or disapproval or a positive or negative attitude towards the Euro. Thus, the collocations prevailing in the texts of this period can be classified according to four collocation areas, to which all frequently recurring and other typical collocations have been assigned:

Examples for collocations referring to the term *Euro* for the common European currency:

> *die Bezeichnung, die Währungsbezeichnung, der Name Euro*
> *die neue Währung Euro nennen, taufen*
> *die neue Währung, das Kind soll / wird Euro heißen*
> *Euro sei dein Name* (see Example 1 below)
> *an den Euro die alte Währung anhängen*
> *Euro ist polysem, hat kein Geschlecht*
> *ein mit 'Euro' bedruckter Geldschein*

Example 1:
> Der portugiesische Regierungschef Antonio Guterres fand auf dem EU-Gipfel vor ein paar Tagen die richtigen, weil biblischen Worte dafür: 'Euro sei dein Name, und auf diesem Euro werden wir unser Europa errichten'. (*taz*, 21 December 1995, p. 10)

[At the EU summit a few days ago, the Head of the Portuguese Government, Antonio Guterres, found the right, because biblical, words for this: 'Euro be thy name and upon this Euro we shall build our Europe'.]

Examples of collocations referring to the introduction of the Euro:

Einführung des Euro, der EU-Währung Euro
Start des Euro
Startschuß für den Euro
Endspurt des Euro
der Euro kommt
der Euro wird Wirklichkeit, wird geschaffen, erblickt das Licht der Welt
den Euro bekommen, kriegen, haben
die Geburtsstunde für den Euro schlägt
für den Euro werben, die Werbetrommel rühren
Übergang zum Euro
Umstellung der Mark auf den Euro
die D-Mark wird zum Euro, soll dem Euro Platz machen
in Euro umrechnen
mit (dem) Euro bezahlen
Rechnungen künftig in Euro schreiben

Examples of collocations expressing the collocation partners' agreement or disagreement with the Euro:

Agreement:
den Euro wollen, liebenlernen, ernst nehmen
an den Euro glauben

Disagreement:
den Euro sabotieren, bereits beerdigt haben
Angst vor dem Euro
ungeliebter Euro
emotionale Blockade gegen den Euro
auf Distanz zum Euro gehen
der Euro ist gescheitert

Examples of collocations expressing the collocation partners' positive or negative attitude towards the Euro:

positive: *der Euro ist eine gute Sache.*

negative: *wenig stabiler* (see Example 2), *weicher, labberiger Euro.*

It is a characteristic feature of the texts of Period 1, that the main focus is on the procedure for finding a name for the new European currency and certain aspects of its introduction, while in this early period (1995/96) – with the real issues concerning the transition to the Euro still rather far ahead – pro and con-statements are comparatively rare. But even at this early point it was feared that the solid, stable Deutschmark would be changed into a weak, unstable Euro:

Example 2:

> Gerade in deutschen Köpfen hat sich die Befürchtung festgesetzt, der Euro werde nie so stabil sein wie die Mark. (*Die Zeit*, 29 December 1995)
> [Especially in the heads of the Germans there is a fear that the Euro will never be as strong as the Deutschmark].

Word Formation

The texts of Period 1 show a range of – mainly nominal – compounds with *Euro* as qualifying element. However, in some cases we cannot always exclude the possibility of a prefix(oid) formation with *euro-*: For instance, does *Eurowährung / Euro-Währung* stand for 'the currency Euro' or simply for 'European currency'? The often inhomogeneous spelling – with or without hyphenation – of one and the same formation type could be partly based on the novelty character and instability of the formation. Generally, hyphenated spellings dominate. It is obvious that the ambiguity of those compounds – including graphematic variance – is sometimes used to play with the language. The compounds with *Euro* as qualifying element can be roughly classified by the meaning of their base words.

Examples of compounds referring to different aspects of the introduction of the Euro:

> *Euro-Einführung, Euro-Projekt, Euro-Idee*
> *Euro-Zeitplan, Euro-Ära, Euro-Tag*
> *Euro-Club, Euro-Bürger*
> *Euro-Umfrage*

Examples of compounds referring to the monetary aspects of the currency Euro. The graphematic variants mentioned above are mainly found in this group:

> *Eurowährung/Euro-Währung, Eurogeld/Euro-Geld, Euro-Geldscheine, Euro-Geldmünzen und -Scheine, Euromünzen und -Scheine, Euro-Knete, Euromark/Euro-Mark, Europfennig/Euro-Pfennig, Euro-Franc, Euro-Lira, Euro-Pfund, Eurocent*

Examples of compounds expressing agreement or disagreement towards the Euro:

Agreement: *Euro-Befürworter, Euro-Fans*

Disagreement: *Euro-Skepsis, euroskeptisch*
                 Euro-Pessimisten, Euro-Skeptiker, Euro-Muffel (see
                 Example 3)

Most occurrences with compounds expressing disagreement refer to the British, e.g.

Example 3:
die als Euro-Muffel verschrienen Briten (*Die Zeit*, 19 January 1996)
[The British as notorious Euro-grousers]

Period 2: Debate on the fulfilment of the convergence criteria and on the eligibility of the participating countries for membership in the EMU (November/December 1997, January/February 1998)

Similar to Period 1, the part of the survey defined as Period 2 also falls into the second stage of the introduction of the EMU. It covers four months representing a significant cross-section of the discussion on central aspects of creating the EMU. To sum up: This period is marked by the struggle for meeting the convergence criteria as fixed in the Maastricht Treaty of 1992 and ratified by the European Council in Amsterdam in the middle of 1997 under an 'Agreement for Stability and Growth', where the statistical data of 1997 should determine the eligibility of the candidates for participation in the EMU starting in 1999, this decision having been scheduled for the first half of 1998. Obviously, collocations and compounds referring to this background, i.e. introduction of the Euro, criteria for participation in the EMU, attitudes towards the Euro and its assessment are the main issues of this part of our survey.

The name for the new currency itself, *Euro*, is no longer considered an important issue. Compared to Period 1 there is a wider discussion on possible effects of the Euro, i.e. on future aspects. We do not only detect a different emphasis with regard to content, but also a difference in quantity between the two periods. For instance, the number of occurrences of *Euro* within a comparable time span of four months has more than doubled (*Die Zeit, taz*). The higher absolute number of occurrences compared to Period 1 is the result of adding the *Berliner Zeitung (BZ)* to the survey. The number of types within the compound words (compounds with *Euro -*) has even multiplied, without doubt due to the increased complexity of the issues dealt with in Period 2. Inevitably, this has led to an increase of tokens within the compounds.

Although below we will list all relevant collocation areas, due to the large number of occurrences we must limit – even more restrictively than in Period 1 – the number of examples to very distinct ones. Still, in accordance with the subject of this volume, those collocation areas expressing attitudes and assessments will be dealt with in greater detail. Let us start with the small area of collocations consisting of a generic concept noun (with a definite article) immediately followed by the currency denominator *Euro*. The concept noun then acts as core element of the constituent (or attribute), the proper name is to be defined as juxtaposition (close apposition) (Duden-Grammatik 1995, p. 648), for example:

> *die Gemeinschaftswährung Euro, die Einheitswährung Euro*
> *die (gemeinsame) europäische Währung / Einheitswährung Euro*
> *die künftige gemeinsame Währung Euro*
> *die Euro-Währung Euro*
> *das Gemeinschaftsgeld Euro*

The largest area in Period 2 contains collocations referring to the introduction of the Euro, for example:

> *Vorbereitung auf den Euro, Weg zum Euro*
> *Einführung, Schaffung, Start des Euro*
> *Übergang zum Euro, Umstellung auf den Euro*
> *Kurs des Euro*
> *der Euro kommt, rollt*
> *den Euro einführen*
> *der Euro ist beschlossen, wird Realität, wird verbindliches Zahlungsmittel*
> *sich auf den Euro vorbereiten, einrichten*
> *auf (den) Euro umstellen*
> *mit / in Euro bezahlen*
> *Rechnungen, Schecks in Euro ausstellen*
> *Preise in Euro auszeichnen, Waren in Euro auspreisen*
> *Mark-Bargeldbestände in Euro umtauschen*
> *Steuererklärungen in Euro akzeptieren, zulassen*
> *den Aktienhandel in Euro abwickeln*

Some collocations – more or less as a thematic sub-group of this area – refer directly to a postponement or non-establishment of the Euro, for instance:

> *Verschiebung des Euro*
> *der Euro kommt zu früh* (see Example 4), *muss / kann verschoben werden*
> *den Euro noch aufhalten, vorläufig stoppen*

Example 4:

> Der Euro kommt zu früh, meinen 155 deutsche Professoren und fordern, die Währungsunion zu verschieben. (*Die Zeit*, 12 February 1998, p. 20)
> [The Euro is too early, such is the opinion of 155 German professors who demand a postponement of the currency union.]

The background for collocations of this kind is the above-mentioned petition by 155 German professors to postpone the currency union and the complaint about infringements of the constitution by four prominent opponents to the Euro, both having taken place in Period 2. However, neither this petition nor the complaint to the Federal Constitutional Court could hinder the scheduled introduction of the Euro on 1 January 1999.

Examples of collocations referring to meeting the so-called convergence criteria as prerequisites for membership in the EMU:

> *Maastricht-Kriterien, Stabilitätspakt, Stabilitätskriterien,*
> *Konvergenzprogramm für den Euro*
> *Qualifikation, Aufnahmeprüfung, Reifezeugnis für den Euro*
> *Teilnahme, Teilnehmer am Euro*
> *am Euro teilnehmen, sich am Euro beteiligen*
> *beim Euro von Anfang an / mit dabei sein, beim Euro mitmachen*
> *fit, reif sein / werden für den Euro, X fit machen für den Euro*
> *sich für den Euro qualifizieren, für den Euro sparen*
> *X (nicht) vom Euro ausschließen*
> *dem Euro beitreten, angehören*
> *den Euro schaffen* (= 'to manage, to accomplish the Euro')

Examples of collocations referring to possible effects of the introduction of the Euro:

> *Vorteile, Chancen, Gefahren, Risiken, Folgen, Auswirkungen des Euro*
> *der Euro eröffnet beachtliche Chancen*
> *der Euro wird Europa radikal verändern*
> *der Euro schafft (keine) neue(n) Stellen / Arbeitsplätze*

der Euro wird den Arbeitnehmern / Verbrauchern eher schaden
der Euro heizt die Immobiliennachfrage an
der Euro verbindet, trennt, lockt
Spaltung durch den Euro
Urlaub mit dem Euro
mit dem Euro rechnen müssen
vom Euro profitieren
Herr über den Euro (see Example 5)

Example 5:
> Wer wird Herr über den Euro? Die Mitgliedsländer der EU ringen um die Spitzenpositionen bei der Europäischen Zentralbank (*Die Zeit*, 13 February 1998)
> [Who will be master of the Euro? The EU member states struggle for the leading positions in the European Central Bank]

The occurrences often refer to expected effects on the economy in general, on banking, on the labour market and on tourism. Whereas sceptical attitudes prevail with regard to the labour market, the effect on the other areas is seen rather optimistically.

The following collocation areas with collocations expressing attitudes towards and assessments of the Euro have both been already detected in Period 1. However, with the political, juridical and verbal debates concerning the establishment of the Euro reaching their climax in Period 2, compared to Period 1 collocations of the above type claim a larger part with regard to the overall number of collocations with *Euro*. On the same level, there is a considerable increase in the variety of the collocation partners.

Examples of collocations expressing the collocation partners' agreement or disagreement towards the Euro:

Agreement:

Befürworter des Euro, pro Euro
den Euro befürworten, wollen, brauchen, zum Erfolg führen
auf den Euro setzen
Entscheidung, Zustimmung, Mehrheit, Argumente, Kampf, Bündnis für den Euro
für den Euro sprechen, argumentieren
sich für den Euro aussprechen, stark machen
Vertrauen in den Euro haben
fest, voll und ganz hinter dem Euro stehen
positiv über den Euro denken

vom Euro überzeugt sein
Bekenntnis, Ja zum Euro
sich zum Euro bekennen, fest zum Euro stehen

Disagreement:

Gegner, kein Freund des Euro
Ablehnung des Euro
der Euro ist ungeliebt, hat viele Gegner, wird scheitern, ist 'out'
den Euro fürchten, scheuen, nicht wollen, geißeln, skeptisch beurteilen (see
Example 6), *noch kippen, in Frage stellen*
dem Euro mit Skepsis entgegensehen
sich dem Euro widersetzen
Absage an den Euro, Kritik am Euro
Widerstand, Abneigung, Wahlkampf, Klage, Verfassungsbeschwerde, Votum,
Volksbegehren, Volksbefragung, Demonstration, Opposition gegen den Euro
Kläger, Agitator gegen den Euro
gegen den Euro sein, klagen, agitieren, mobilisieren, Stellung beziehen
sich gegen den Euro engagieren
Zweifel gegenüber dem Euro
dem Euro gegenüber negativ eingestellt sein
über den Euro streiten, (Dauer)streit um den Euro
vom Euro nicht überzeugt sein, wenig vom Euro halten
Ängste, Warnung vor dem Euro
sich vorm Euro fürchten
Rettung der D-Mark vor dem Euro
wider den Euro
Nein, kritische Haltung zum Euro

Example 6:
Die Mehrheit der Deutschen beurteilt den Euro weiterhin skeptisch. (*BZ*, 30
December 1997)
[The majority of Germans is still sceptical towards the Euro.]

Even this limited selection clearly shows that the collocations
expressing disagreement are far more frequent and varied in expression
than those expressing agreement, one reason being the influence of the
above-mentioned petitions and complaints, not to mention decisions and
referenda which have massively affected the press texts throughout the
whole period.

Examples of collocations expressing the collocation partners' positive or
negative attitude towards the Euro;

positive:

harter, stabiler, starker, gesunder Euro
erfolgreicher, konkurrenzfähiger Euro
Härte, Stabilität des Euro
Erfolg, Vorteile des Euro

negative:

weicher, schwacher Euro (see Example 7)
der Euro wird nicht so stabil wie die D-Mark sein
der Euro wird weniger hart als die D-Mark sein
der Euro ist risikoreich, riskant, hochinflatorisch, politisch verhängnisvoll
der Euro hält nicht, was man sich von ihm verspricht
Instablität, Unflexibilität, Werteverlust des Euro

Example 7:

> In der jüngsten Entwicklung der Mark sehen die Professoren schon eine Bestätigung ihrer These vom kommenden schwachen Euro. (*taz* 10 February 1998, p. 2)
> [The professors see their prophecy of a weak Euro confirmed by the recent development of the Deutschmark.]

Word Formation

In Period 2 not only the collocations with *Euro*, but also the types and tokens of word formations with *Euro* have clearly increased compared to Period 1. The variety of the aspects discussed above has obviously led to a greater demand for nominal compounds with *Euro* as the modifier; with the occasional occurrence also of adjectival compounds. Constructions with *Euro* acting as base word are extremely rare.

The problem of graphematic variants with or without hyphen, already discussed in the word-formation section of Period 1 above, also exists in Period 2; here too, the hyphenated spellings dominate.

The compounds with *Euro* as qualifying element can be roughly classified by the meaning of their base words. In addition to the three groups known from Period 1, where the compounds refer to monetary issues and aspects of procedure and attitude, we may classify a new group of compounds which – in accordance with a corresponding collocation area – refer to aspects of meeting the so-called convergence criteria as a prerequisite for membership in the EMU.

Examples of compounds referring to the different aspects of establishing the Euro:

Euro-Debatte, Eurodiskussion, Euro-Referendum, Euro-Abstimmung
Euro-Entscheidung, Euro-Beschluß
Euro-Einführung, Euro-Start, Euro-Umstellung, Euro-Umtausch, Euro-
Verwendung, Euro-Fragen, Euro-Details, Euro-Regularien
Euroeinführungsgesetz / Euro-Einführungsgesetz
Euroverschiebung / Euro-Verschiebung, Euro-Kalender, Euro-Zug (see
Example 8)
Euro-Zeitalter, Euro-Ära, Euro-Jahr (= 1998), *Euro-Phase*
Euro-Beauftrager, Euro-Fachmann, Euro-Stäbe, Euro-Kompetenz
Euro-Bürgertelefon, Euro-Informationsforum, Euro-Hotline

Example 8:
'Der Euro-Zug rollt' – davon sind die Analysten spätestens seit Freitag
überzeugt. (*BZ*, 28 February 1998)
['The Euro train is on its way' – such is the conviction of the analysts at least since
Friday.]

Examples of compounds referring to the monetary aspects of the currency
Euro:

Euro-Währung, Euro-Bargeld, Euromünzen / Euro-Münzen, Euro-Banknoten,
Euro-Scheine
Euro-Aktien, Euro-Kredite, Euro-Pfandbrief, Euro-Wertpapiere, Euro-Steuer,
Euro-Zins, Euromieten, Euro-Gehalt, Euro-Konto
Euro-Bank, Euro-Zentralbank, Eurobanker, Eurotower / Euro-Tower
Euro-gefördert, Euro-kompatibel

A remarkable difference to Period 1 is the fact that the coming up of
practical issues concerning the transition to the Euro led to a majority of
those base words referring to various aspects of monetary policy and the
financial market.

The formation *Eurotower / Euro-Tower* (see Example 9), describing
the premises of the European Central Bank (ECB) in Frankfurt/M., is not
self-explanatory:

Example 9:
Noch ist die Bezeichnung Eurotower für das 150 Meter hohe Domizil des
EWI wenig populär. (*Die Zeit*, 26 February 1998)
[The name 'Eurotower' for the domicile of the ECI, which is 150 metres high, is still
not very popular.]

Examples of compounds referring to meeting the so-called convergence criteria as a prerequisite for membership in the EMU:

> *Euro-Kriterien, Euro-Teilnahme-Kriterien, Euro-Kennzahlen, Euro-Marke, Euro-Gutachten*
> *Eurotauglichkeit / Euro-Tauglichkeit, eurotauglich / Euro-tauglich, Euro-Fähigkeit, Euro-Reife, euroreif*
> *Euro-Kandidaten, Euro-Bewerber, Euro-Aspirant, Euro-Qualifikanten*
> *Eurobeitritt / Euro-Beitritt, Euro-Teilnahme*
> *Euroteilnehmer / Euro-Teilnehmer, Euro-Teilnehmerländer, Euro-Teilnehmerstaaten, Euro-Teilnehmergruppe, Euro-Teilnehmerkreis, Euro-Staaten (*also: *Nicht-Euro-Staaten), Euro-Gruppe, Euro-Start(er)gruppe, Euro-Startteilnehmer, Euroländer / Euro-Länder* (see Example 10), *Euro-Mitglieder, Euroclub / Euro-Club, Euro-Club-Mitglieder, Euro-X, Euro-X-Klub, Euro-11, Euro-Partner, Euro-Liga, Euro-Union, Euro-Truppe, Euro-Kreis*
> *Euro-Gebiet, Euro-Zone, Euro-Raum, Euro-Währungsraum, Euroland / Euro-Land* (see Example 11), *Euro-Markt, Euro-Binnenmarkt*

For reasons of space, we have to restrict our comments to a particularly interesting compound: *Euroland / Euro-Land*

As early as during the preparation stage for the EMU there was a need for a concise, attractive term for the territory of those members of the European Union taking part in the currency union. Generic, common terms such as *die Euro-Staaten* or *die Euro-Länder* seemed unsatisfying. Hence, other terms, such as *Euro-Zone* were discussed.

However, another word won the race: *Euroland*. It has been suggested that the economic expert and publicist Claus Noé was the first to use this term (cf. *Die Zeit*, 29 October 1998, p. 28).

Since then, corpus evidence shows two clearly distinctive interpretations of the compound *Euroland / Euro-Land* (see also the relevant article in Duden – Das große Wörterbuch 1999):

> *Euro-Land*, das (Genitive Singular: *Euro-Land(e)s*; Plural: *Euro-Länder*) meaning 'one of the countries participating in the Economic and Monetary Union' as in:

Example 10:

Die Entscheidung über die Euro-Länder soll Anfang Mai fallen. (*BZ*, 2 January 1998)

[The decision regarding the Euro-Länder is scheduled for the beginning of May.]

Euroland (mostly without article; no plural) meaning 'all countries participating in the Economic and Monetary Union', as in:

Example 11:
Beide [Trichet und Duisenberg] stehen im Rennen um den Job des obersten Währungshüters in Euroland. (*Die Zeit*, 14 January 1997, p. 3)
[Both [Trichet and Duisenberg] are among the front runners for the job of first custodian of the currency in Euroland.]

Unfortunately, this semantic difference is not as clearly distinguished in real language as may be suggested by the above extracts. They are – albeit relatively rare – hyphenated spellings for variant 2, as well as compound spellings for variant 1. However, the adoption of variant 2 in common language use results in a preference for the compound forms.

Examples of compounds expressing agreement or disagreement towards the Euro;

Agreement:

Euro-Bekenntnis, Euro-Aufruf, Euro-Kampagne
Euro-Erfolg, Euro-Boom, Euro-Euphorie (also as pun using contamination: *Euro-phorie*, see Example 12)
Euro-freundlich, euroselig
Euro-Befürworter, Euro-Sympathisanten, Euro-Freund, Euro-Fan

Example 12:
Euro-phorie in Brüssel (*Die Zeit*, 5 December 1997)
[Euro-phoria in Brussels]

Disagreement:

Eurofeindlichkeit / Euro-Feindlichkeit, Euro-feindlich, Euroskepsis / Euro-Skepsis, euroskeptisch / Euro-skeptisch, Euroskeptizismus, Europessimismus, Euro-Protest, Euroangst / Euro-Angst, Euro-Müdigkeit
Euro-Protest, Eurostreik, Euronörgeleien
Euro-Kritik, Euro-Klage, Euro-Streit, Euro-Terror
Euro-Sackgasse, Euro-Krise, Euro-Zwänge, Euro-Unheil
Eurogegener / Euro-Gegner, Euroskeptiker / Euro-Skeptiker (see Example 14), *Euro-Kritiker, Euro-Kläger, Euro-Blockierer, Euro-Rebell, Euro-Dissident*

Period 2 shows the first appearance of a new formation type among the compounds expressing approval or disapproval by placing the constituents *Pro-Euro-* or *Anti-Euro-* respectively in front of base words that themselves are neutral with regard to the Euro, such as:

> *Pro-Euro-Kampagne, Pro-Euro-Manifest, Pro-Euro-Stimmung*
> *Anti-Euro-Initiative, Anti-Euro-Klage, Anti-Euro-Erklärung, Anti-Euro-Diskussion, Anti-Euro-Werbung, Anti-Euro-Kurs, Anti-Euro-Linie, Anti-Euro-Volksbegehren* (see Example 13), *Anti-Euro-Partei*
> *Anti-Euro-Kämpfer, Anti-Euro-Kläger*

Example 13:
> Vom 24. November bis 1. Dezember liegt sein (= Jörg Haiders) Anti-Euro-Volksbegehren zur Unterschrift aus (*taz* 24 November 1997, p. 11)
> [From 24 November until 1 December his (= Jörg Haider's) petition for a referendum against the Euro is on display for people to sign.]

In period 2, the total number of types and tokens expressing disapproval clearly exceeds those expressing approval. Compared to period 1, there is a significant difference with regard to content. Whereas in period 1 most occurrences deal with the topic of disagreement as a matter of principle (especially from the British side), in period 2 the texts reflect the opposition and scepticism within the potential participants of the EMU, for instance:

Example 14:
> Frankreichs Euro-Skeptiker machen erneut gegen den EU-Vertrag von Amsterdam mobil. (*taz*, 3 January 1998, p. 5)
> [Again, the French Euro-Sceptics mobilise against the EU Treaty of Amsterdam.]

Our corpus evidence shows only three occurrences of compounds with *Euro* acting as base word in period 2: '*Silber-Euro*', '*Probe-Euro*' und '*Peterseuro*' (see Example 15), two of them expressing their singular and novel character through quotation marks.

Example 15:
> Die Umwandlung des Peterspfennigs in einen 'Peterseuro' (*Die Zeit*, 26 December 1997, p. 16)
> [The conversion of St. Peter's Penny into 'St. Peter's Euro']

Period 3: Introduction of the Euro as 'ledger currency' on 1 January 1999 (November/December 1998, January/February 1999)

On 1 January 1999 the third and last stage of the EMU began. On this day, the eleven participants of the European Currency Union centralised their financial policy under the European System of Central Banks (ESCB) and introduced the Euro as common currency: until the end of 2001 as a so-called 'ledger currency' parallel to their local currencies, from 1 January 2002 as legal tender, with local banknotes and coins being abolished from 1 March 2002. The survey section defined as Period 3 ranges from two months ahead of 1 January 1999 to two months after that date, so that the reflection of the transition process - the final preparation for the transition, the deadline, the first weeks with the new 'ledger currency' Euro - in the chosen press media will be fully covered by the survey. The majority of the collocations and compounds in Period 3 deal with aspects of the introduction and in particular with the monetary aspects of the Euro currency, now for the first time appearing in reality. Aspects of attitude and assessment are also frequent subjects of discussion in this period. Collocations following the pattern 'generic concept noun+*Euro*' or referring to aspects of participation in the EMU or possible consequences show only small areas.

The large number of collocations and compounds made it again necessary to choose only a very limited set of distinctive examples for illustration.

To ensure a maximum comparability of results, the arrangement of collocation is the same as in Period 2. The extensive collocation area dealing with monetary aspects, appearing here for the first time, follows the one dealing with aspects of the introduction of the Euro, as both belong to the same context.

Let us again begin with the small area of collocations consisting of a generic concept noun (with a definite article) immediately followed by the currency denominator *Euro*. Examples:

> *die Gemeinschaftswährung Euro, die Einheitswährung Euro*
> *die europäische Währung/Einheitswährung Euro*
> *die einheitliche/gemeinsame/neue Währung Euro*

Next follow the by far largest collocation areas dealing with aspects of the introduction of the Euro. Due to the large number of aspects, we have decided – different to Period 2 – to structure the overall area by distinguishing between general collocations and those referring to concrete monetary and banking aspects in two different sub-groups. There is no need to comment on these collocations as they are self-explanatory.

Examples of collocations referring to the introduction of the Euro:

> *Einführung, Schaffung, Start, Ankunft, Beginn, Geburt(sstunde), Jahrzehnt, Zeitalter, Europa des Euro*
> *Vorläufer des Euro* (= Ecu)
> *Stadt* (see Example 16), *Hauptstadt, Kapitale des Euro* (= Frankfurt/Main)
> *der erste Tag, das erste Jahr des Euro*
> *der Euro kommt, rollt, startet, gilt, tritt in Kraft*
> *der Euro steht vor der Tür, ist auf den Weg gebracht, hat seinen Einzug gehalten*
> *der Euro existiert, ist da, wird konkret, ist Realität*
> *der Euro lebt, ist geboren, hat das Tageslicht erblickt, wurde zum Leben erweckt*
> *der kommende, nahende, frische, neugeborene Euro*
> *die ersten Euros*
> *dem Euro gelassen entgegensehen*
> *den Euro einführen, begrüßen*
> *sich an den Euro gewöhnen*
> *sich auf den Euro einstellen, vorbereiten*
> *Vorbereitung, Aussicht, Warten auf den Euro*
> *für den Euro fit, gerüstet sein*
> *der Umgang mit dem Euro*
> *Volksabstimmung über den Euro*
> *Aufwand, Diskussionen rund um den Euro*
> *Übergang, Vorbereitungen zum Euro*
> *Fragen, Antworten, Infos zum Euro*

Example 16:
> 'Stadt des Euro', wie sich Frankfurt nennt (*Die Zeit*, 28 January 1999)
> ['City of the Euro', as Frankfurt calls itself]

Examples of collocations referring to monetary and banking aspects of the Euro:

> *2 Euro, ein halber Euro, mehrere Milliarden Euro*
> *der Euro fällt, wertet ab, gibt nach*
> *den Euro testen, verwenden*
> *Kurs, Wert, Preis des Euro*
> *Anschub, Aufwertung, Überbewertung, Wertzuwachs, Kursrückgang des Euro*
> *Produktion, Erstausgabe des Euro*
> *Herr des Euro* (= Wim Duisenberg), *Verwalterin des Euro* (= European Central Bank)

> *Wettbewerbsvorteile des Euro*
> *sich am Euro orientieren*
> *auf Euro umschreiben, umstellen, umrechnen*
> *auf Euro lauten, laufen*
> *Umstellung, Umrechnung auf Euro*
> *Zinssatz, Quotierungen, Zielzonen für den Euro*
> *in Euro (be)zahlen, abrechnen*
> *Konten in Euro führen*
> *Rechnungen in Euro ausstellen, transferieren*
> *Schecks in Euro ausfüllen, akzeptieren*
> *Beträge in Euro überweisen, umrechnen, ausweisen, angeben*
> *Einlagen, Kurse, Preise, Forderungen in Euro*
> *Auszeichnung, Bezahlung, Handel, Umrechnung in Euro*
> *Noten, Scheine, Münzen in Euro*
> *mit Euro zahlen*
> *Handel, Umsatz mit Euro*
> *Nachfrage nach Euro*
> *Kontrolle, Kommando über den Euro*
> *Umtauschkurs, Wechselkurs zum Euro*

Examples of collocations referring to aspects of membership in the EMU:

> *Qualifizierung für den Euro*
> *(Nicht)Teilnahme am Euro, Beitritt zum Euro* (see Example 17)
> *Teilnehmerländer des Euro / am Euro*
> *Außenvertretung des Euro*
> *noch nicht am Euro teilnehmen*
> *beim Euro mitmachen*
> *dem Euro vorerst fernbleiben*

Example 17:
> Blair bereitet britischen Beitritt zum Euro vor [Überschrift] (*Die Zeit*, 28 January 1999)
> [Blair prepares for British participation in the Euro [Headline]] (*BZ*, 24 February 1999)

It is not surprising that with the participants of the EMU already fixed and the actual transition to the Euro being the centre of interest, the above collocation type plays a minor role compared to Period 2.

The possible consequences of the introduction of the Euro are still a matter of debate in Period 3, however, the prognostical aspects are clearly dominated by those dealing with the concrete transition to the Euro.

Examples of collocations referring to possible consequences of the introduction of the Euro:

Folgen, Folgewirkungen, Wirkungen, Auswirkungen des Euro
Chancen, Risiken des Euro
die (internationale) Rolle, die Zukunft des Euro
der Euro als Motor der Integration
den Euro als Chance begreifen
der Euro bringt Nutzen, Vorteile
der Euro begünstigt Investitionen, treibt Investitionen an
der Euro macht uns stark (see Example 18)
der Euro schafft Unsicherheit

Example 18:
> Eine breite Werbekampagne mit dem Slogan 'Der Euro macht uns stark' (*taz*, 15 January 1999, p. 4)
> [A broad publicity campaign with the slogan 'The Euro will make us strong']

A remarkable fact is the lesser frequency of negative articulations compared to positive ones – a clear difference to Period 2. This is obviously a result of the advancing and irrevocable introduction of the Euro in the member states of the EMU: there is not much sense anymore in evoking pessimistic prognoses as a warning against the Euro.

Both the following collocation areas expressing the same aspects with regard to attitudes and assessments already mentioned in Period 1 and 2, draw a strikingly different picture compared to earlier periods, in particular to Period 2. Apart from a decreasing frequency of such collocations in general, there is a significant majority of collocations expressing agreement or a positive attitude, one plausible reason being that with the Euro now a reality, the warning and equivocal voices obviously step back behind those who bear in mind the inevitable facts and try to seek the positive aspects of the Euro.

Examples of collocations expressing the collocation partners' agreement or disagreement towards the Euro;

Agreement:

Beliebtheit, Popularität, Begrüßung, Glaubwürdigkeit des Euro
Anhänger, Freunde, Befürworter des Euro
den Euro befürworten, loben, feiern, akzeptieren, unterstützen, stärken, wollen
der Euro ist in, erzeugt Hoffnungen
große Erwartungen an den Euro
positive Reaktionen auf den Euro

> *optimistisch auf den Euro blicken, sich auf den Euro freuen*
> *für den Euro sein*
> *Sympathie, Begeisterung, Hauptargumente, Kampagne für den Euro*
> *sein Heil im Euro suchen* (see Example 19)
> *Zustimmung zum Euro*

Example 19:

> Diesmal könnten die roten Zahlen Blair dazu verleiten, doch noch sein Heil im Euro zu suchen. (*taz*, 5 November 1998, p. 2)
> [Being in the red, Blair could be tempted to seek his salvation in the Euro after all.]

Disagreement:

> *unpopulärer Euro*
> *den Euro ablehnen, nicht wollen, nicht brauchen*
> *dem Euro nicht über den Weg trauen*
> *der Euro erzeugt Ängste, scheitert*
> *Vertrauensverlust für den Euro*
> *gegen den Euro sein, stimmen*
> *Mißtrauen, Vertrauensschwund in den Euro*
> *Angst, Panikmache vor dem Euro*

Examples of collocations expressing the collocation partners' positive or negative attitude towards the Euro;

positive:

> *harter, stabiler, starker, fester, steigender Euro*
> *Stabilität, Stärke des Euro*
> *Erfolg, Vorteil, Vorzüge, Glanz des Euro*
> *vom Euro profitieren*

negative:

> *weicher, schwacher, geschwächter, instabiler, leichter Euro*
> *Schwäche, Probleme, Kehrseite des Euro*
> *den Euro schwächen*

Word Formation

The same four content-defined groups detected for Period 2 also appear in Period 3. However, a certain shift in quantity can be stated for those compounds having a parallel within the collocation areas, i.e. a strong increase in compounds referring to monetary and banking aspects. There is also a rather striking number of compounds referring to aspects of membership in the EMU. In particular, there is a large number of those types of compounds representing the EMU member states as a whole. This comes as no surprise given the communicative need for formations illustrating the unifying power of the Euro just at the time when the common European currency finally becomes reality. As in the previous period, nominal formation and hyphenation prevails.

Examples of compounds referring to the different aspects of the establishment of the Euro:

Euro-Debatte, Euro-Informationen, Euro-Fragen, Euro-Vorbereitungen, Euro-Aspekte, Euro-Projekt, Euro-Experiment, Euro-Erwartungen
Euro-Entscheidung, Euro-Initiative
Euro-Rhetorik, Euro-Vokabular
Euroeinführung / Euro-Einführung, Euro-Test, Eurostart/Euro-Start, Euro-Debüt,
Euroumstellung/Euro-Umstellung, Euro-Stufenfahrplan, Euro-Terminkalender, Euro-Übergangszeit, Euro-Einführungsgesetz
Euro-Erstausstattung, Euro-Automat, Euro-Update
Eurobeauftragter / Euro-Beauftragter, Euro-Experte, Euro-Spezialist, Euro-Projektleiter, Euro-Macher
(erster) Euro-Tag, (erste) Euro-Wochen, Euro-Ära
Euro-Feier(lichkeiten), Euro-Party, Euro-Dinner
Euro-Symbol, Eurozeichen/Euro-Zeichen
Euro-City, Euro-Metropole (= Frankfurt/Main)
Eurotower / Euro-Tower, Euro-Turm
Euro-Briefmarke, Euro-Uhr (see Example 20), *Euro-Schlips, Euro-Weste*
eurotauglich, eurofähig / Euro-fähig, eurokompatibel

Example 20:
Die Euro-Uhr in Frankfurt zeigte den Countdown bis zur Währungsunion.
(*BZ* 2 January 1999)
[The Euro-Clock in Frankfurt displayed the countdown to the currency union.]

Examples of compounds referring to monetary aspects of the currency Euro:

*Euro-Währung (*also: *Nicht-Euro-Währungen), Eurogeld / Euro-Geld, Euro-Bargeld, Euro-Beträge, Euro-Summen, Euromünzen/Euro-Münzen (*also: *Zwei-Euro-Münze, Zwei-Euro-Stücke), Euro-Banknoten, Euro-Noten, Euro-Geldscheine, Euro-Scheine*
Euro-Zahlung(en), Euro-Überweisung, Euro-Buchungen, Euro-Umtausch, Euro-Konto, Euro-Bank, Euro-Zentralbank, Euro-Notenbank, Euro-Zentrale, Euro-Haushalt, Euro-Geldpolitik, Euro-Vermögen, Euro-Werte, Euro-

*Außenwert, Euro-Finanzmarkt, Euro-Geldmarkt, Euro-Aktienmarkt, Euro-Rentenmarkt, Eurokurs(e) / Euro-Kurs(e) (*also: *Euro-Dollar-Kurs), Euro-Wechselkurs, Euro-Umrechnung(skurs), Euro-Niveau, Euro-Aktien, Euro-Anleihe(n), Euro-Aktienbarometer, Euro-Aktienindex, Euro-(Stoxx-)Index, Euro-Libor, Euro-Fixing, Euro-Anpassung, Euro-Überbewertung, Euro-Wertpapiere, Euro-Pfandbrief, Euro-Darlehen, Eurobonds/Euro-Bonds, Euro-Schuldschein, Euro-Tagesgeld, Euro-Börsen, Euro-Zinsen, Euro-Leitzinsen, Euro-Tarife, Euro-Transaktionen, Euro-Orders, Euro-Reserve, Euro-Preisauszeichnungen, Euro-Steuererklärungen*
Eurohüter, Euro-Währungshüter, Eurobanker, Euro-Koordinator, Euro-Schuldner
Euro-Taschenrechner, Euro-Taste (see Example 21)
Euro-spezifisch

Example 21:

Für den Ausnahmefall sind die Kassen seit Anfang des Jahres mit einer Euro-Taste ausgestattet. Ein Knopfdruck genügt und der Mark-Betrag wird umgerechnet. (*BZ*, 5 January 1999)
[For this exceptional case, the cash points have (since the beginning of the year), been equipped with a special Euro-button. One touch of the key and the amount in Deutschmarks will be converted.]

Examples of compounds referring to aspects of membership in the EMU:

Euro-Kriterien, Euro-Anforderungen, Euro-Tauglichkeit, euro-fähig
Euro-Beitritt, Euro-Abstinenz, Euro-frei (see Example 22)
Euro-Anwärter, Euro-Aspiranten, Euro-Bürger (also: *Nicht-Euro-Bürger)*
Euro-Abstinenzler, Euro-Außenseiter, Euro-Outsider, Euro-Nachzügler
Euro-Teilnehmer, Euro-Teilnehmerstaaten, Euro-Teilnehmerländer,
*Eurostaaten / Euro-Staaten (*also: *Nicht-Euro-Staaten)*
*Euroländer / Euro-Länder (*also: *Nicht-Euro-Länder), Euroland / Euro-Land, Euro-Kernländer, Euro-Mitgliedsländer, Euro-Mitgliedstaaten, Euro-Nationen, Euro-Regierungen, Euro-Partner(staaten), Eurozone / Euro-Zone, Euroraum / Euro-Raum, Euro-Gebiet, Euro-Währungsgebiet, Euro-Bereich, Euro-Welt, Euro-Europa, Euro-Klub / Euro-Club, Euro-Block, Euro-Verbund, Euro-Gruppe, Euro-Kartell, Euro-Gilde, Euro-11 / Euro-Elf, Euro-11-Gruppe / Euro-Elf-Gruppe, Euro-11-Zone, Euro-11-Partner*
Euro-Ausland
Euro-Welthandel, Euro-Stabilitätspakt, Euro-Vertretung, Euro-Gipfel, Euro-Elf-Rat, Euro-11-Präsidentschaft
euro-weit
Euro-Zeitalter, Euro-Zeit

Example 22:
Großbritannien noch lange Euro-frei [Überschrift] (*taz* 4 November 1998, p. 11)
[Great Britain will remain Euro-free for some time to come[Headline]]

Examples of compounds expressing agreement or disagreement towards the Euro:

Agreement:

Euro-Begeisterung, Euro-Enthusiasmus, Euro-Euphorie (see Example 23; also realised as pun using contamination: *Europhorie / Euro-Phorie, europhorisch)*
Euro-Manie, Eurowahn
Euro-freundlich, europhil
Eurobefürworter / Euro-Befürworter, Euro-Anhänger, Euro-Anhängerschaft, Euro-Optimisten, Euro-Enthusiasten, Euro-Konvertit (= Blair)

Example 23:
Die vorgesehene Übergangszeit von drei Jahren bis zur Ausgabe des neuen Geldes sei angesichts der Euro-Euphorie 'vielleicht eine zu lange Zeit'. (*BZ* 11 January 1999)
[The envisaged transition time of three years until the new banknotes and coins are issued could be considered 'perhaps too long' with regard to the prevailing Euro-euphoria.]

Also belonging to the above group regarding their content are the formation *europhil*, which we consider as a confix compound (for an explanation of this term cf. Fleischer 1995, p. 64) and the derivation *Eurotiker*, a pun based on *Neurotiker* which had been used as the counterpart of *Euroskeptiker* in a '*taz*-Euro-quiz' (*taz*, 30 December 1998).

Examples of disagreement:

Euro-Verweigerung, Euroskepsis / Euro-Skepsis, Euroskeptizismus, euroskeptisch / Euro-skeptisch, eurofeindlich, eurokritisch, Euro-Angst, Euro-Ängste, Europhobie / Euro-Phobie, Euro-Gegner, Euro-Kritiker, Euroskeptiker / Euro-Skeptiker

Although remarkably less frequent than in Period 2, Period 3 also contains some types of compounds expressing approval or disapproval through the constituents Pro-Euro- or Anti-Euro- respectively:

Pro-Euro-Entscheidung
Anti-Euro-Wahlkampf, Anti-Euro-Tumulte

First occurring in Period 3 is the small group of compounds expressing a positive or negative attitude towards the Euro through positive or negative features of the base word; a function predominantly – in Periods 1 and 2 even exclusively – covered by collocations.

Examples of compounds expressing a positive or negative attitude towards the Euro;

positive: *Euro-Stabilität*

negative: *Euro-Schwäche*

Compounds with *Euro* as base word are isolated cases also in Period 3. It seems, however, that the formation pattern is no longer regarded as very unusual as none of the three occurrences is put between quotation marks:
EU-Euro does not need any further explanation. *Schokoladen-Euros* were handed out at the so-called 'changeover weekend' in Frankfurt/Main. *Uni-Euro* is a term often used in the discussion on the introduction of the European Credit Transfer Scheme (ECTS) at German universities.

Conclusion

The decision made at the end of 1995 to assign the name *Euro* to the new European currency led to the coining of a European neologism which in the following years was to act not only as a currency designation, but outside its own scope serve as a theme word and nucleus for aspects of European integration. With the lexeme *Euro* itself being neutral and impartial, attitudes and assessments towards the Euro can only be expressed by using the relevant collocation partners or constituents. The same applies to all other usage aspects, where the communicative power of this neolexeme is evident in its collocations and constructions. For our analysis of the dynamic use of the lexeme *Euro* we have chosen three cross-sections illustrating common language use with reference to historic dates, events and developments in the years 1995 to 1995. Each of these sections corresponds to a survey period of four months based on texts taken from the newspapers *Die Zeit, die tageszeitung (taz)* and *Berliner Zeitung (BZ)*, thus reflecting the common language use of the period in question. The results from these analyses, referring to the expressions based on the lexeme *Euro* have been presented in three sections of a similar internal structure.

Unlike collocations, which may contain nearly all aspects, compounds are subject to various restrictions. For instance, the aspects of the name and the possible effects of the *Euro* are exclusively represented by collocation areas, not by compounds.

With regard to word formation, compound nouns predominate, most of them hyphenated. Compounds using *Euro* as base word are rare exceptions, as are derivations of *Euro*.

Among the eight collocation areas and compound groups that have been structured by their content, the following two appear to be most relevant with regard to communicative powers: those referring to various aspects of the introduction of the Euro and those expressing approval or disapproval of the Euro. Both groups are widely represented in all three periods both with collocations and compound forms.

With the other areas or groups we may observe a sometimes striking clustering in relation to the historic events taking place in the relevant periods. For instance, *Euro* as currency denominator is only discussed in Period 1, the aspect of meeting the convergence criteria as a prerequisite for membership in the EMU, however, is not yet considered an important issue during that period, but is dominant in Period 2. Due to the nature of the subject, monetary and banking aspects prevail in Period 3, when the transition to the Euro became reality.

The survey period clearly shows two distinctive phenomena with regard to the aspects of attitude and assessment. These aspects can easily be classified by their content: agreement/disagreement; positive vs. negative assessment; possible effects of the Euro.

The first phenomenon is the distinct shift from con to pro through the periods: Whereas periods 1 and 2 show a mainly negative, disapproving or at least reluctant attitude, this changes in the course of periods 2 and 3, displaying an increasing number of occurrences expressing a more positive, approving and optimistic attitude. This change is apparently due to the power of fact, i.e. the actual realisation of the currency union.

Secondly, we may observe that within Period 1 – representing a comparatively early stage of the discussion about the pros and cons of a common currency – occurrences expressing a negative or disapproving attitude tend to be attached to potential 'opt-out'-countries such as Britain, whereas in period 2, which shows a vast increase of those negative occurrences, they are more related to arguments within 'Euroland' or individual member states. For instance, in Germany the predominance of occurrences expressing negative attitudes is most certainly due to the professors' petition and the complaint about a violation of the constitution brought to court by four prominent opponents to the Euro.

The present survey has been strongly motivated by the author's belief that the currency designated by the lexeme *Euro* will rise above itself in playing an important role in the creation of a common European identity. A final quote from the *Berliner Zeitung* will serve to emphasise this:

> Dabei ist die Einführung der Einheitswährung selbst ein erster Schritt zur Schaffung dieses neuen Gefühls der Zusammengehörigkeit. Der Euro könnte zu einem wichtigen Identifikationssymbol für Europa werden. Denn zum ersten Mal werden alle Europäer gemeinsam etwas besitzen. Allein die sinnliche Erfahrung, in ein anderes Land zu kommen und mit seinem »eigenen« Geld bezahlen zu können, verändert das Gefühl von Fremde und Heimat. Bisher speiste sich europäische Gemeinsamkeit vor allem aus der Idee, zusammen neue Kriege zu verhindern. Jetzt kommt etwas sehr Konkretes hinzu. Identität entsteht auch durch die Alltäglichkeit des Umgangs mit Dingen. Der Euro macht Europa anfaßbar. (*Berliner Zeitung* 30 December 1998)
>
> [The introduction of a common currency is itself a first step towards a feeling of togetherness. Thus, the Euro could become an important symbol for the identification with Europe, as for the first time, all European citizens share a common possession. Just the emotional perception of entering a foreign country and still being able to pay with one's »own« money will change the feeling of home and abroad. Until now, the idea of a common Europe has mainly been based on the common obligation to prevent a new war. But from now on, there is something else, something concrete. Identity also develops from the things of daily life. The Euro will make Europe tangible.]

References

Bertelsmann-Fremdwörterlexikon (1999): Wahrig-*Fremdwörterlexikon*. Neuausgabe, Bertelsmann Lexikon Verlag Gütersloh/München.

Bertelsmann–Rechtschreibung (1999): *Die deutsche Rechtschreibung*, Bertelsmann Lexikon Verlag Gütersloh, München.

Born, J. (1995), 'Wortbildung im europäischen Kontext – "euro-" auf dem Wege vom Kompositionselement zum Präfix', *Muttersprache*, vol.105, pp. 347 - 359.

Duden – Der Euro (1998): *Der Euro: Das Lexikon zur Währungsunion*, Dudenverlag Mannheim, Leipzig, Wien and Zürich.

Duden – *Deutsches Universalwörterbuch* (1996), 3rd ed., Dudenverlag Mannheim, Leipzig, Wien and Zürich.

Duden – Grammatik (1995): *Grammatik der deutschen Gegenwartssprache,* 5th ed., Dudenverlag Mannheim, Leipzig, Wien and Zürich.

Duden – Rechtschreibung (1996): *Rechtschreibung der deutschen Sprache*, 21st ed., Dudenverlag Mannheim, Leipzig,Wien and Zürich.

Fleischer, W. (1995), 'Konfixe' in Pohl, Inge, Ehrhardt, Horst (eds), *Wort und Wortschatz. Beiträge zur Lexikologie*, Niemeyer, Tübingen, pp. 61-68.

Herberg, D. (1999), 'Der Euro – sprachlich betrachtet', *Sprachreport,* no. 4, pp. 2-7.

Herberg, D. / Steffens, D. and Tellenbach, E. (1997), *Schlüsselwörter der Wendezeit: Wörter-Buch zum öffentlichen Sprachgebrauch 1989/90*, de Gruyter, Berlin and New York.

Heyne-Wörterbuch (1997): *Das neue deutsche Wörterbuch für Schule und Beruf*, Heyne, München.

Langenscheidt-Internet (1999): http://www.langenscheidt.aol.de (seen 2 September 1999).

Stötzel, G., Wengeler, M. (1995), *Kontroverse Begriffe: Geschichte des öffentlichen Sprachgebrauchs in der Bundesrepublik Deutschland*, de Gruyter, Berlin and New York.

Werneke, G. (1998), *Politische Lexik in der Diskussion um die Europäische Währungsunion, untersucht an deutschen Pressetexten von September bis November 1997*, M.A. thesis, University of Heidelberg.

Wurzel, W. U. (1994), *Grammatisch initiierter Wandel*, Universitätsverlag Dr. N. Brockmeyer, Bochum.

PART III: COMPARATIVE STUDIES

6 The European Debate in and between Germany and Great Britain

COLIN GOOD

Introduction

In a discussion of differences in the meaning of *federalism* in various European countries one commentator wrote:

> Diese babylonische Sprachverwirrung ist auf das Fehlen *eines europäischen, öffentlichen Diskurses* zu wichtigen Fragen der gemeinsamen Zukunft zurückzuführen. (Müller-Brandeck-Bocquet, 1991, p.14)
> [We have this veritable Tower of Babel because of the lack of an European, public discourse about important questions of our common future.][1]

The following discussion describes some of the problems impeding the development of an 'European, public discourse'. The material for the discussion includes extracts from debates in the German Lower House (as reproduced in *Das Parlament,*), the Hansard transcription of a House of Commons debate of June 1997 (all references to *Hansard* in the following are to the official records of this debate), other German political statements - as reproduced in the Bulletin - and a series of German and English newspaper articles on the European issue. Because it was my aim to reveal tendencies of 'national debates', the identities of the speakers quoted in the two debates and elsewhere are given only when germane!

Some Features of the Domestic Debates

Europa/Europe and Related Ideas

> Erst das Bewußtsein unserer gemeinsamen *Werte* und erst die *kulturelle* Dimension Europas geben unserem Kontinent und unserer Gemeinschaft die Identität. (*Bulletin*, 29 April 1998)

151

[The real identity of our continent and our community is found in the consciousness of our common *values* and in a European *cultural* dimension.]

The utterances of both British and German politicians and journalists suggest that the very idea of 'Europe' is differently construed in the two political cultures. Debates about Europe concern both its 'existence' and its size and shape. For instance, the extract quoted a few lines earlier appears to take Europe for granted, assuming its existence in an unproblematical way. (It also proposes some of the components which constitute this entity; some of these are returned to below.) The 'thematisation' of this position in the following lends the 'presupposition' greater weight: 'Warum soll man sich, so fragen wohl viele, für etwas einsetzen, *das ohnehin schon Realität ist*'. [Why should we, some people must be asking themselves, fight for something *that already exists* anyway.] (*Bulletin*, 15 June 1996)

The logic of both of the following - fascinatingly similar - extracts, although problems are acknowledged, similarly presupposes the entity 'Europe':

Gerade *weil es so selbstverständlich erscheint*, hat Europa es in der öffentlichen Diskussion manchmal schwer. (*Die Zeit*, 15 June 1993)
[Its precisely *because the idea seems so obvious* that Europe sometimes fares so badly in the public debate.]
Gerade auch diejenigen, die Europa als *Selbstverständlichkeit* begreifen, sehen den konkreten Prozess der Einigung mit gewissem Unbehagen. (*Das Parlament*, 25 December 1998)
[Its precisely also those who *take Europe for granted* who regard the process of unification with a certain amount of unease.]

This kind of 'ontological' certainty about Europe appears to be less evident in the British debate, as does the conviction that there are a common European culture, history and values. The British answer to the historically resonant question: 'Europa, aber wo liegt es?' (*Die Zeit*, 9 December 1999) literally: ['Europe, but where does it lie?'], was suggested in the self-assured assertion of the British Prime Minister that the 1999 Cardiff summit had brought about a 'transformation of our own relations with Europe' (*The Guardian*, 17 June 1998), which betrays no comparable insecurity about Britain's boundaries!

Extracting possible answers to the same troubled question from a number of German texts reveals an interesting bias in the German definition of Europe, which may be geographical, economic or even military. Whilst what we may justifiably regard as the *dominant* British attitude is, as we noted above, to conceive of Europe as beyond/not part of Britain, the German discussion bespeaks a number of different 'Europes'. As is the case with *Kontinent* also (see above), Europe's geographical boundaries 'move'! This is most strikingly the case in relation to its easternmost boundaries, in particular to the inclusion or exclusion of Russia; for instance, the 'Europe' referred to in the phrase 'Mauerfall und Einigung Europas (*auf unserem Kontinent*)' ['the fall of the wall and the unification of Europe (*on our continent*)'] (*Bulletin*, 3 April 1998) is 'open' and includes Russia, as also does Waigel's 'neighbours' in:

> Wir können die politische Union besser gemeinsam mit unseren *Nachbarn auf dem alten Kontinent* verwirklichen. (*Bulletin*, 15 June 1993)
> [We can achieve political union more easily if we act together with *our neighbours on the old continent*.]

whereas elsewhere 'Europe' is 'closed', occupied by and identical with 'the West', leading to such apparently illogical texts as the following:

> Der Erfolg *Europas im Westen* gegen die früheren kommunistischen Machthaber im Osten. (*Bulletin*, 15 June 1993)
> [The success of *Europe in the West* against the old communist leaders in the East.]

> Konflikte sind in Europa und an seiner Peripherie ausgebrochen. Darüber hinaus tragen politisch-soziale Spannungen in einigen Ländern Mittel-, Ost- und Südosteuropas zur Instabilität in und um Europa bei. (*Bulletin*, 16 February 1994)
> [Conflicts have broken out in Europe and on its boundaries. And political and social tensions in a number of countries in central, eastern and south-east Europe are contributing to instability in and around Europe.]

Here there is a distinct sense that the real Europe lies in the West, the locus of European democracy and market economies. Indeed 'Europe' may sometimes be limited 'referentially' to the Western Alliance, NATO, which is described as a *Wertegemeinschaft* ['community of shared values'], a kind of higher or 'ideal' Europe now becoming available to previously benighted others. *Wertegemeinschaft*, it is suggested later in this essay, is commonly *instrumentalised* to preempt possible accusations of Western/German hegemony or imperialism. Party-political disagreement surrounding this issue of Europe's boundaries sometimes involves the concept *gesamteuropäisch*, a term which has been employed by detractors of the dominant discourse. Here is Gysi, on the far left, for the PDS (the

'Party of Democratic Socialism', the successor of the old 'communist' Socialist Unity party) making this point in an explicitly linguistic comment on the subject of this essay, European discourse:

> Denn wer spricht heute noch vom *gesamteuropäischen Haus*, von einer europäischen Friedensordnung? Waren das also nur Zweckerklärungen oder war es wirklich Absicht? Im gegenwärtigen Europakonzept der Bundesrepublik kommen das Zusammenwachsen von Ost und West und damit *Gesamteuropa* für die nächsten 10 Jahre lediglich als Nebenschauplatz vor. Zumeist sind es Worthülsen ohne praktische Gestaltung. (*Das Parlament*, 18 March 1994)
> [Who is talking about the *pan-European House* these days, or about an European peaceful order? Were these just expedients, then, or was there a genuine intention? In Germany's current ideas on Europe, the rapprochement of East and West over the next 10 years, the *pan-European ideal* in other words, is a side-show. The language is hollow, with no practical implications.]

The same charge was put even more explicitly by another member of the PDS, Hans Modrow, who saw the Europe of Maastricht 'als ein auf *Westeuropa* begrenzter Interessenblock unter Ausschluss Osteuropas' ['as a self-interested bloc, limited to *Western Europe* and excluding eastern Europe'] (*Das Parlament*, 18 March 1994) -a view repudiated in the same debate by Klaus Kinkel, the then foreign minister:

> Die Bundesregierung hat sich nie mit einem Konzept der *Westunion* oder einer *Südwestunion* identifiziert; sie hat sich stets zum *gesamten Europa* bekannt. (*Das Parlament*, 18 March 1994)
> [The government has never identified itself with the concept of a *Western Union* or a *South-western Union*; it has always espoused the idea of *'Europe as a whole'*.]

Such havering between different 'European entities' is not uncommon in the German debate. Such open rejections of the charge of a bias towards the West are implicitly denied in usages which are both open *and* biased at one and the same time:

> Erstens freuen wir uns über diese Bereicherung durch die Eigenarten dieser Länder, die *Europa, das Europa der Europäischen Union*, erzielt. (*Das Parlament*, 8 March 1994)
> [Firstly we welcome the enrichment of *Europe, the Europe of the European Union* through the special characteristics of these (the Scandinavian, CG) countries.]

In many respects, of course, the kind of polysemy we have illustrated is harmless. But, firstly it must be remembered that quite casual formulations can contain biased interpretations - and secondly, only a close study of the words in context will reveal whether speakers may be exploiting polysemy in order to obfuscate, for instance, by talking apparently about one thing, whilst at the same time pursuing some tacit agenda. The fluctuating senses of 'Europe' are deployed in conflictual situations in the German debate, other terms - such as Gysi's *gesamteuropäisch* - being brought in to challenge the imprecision of the basic word. A cynic might - indeed, people on the left do - see in the exploitation of *Europe's* 'elasticity' the pretence of a visionary view of a greater Europe, which is actually serving to legitimise the 'westernisation' of the economies of countries in Eastern Europe. Not surprisingly, because of a dominant strand in Britain's whole attitude towards Europe, this feature is almost lacking in the British political discussion, the point about varying interpretations being raised only very occasionally.

Kontinent, like, but to an even greater degree than *Europe*, is not tied into any obvious structures. Like the latter, therefore, it may be invoked for the discursive gain it affords. We have already heard Waigel who proposes acting *'together with our neighbours on the old continent'* (see above). Predictably, British discourse puts *continent* in the same category as Europe (and 'culture'!), that is, excluding Britain:

> As you, Mr. Deputy Speaker, will understand from your background, there is a cultural problem between the United Kingdom and the *continent of Europe*. (Teddy Taylor, Conservative MP; *Hansard*)

The previous Prime Minister, John Major's sentiment that Britain had 'historical obligations to countries such as Poland, Hungary and the Czech Republic' (*Hansard*), is most unusual (although it does remind us that there is not one, single, homogenous discourse, a point which needs to be constantly borne in mind!).

Taylor (see above) is clearly of the mind that British and 'continental' cultures are quite different. In any case, 'culture' is simply not written large in the British debate on Europe; the concept, subsumed in the idea of 'history', as it were, was commented on by a German newspaper, which, in turn, was quoting from *The News of the World*, as follows:

Sie [die Europäer [sic!], CG] bedrohen unsere 1000jährige, unabhängige *Geschichte* ebenso ernsthaft wie einst Napoleon und Hitler. (*Die Welt*, 6 May 1996)
[The Europeans [sic!, CG] are as great a threat to our thousand -year old history as once were Napoleon and Hitler.]

In the German debate *Kultur* is invoked frequently and, it will be suggested, for a variety of ends. As the extract quoted at the beginning of this section suggests, a 'common European culture' may also be taken for granted. 'Naive' invocations of *'Kultur'* as a bond are frequent:

Europa ist aber mehr als Politik und Wirtschaft. Es steht vor allem für ein grossartiges *kulturelles Erbe: Antike, Humanismus, Aufklärung und Christentum.* (Kohl, *Bulletin*, 21 June 1996)
[Europe is more than just politics and the economy. Above all it represents a magnificent *cultural heritage: Classical Antiquity, Humanism, the Enlightenment and Christianity.*]

This dimension is, it appears, missing from the British debate. When something like 'common ideals' are invoked, it tends to be rather in the more pragmatic guise of the 'shared values' held to inform the present political/economic 'arrangement', such as those advanced by Robin Cook (British Foreign Minister), who spoke of 'our shared values of fairness, democracy and opportunity' during the *Hansard* debate referred to. Note how significantly different in emphasis this is from Herzog's in some sense similar:

Als Indizien für die Existenz einer *historischen europäischen Kultur* nannte Herzog den *Freiheitsgedanken* und die Achtung der Menschenrechte, die sich im Westen mittlerweile durchgesetzt hätten. Die östlichen Länder vollzögen dies nun nach. (*Das Parlament*, 5 March 1999)
[As evidence of the existence of an *historical European culture* Herzog cited the *idea of freedom* and the protection of human rights, which he thought, had now been established in the West. The countries in the East were now following in this process.]

Confirmation of the more pragmatic 'mind-set' of the British came from the British Ambassador, Sir Paul Lever, who, in an important lecture to the German-Atlantic-Society in 1998, in London, was reported as follows:

London, dies zog Lever als Fazit, stehe nicht weniger zu Europa als jeder andere EU-Staat. Das europäische Engagement betrieben die Briten jedoch

eher mit Kopf und Verstand, 'weniger mit dem Herzen'. Eine Entwicklung zu
dieser Position stelle er auch bei den Deutschen fest. Botschafter Lever:
'Gefühle und Erinnerungen an die Vergangenheit sind vielleicht nicht die
besten Grundlagen für Europa'. *Vernunft und Realitätssinn* sollten dabei eine
wichtigere Rolle spielen. (*Das Parlament*, 27 November 1998)
[London, Lever concluded in summing up, was no less in favour of Europe than any
other EU state. But the European commitment of Britons was a matter of the *head and
the mind, 'less of the heart'*. He also discerned a move towards this attitude on the part
of the Germans. He went on to say that 'sentiments and memories of the past are
perhaps not the best basis on which to build Europe'. *Reason and a sense of reality*
should play a more important part.]

Particularly away from the narrow political context, German speakers
undertake the task of *establishing* a common culture, in statements which
are not so much descriptive as *normative-constitutive*: 'Die Frage der
Zukunft Europas stellt sich deshalb als die Frage: Gibt es eine *europäische
Kultur*?'. [The question of the future of Europe assumes the form of the
question: Is there a *European culture*?] (*Bulletin*, 10 March 1999)

When John Major spoke of the European Union overriding 'the
instinctive wishes, habits and traditions of the United Kingdom' (Hansard),
his words were instructive for us not merely because the terms he deployed
(see emphases) are so peculiarly and profoundly 'pragmatic' in the context
of the UK-'Europe' divide and, specifically, compared with the way
Herzog framed the issue (see above), but also because he appears not to
feel the need to invoke an idea called 'political culture' which might not
include such characteristics as the 'British instinct' (referred to a few lines
later in the same speech). It is a strand in Major's thinking - and, beyond
him, of many on the right in Britain - that 'being British' simply includes
all of the activities Herzog cites, and includes 'doing politics' in our own
peculiar, 'instinctive' way. The distinctions which might apply in alien
cultures between 'culture' and 'political culture' - given the relative rarity
of these terms in the British debate, already mentioned - are not relevant for
the British!

Taking 'culture' in the different sense of present and future official
'non-political', cultural activity, we note that one speaker in the House of
Commons refuses to contemplate the interference of Europe: 'It is even
proposed to extend the role of the EU in culture, believe it or not!'
(Hansard), whereas Herzog, speaking on a related idea, expressed no
similar misgivings: 'Vor uns steht die Aufgabe der Einigung von Bildung
und Kultur'. [We are faced with the task of unifying education and culture.]
(Bulletin, 2 November 1998)

We have so far exemplified both the unquestioning assumption of *a common European culture* in the German debate as against its relative unimportance, even outright denial in the British discussion. A further aspect of the role played by '*Kultur*' in the European debate is what some detractors clearly regard as its *instrumentalisation* in the German context.

For instance, Lafontaine drew attention to this phenomenon when he accused Chancellor Kohl of obfuscating the real *economic* and other difficulties involved in *Osterweiterung* ('eastwards expansion'), by shifting the focus onto a vague common cultural heritage and framing the issue generally in other than economic terms. Certainly the stressing of the 'cultural' 'alongside more hard-nosed calculations seems both suspiciously frequent and *de rigueur* and to carry with it a more placatory than substantive significance; the following extract (from a speech by Waigel) is typical and representative (the reference in the following is not to countries further East but to Scandinavian countries):

> Es ist ein Erfolg, weil diese Länder in die EU wollen und diese Union damit bereits eine *Bereicherung* erfährt. Und zwar *zunächst einmal in kultureller Hinsicht*, wie ich meine. (*Das Parlament*, 18 March 1994)
> [This is a success, because these countries want to join the EU and the Union is thereby *enriched. Firstly*, I would argue, *in a cultural sense.*]

Such textual evidence as this is not, of course, sufficient to sustain the thesis that Germany's aim is expansionist (but see e.g. Santo, 1993), but there does seem to be something disingenuous about the structure and ordering of the arguments, which in turn raise suspicions about the precise priorities of the West in general, as what for many commentators are the real motives are played down:

> *Erstens* freuen wir uns über die *Bereicherung* durch die Eigenart dieser Länder, die Europa, das Europa der EU, erfährt. *Zweitens* freuen wir uns aber auch darüber, *dass diese Länder ein politisches Europa wollen.* (ibid)
> [*Firstly*, we welcome the *enrichment* of Europe, the Europe of the EU, through the peculiar characteristics of these countries. *Secondly*, however, we are also delighted *that these countries want a political Europe.*]

One more example must suffice to support the argument that playing the cultural card is mere lip service:

Die neuen Länder werden die Gemeinschaft *durch ihre Kultur, aber auch* ihre wirtschaftliche Leistungsfähigkeit und ihre hochentwickelten Volkswirtschaften stärken. (*Das Parlament*, 18 March 1994)
[The new countries will strengthen the Community *through their culture, but also* through their economic performance and their highly developed economies.]

Such rhetorical *instrumentalisation* of 'culture' and other terms is not restricted to Germany. The reaction to it by Lafontaine and others does, however, carry a particular resonance in the context of Germany's feared hegemony, the recent move to Berlin and so on and so forth!

Nation and related vocabulary

The vocabulary of 'nationhood' which had been problematical in mainstream German political debate since the Nazi era was certainly partly rehabilitated in the early 1980's, when a Conservative government returned to power in Germany. The picture at the moment seems to involve, however, a certain ambivalence. Thus we can still hear a German politician speaking enviously of:

[...] die skandinavischen Länder mit ihrem ungebrochenen, ungezwungen natürlichen Verhältnis zu ihren *Nationen*. (*Das Parlament*, 18 March 1994)
[the Scandinavian countries and their continuous, naturally easy relationship to their *nations*.]

whereas Waigel's use of the German translation of de Gaulle's concept of *l'Europe des patries* betrays no more embarrassment on his part than does a similar term used on the British right, *Europe of Nations*. The differences between the two cultures in this area is more subtle: whereas such language in Germany remains, for some, simply unacceptable, because of recent history (here, for instance, is a *Zeit* journalist commenting on Waigel's term that he just he has just cited in his article):

Waigel hält es mit einem *'Europa der Vaterländer'* mit dem besonders grossen deutschen Vaterland in der Mitte. (*Die Zeit*, 18 June 1998)
[Waigel is after a *'Europe of Fatherland'* with the particularly big German fatherland in the middle.]

British criticism castigates not the language, which is out 'in the open' and can be used far less self-consciously, but particular versions of its interpretation: 'What I find depressing about the Opposition's stance is what a tim'rous wee beastie is their version of *nationalism* - a Britain constantly *in fear of the continentals'* (Robin Cook, *Hansard*).

Images involving 'white flags' and 'surrender' are frequent in the British debate, where 'battle is joined' very publicly around these issues: 'We can now see that the international government conference is not about the Battle of Britain or the *Nation State* as we know it and as we have heard from some Conservative members' (*Hansard*).

Such a tone is a long way from the 'apologetic' strain running through German discussion; a single example will give a sense of the need that is clearly felt to 'legitimise':

> *Patriotismus* und europäische Gesinnung gehören untrennbar zusammen. [...]
> die Deutschlandstiftung hat stets für einen *Patriotismus* geworben, der die
> *Vaterlandsliebe* anderer Völker achtet und die Einigung Europas bejaht. [...]
> *Europäische Identität ist kein Gegensatz zu unserer nationalen Identität.*
> *Liebe zum Vaterland,* Liebe zu Freiheit, *Patriotismus* und einer *europäischen*
> *Gesinnung* dürfen in Deutschland nie wieder getrennte Wege gehen. (Kohl, in
> a speech to the 'Deutschland- Stiftung', *Bulletin*, 21 June 1996)
> [*Patriotism* and a European mentality are inseparable from one another. [...] The
> 'Germany Foundation' has always promoted a *patriotism* which respects *the love of*
> *other peoples for their fatherlands* and welcomes the unification of Europe. *European*
> *identity and our national identity do not contradict one another. Love of the*
> *fatherland,* love of freedom, *patriotism* and *a European mentality* must never again be
> allowed to go their separate ways in Germany.]

The 'Nation State' extract above which stresses the *continuity* of this concept ('as we know it'), is quite at odds with a frequent - fragile - German line of argument, according to which many concepts are precisely not traditional or received, but represent a break with the past:

> Klar gesagt, die EU wird ganz selbstverständlich *Nationalstaaten* haben. Es
> werden andere *Nationalstaaten als Nationalstaaten im früheren Sinne* sein.
> (*Bulletin*, 29 April 1998)
> [To be quite clear here, naturally the EU will have Nation States. But these will be
> different Nation States than they used to be, in the old sense of the word.]

Renationalisierung

British commentators on the Cardiff Conference of Ministers in summer 1998 reported a general 'reassessment of the role of national governments (sic! - *not* 'nations' or 'nation states', CG) and a concomitant critique of once fashionable federalism', as *The Guardian* (17 June 1998) put it of

Blair's position. The shift in positions had to be registered with greater concern in Germany, given the problems we have just described! For critical voices there this 'reassessment' was, predictably, a *Renationalisierung*,[2] a negative term tapping into the problematic 'nation state' issue discussed above. *Renationalisierung* was doubly, perhaps trebly, negative: firstly, because of the problematic nature generally of vocabulary around 'nationhood', secondly - although one is actually the function of the other - because it was seen as a particular reaction of Kohl to his own right wing and to pressures from the right in Germany as a whole. And the whole thing was compounded by the specific charge of 'electioneering'. Joschka Fischer's (BÜNDNIS 90/DIE GRÜNEN) criticism was described as follows:

> Joschka Fischer kritisiert den Versuch, das drängende Problem der EU-Finanzreform unter dem Eindruck des *Wahlkampfes* innenpolitisch zu *instrumentalisieren*. Das Argument, dass Deutschland ein zu starker Nettozahler sei, bedeute entweder, 'dass Sie schon vorher versagt haben, da die Beschlüsse im Ministerrat einstimmig gefasst worden sind, oder aber, dass es sich hier um rein *nationale Töne* handelt zum Zweck der Mobilisierung *des rechten Randes*, zum Zweck der Beruhigung'. (*Das Parlament*, 26 June 1998)
> [Joschka Fischer criticised the attempt to *instrumentalise* the pressing problem of financial reform in the EU *for domestic electioneering purposes*. For Fischer the argument that Germany was making net overpayments to Europe meant either 'that you failed earlier, because the decisions were taken unanimously in the Council of Ministers, or, however, that the real reason you're making these *nationalistic noises* is to mobilise and pacify those on the *extreme right'*.]

Commentators identified a gradual loss of what some saw as the 'visionary' rhetoric in German discourse (such as we have heard a number of times from Herzog) at the same time as a discourse emanating directly from the Bavarian right gained ascendance:

> Bayerns Regierungschef Edmund Stoiber verlangt deshalb mehr Entscheidungsfreiheit in der Agrar- und Regionalpolitik. Der Leiter der Staatskanzlei ... erklärt, 'wir müssen die Entwicklungsunterschiede im eigenen Lande ausgleichen dürfen, sonst können wir gleich eine *Verwaltungsprovinz von Brüssel* werden'. (*Die Zeit*, 18 June 1998)
> [Bavaria's head of government is demanding greater autonomy in agricultural and regional policy decisions. Stoiber declares. 'we must be able to equal out the different stages of development in our own Land, or else we'll simply become an *administrative province of Brussels*.]

Once the negatively charged term *Renationalisierung* had been introduced into the debate, Kohl was forced to repudiate criticism against him *precisely 'in those terms'*, by using the word himself. It seems to be a characteristic of public/political debate that it be conducted with the dominant symbols which have emerged, even if they are disadvantageous to one side (as is *Renationalisierung* here); the apparent alternative of reframing the issue may be felt to run the risk of sounding like evasion. Note Kohl's insistent 'foregrounding' in:

> Bei all diesen Fragen - *auch das muss klar ausgesprochen werden* - geht es überhaupt nicht um *Renationalisierung*, wie das von einigen behauptet worden sei. (*Bulletin*, 29 April 1998)
> [All of these matters have - and *this is something which needs to be stated very clearly* - nothing whatever to do with renationalisation, as some people have claimed.]

It underlines the fact that 'renationalisation' does not simply denote certain measures, but classifies them, as part of a negative, 'voter-orientated' discourse, which also involved the negative *instrumentalisation* of 'Europe' as a scape-goat in an attempt to legitimise the 'reassessment':

> Nun inszeniert man auch noch den *ideologisch überhöhten Streit mit dem europäischen Moloch*, um vom eigenen Versagen abzulenken. (*Die Zeit*, 18 June 1998)
> [Now they're even staging an *ideologically hyped argument with the evil European giant* in an attempt to divert attention away from their own failures.]

Part of Kohl's rejection of the charge of *Renationalisierung* was to subsume the measures referred to under the related headings of *Subsidiarität* and *Bürgernähe*, often, revealingly, in the context of the 'rejection':

> Das hat überhaupt nichts mit *Renationalisierung* zu tun, wie manches mal behauptet wird. Wir wollen eine *bürgernahe* EU. (*Bulletin*, 29 April 1998)
> [That has got nothing to do with *renationalisation*, as is often claimed. We want a *'people's Europe'*.][3]

Both of these concepts (*Subsidiarität* and *Bürgernähe*), and, indeed, *Föderalismus*, have been in the European debate for almost a decade. The first two express - on this there is reasonably widespread agreement - countervailing values to the idea of an 'anonymous, bureaucratic superstate'; 'federalism', which will be discussed later in this essay, is more contentious. Both *Subsidiarität* and *Bürgernähe* became contentious in the post-Cardiff debates to a much higher degree in Germany than they did in Britain.

Bürgernähe, a concept apparently introduced already during the Maastricht negotiations, in 1992, by Germany - it is easy to read this as a token introduced at that time to allay suspicions of 'centralism' on the part of Germany's European neighbours - became revitalised in the Kohl/Chirac letter to Blair, as Chairman of the European Council, in advance of the Cardiff meeting of heads of government. The idea was indeed taken up and developed; the British press repeated Blair's notion of a 'people's Europe'. The difference lay in the way this was commented on: in the British debate the putative 'gap between Europe and the people' was treated simply as an 'issue' - and the project reported on merely 'descriptively'. Both of the following short extracts read 'neutrally': 'Blair's call for political reforms to bring Europe closer to its people' (*The Independent*, 15 June 1998) and even: 'The new nation-state rhetoric of Cardiff [...] and the idea that Europe will be brought closer to its people by rallying behind the privileges of the nation-state (*The Guardian*, 17 June 1998). *Bürgernah* and *Subsidiarität*, however, resonate quite differently in the German post-Cardiff debate. A brief extract from *Die Zeit* sums up one powerful interpretation:

Eine wachsende Zahl von deutschen Politikern hat Angst vor einem Bedeutungsverlust. Sie wird verhüllt in angebliche Sorge um mehr *Bürgernähe* - als seien die Bundesregierung, die deutsche Verwaltung insgesamt Gralshüter bürgerfreundlichen Handelns [...] *Renationalisierung* statt fortschreitender Integration ist die Leitidee, die sich hinter der *hübschen Formel von der Subsidiarität* verbirgt - auch wenn Kohl das heftig abstreitet. (*Die Zeit*, 18 June 1998)
[A growing number of German politicians are frightened of becoming less important. The fear is dressed up as alleged concern that politics should be brought *closer to the people* - as if the German government, perhaps the administration as a whole, were the champion of people-friendly behaviour. [...] The main idea is *renationalisation* instead of increasing integration, although the idea is hidden behind the *nice little word 'subsidiarity'.*]

Bürgernähe and *Subsidiarität* are held by many German commentators, but by others also, to be a version of 'double-speak', legitimising a transfer of many competencies from Europe back to the nation-state. Again there is welcome evidence in the explicitness of the need apparently felt by the government to counter the negative characterisation of a 'nationalist discourse' which created, as we have seen, many fewer problems in the context of British political culture (and where, furthermore, the terms did not generate so much conflict!):

> Das [ein recht verstandenes *Subsidiaritätsprinzip*, CG] hat nichts - um es klar auszusprechen - mit dem Willen zur *Renationalisierung* zu tun. *Ich finde dieses Schlagwort ist völlig fehl am Platz.* (*Bulletin*, 29 April 1998)
> [A properly understood principle of subsidiary has - and this needs saying very clearly - nothing to do with a desire for renationalisation. I think this slogan is quite inappropriate in this context.]

The terms in which the German debate over Europe is conducted suggest that the federalist structure and sensibilities of the country constitute another reason for difficulties . For, whereas in Britain the ideas of a 'people's Europe' and 'subsidiarity' can still express (only) acceptable aspirations, the conditions already 'given' in Germany, of devolution of power, and local and regional autonomy - processes just beginning, we note, in the British polity - present an ever-present, real structure, against which the sincerity of the intention to implement *Subsidiarität, Bürgernähe* and so on can be challenged and tested. Something like this surely underlies Joschka Fischer's view on Kohl's post-Cardiff domestic speech:

> Herr Bundeskanzler, Sie haben es am Beispiel der *Bürgernähe* mit dem Begriff der *Subsidiarität* versucht. Ich habe eben sehr genau zugehört. *Subsidiarität* dort, wo es heisst, die Kirche im Dorf zu lassen, ist völlig richtig. Die Frage ist die Abgrenzung. Darauf ist die Bundesregierung mit keinem Wort eingegangen. (*Das Parlament*, 24 June 1998)
> [Chancellor, you've just tried to say something about *subsidiary* by using the example of *'closeness to the people'*. And I listened very carefully to what you had to say. *Subsidiarity* is fine, if you don't want too many changes. The question is one of demarcation [of competencies, CG]. And the government didn't have a word to say on that score.]

Fischer sees his suspicions borne out by the 'abstractness' of the government's expression, as it were (the only mode of understanding the terms in the British system, it is suggested). And indeed, although there is much talk of *Subsidiarität* as including the participation of individual citizens right down to the lowest level:

> Sie [Harmonisierung der Sozial-, Einkommens- und Steuerpolitik, CG] würde das *Subsidiaritätsprinzip verletzen.* Sie wäre das Gegenteil von dem, was wir wollen, nämlich ein Europa, in dem Bürgerinnen, Bürger, Unternehmen und Regionen *ihre eigene Aufgabe selbstverantwortlich in die Hände nehmen.* (*Bulletin*, 29 April 1998)

[Harmonising social, incomes and tax policies would break the principle of *subsidiarity*. It would be the exact opposite of what we want, that is, an Europe where men and women, firms and regions take over *the responsibility for running their own affairs*.]

Wir können auch nicht fehlgehen, wenn wir uns zunächst um unsere *Verwandten und Freunde* kümmern und nach dem Staat nur dann rufen, wenn wir in der *kleinen Gemeinschaft* nicht mehr weiter kommen. (*Bulletin*, 15 June 1993)
[We won't go far wrong if we look after our *relatives and friends*, first and foremost, and only look to the state if we can't manage things in the *small community*.]

much of the 'talk' must strike Fischer et al. precisely as being no more than that - talk - , when in fact already extant conditions in Germany would allow a greater degree of 'institutionalisation'.

In the Maastricht and Amsterdam treaties the two concepts appear without any emotional accompaniment, so to speak. It is precisely their 'emotionalisation' in the aftermath of Cardiff which strikes commentators as marking their degeneration into a kind of mere 'mood music' There is evidence to justify my - and Joschka Fischer's! - sense of unease. For instance, in many cases when the speaker goes beyond the 'fine phrases' and perhaps begins to specify 'institutions' which would facilitate the two ingredients we are discussing, in an attempt to correct perceived *'Fehler im Dialog mit den Bürgern'* (Kohl, *Bulletin*, 18 March 1994) the language and context are sometimes revealing:

Dieses Europa darf nicht fern von den Menschen sein; [...] dass im nationalen Bereich in Bonn das entschieden wird, was dort für Deutschland am besten, bürgernah entschieden werden kann. (*Das Parlament*, 22 June 1998)
[This Europa must not be far removed from ordinary people; [...] that we decide nationally, in Bonn, those things that are best decided there for Germany, close to the people.]

Formulations, in other words, which move beyond the abstract seem to fix on Germany/Bonn as the ultimate locus of *Bürgernähe*.

In short, the following rhetorical question posed by a *Zeit* journalist does appear to spring from a certain sense of insincerity regarding the commitment to implement the principles we have been discussing (indeed the comment could relate directly to this last passage!):

Ist die *Subsidiarität* nicht eher ein Vorwand für *nationale* Regierungen, die um ihre Stellung zwischen Brüssel und den Regionen bangen? (*Die Zeit*, 10 June 1998)
[Maybe *subsidiarity* is only a pretext for *national* governments, worried about their position between Brussels and the regions?]

In Britain, the idea of returning responsibility to the nation-state does not necessitate problematising the term.

It is because of the peculiar German conditions that Scharping could argue:

Wenn es darum geht, Europa *bürgernah* zu gestalten, dann sollten wir uns in Deutschland vornehmen, zunächst bei uns einzulösen, was Sie von Europa verlangen. Die Reform wesentlicher Politikbereiche, und zwar nach dem Prinzip der *Subsidiarität*, schafft die Voraussetzung dafür, dass wir Europa erweitern können. (*Das Parlament*, 24 June 1998)
[If we want *to bring Europe closer to its peoples* we should determine to deliver here in Germany what you are asking of Europe. Reforming a number of essential areas of politics according to the *subsidiarity* principle is a pre-condition of our being able to extend Europe.]

The accusation underlying this is that the concepts under discussion here are being *instrumentalised*, that is, are serving merely to support and enhance the prospect of the extension of the EU, perhaps to oil the wheels of negotiation, whilst committing the then government to no action beyond their utterance!

Typically, it is in more visionary texts that an answer to the substantive questions is indicated:

Die andere ist die Frage der *Bürgernähe*, und zwar zunächst die der *örtlichen Nähe des Bürgers zu 'seinem' Europa-Abgeordneten*. (Herzog, *Bulletin*, 4 May 1998)
[The other question concerns bringing Europa closer to the people, first and foremost therefore the geographical proximity of the ordinary citizen to 'his' European MP.]

(Unfortunately, this may be utopian in more senses than one, for, although the constituency principle operates in the UK, Europe seems to many citizens there to be as remote as it apparently does in Germany!)

Opponents of the, as they see it, duplicitous discourse, have called for - and criticised the government for rejecting - *plebiscites* and other similar, more *participatory*, expressions of democracy as ways of giving real meaning to the twin principles of *Subsidiarität* and *Bürgernähe*.[4] Since referenda are problematical in the British polity also, we can possibly understand the failure of many terms in a potentially fulfilled European discourse to establish themselves as lying ultimately precisely in the often tacit conflict between two forms of democratic practice, the representative and the participatory, practice, as it were, lagging behind linguistic potential.

To sum up the argument on these and similar central terms: we have argued that *Subsidiarität* and *Bürgernähe* seem to function in German political discourse about Europe more as 'emotive' terms, with little by way of stable reference. The equivalents do this also in British discourse, but whereas, for the reasons suggested above, that is a tolerable position, the strong federalist impulse in Germany often generates argument about their sincerity.

The adaptability of the terms has been demonstrated again under the new leadership of Chancellor Schröder, who came to power in the 1998 election. Some of his pronouncements in the area have given a surprising pragmatic twist to an application of the concepts already encountered in the language of the FDP (the German 'Liberal' party): 'Europa kann dem kleinen Mann helfen durch stabile Preise und niedrigere Zinsen, das ist *Bürgernähe*'. [Europe can help the little man, through price stability and lower taxes. That's *'closer to the people'*.] (*Das Parlament*, 24 June 1998) ('User-friendly' policies, is the suggestion here, are more genuinely 'popular' than any form of institutionalised participation or 'empowerment of the individual'.)

Schröder has attempted a similar 'inversion': whilst for most of those involved *Subsidiarität* and *Bürgernähe* point downwards, as it were, in the hierarchy, Schröder has incorporated both concepts into his discourse in a way which relates the individual to Europe in an ideologically novel construct, according to which 'European' is, by definition, of itself, 'popular', directly representing 'the little man':

Das heisst, diejenige institutionelle Ebene soll eine Aufgabe anpacken, die sie am besten - d.h. *am nächsten an den Problemen* - zu lösen imstande sind. [...] Das verstehen wir unter aktiver Europapolitik, die die Nöte und *Interessen der Menschen* in den Mittelpunkt stellt. (*Das Parlament*, 25 December 1998) [In other words problems should be tackled at the institutional level which can solve them most easily, that is, are *closest to them*. [...] What we understand by active European policies are those which put the needs and the *interests of the people* at the centre of things.]

Note how, in this highly self-conscious language, the 'ideologeme' 'near to the people' has been replaced by 'near to the problems'! This emphasis allows the 'logical' next step in the argument: 'In den dringenden Fragen wollen die Menschen nicht unbedingt weniger Europa, sondern mehr'. [In urgent matters people don t want less Europe, but more.] (ibid)

The terms of this new line of argument have clearly been dictated by the discussion generated around the demand in the Kohl/Chirac letter, sent to Blair in advance of the Cardiff heads of government conference in 1998, for greater *Bürgernähe*: whilst Schröder may reinterpret this and other related concepts *he needs to retain them* as the dominant - and at least partly established - ideas in international discussion about Europe, framing his arguments in relatively established patterns of thought. Schröder is 'talking about' the important issue of 'harmonisation' at the European level, but casting it - and thereby lending it a degree of legitimisation? - in the 'close to the people' paradigm. Note how self-consciously he again creates the logical link in:

> Es geht uns vor allem darum , den Abbau der Jugend- und Langzeit-arbeitslosigkeit auch auf europäischer Ebene - *ich sage noch einmal, das ist kein Ersatz, sondern eine Ergänzung nationaler Massnahmen* - voranzubringen. (*Das Parlament*, 25 December 1998)
> [Our main aim is to continue reducing youth and long term unemployment on the European level as well - *let me repeat, that is not a substitute for, but a natural extension of national policies.*]

We have already seen Kohl defending himself against the charge of 'renationalisation'. Schröder 'de-nationalises', as it were, but subsumes Kohl's discourse within his own.

Föderalismus/Federalism

A third term, alongside *Bürgernähe* and *Subsidiarität*, is *Föderalismus*. Much has been written on this central idea in the European debate (e.g. Good, 1996) and will not be repeated here. However, the *'F*-word' needs to be mentioned in the context of the present argument also. Many commentators have argued that the references to this in the Maastricht Treaty of 1992 represented no more than a 'Schutzbehauptung' of the negotiators, who failed precisely to allow themselves to be guided by, for example, *föderalistische Einsichten und Rücksichten* (Bohley, 1993). Similar doubts are raised by Bohley and others also over the degree of real commitment to *Subsidiarität* (thus lending welcome support from within a variety of disciplines to the conclusions arrived at in this paper on primarily linguistic grounds):

> Das in Maastricht aufgenommene *Subsidiaritätsprinzip* ist *juristisch wertlos*. (an economic lawyer writing in the *Frankfurter Allgemeine Zeitung*, 12 September 1992)
> [The principle of subsidiarity adopted in Maastricht is *legally vacuous*.]

> Der Kernbegriff von Maastricht (= *Subsidiarität*, CG) ist eine Leerformel. (a constitutional lawyer, *Frankfurter Allgemeine Zeitung*, 17 September 1992)
> [The key concept of Maastricht is *a hollow formula*.]

> Die allseits abgegebenen Bekenntnisse zu ihm haben wohl kaum mehr als *Beschwichtigungscharakter*. (ibid)
> [The ubiquitous expressions of loyalty to the principle seem to be there chiefly to *mollify* people (= to calm potential opposition? CG).]

These reactions are, it should be noted, to be found in a piece which is distinctly *pro-federalist*, arguing the case for transferring a well-tried German principle onto the European level. These early misgivings with regard to *Föderalismus* and *Subsidiarität* appear to confirm the argument advanced here that such 'abstract' concepts, although they are a constant theme in the European debate, tend to remain at a level of abstraction, failing agreement about their precise application/implementation. (Maybe it is precisely by remaining at a level of abstraction that international agreement becomes at all possible?) A sharp distinction exists here between Germany and Great Britain, for, whereas we learn that, in German culture:

> Das *Subsidiaritätsprinzip* ist auf Interpretationshilfe aus der *Föderalismus-theorie* angewiesen. (Bohley 1993, p. 37)
> [The principle of *subsidiarity* needs to be interpreted in relation to the theory of *federalism*.]

The two principles mentioned here are quite incompatible in Britain.

Language in the International Domain

Given the problematical nature within the national cultures of certain terms crucial for a European discourse discussed above, it might seem obvious that the attempt to use such terms in an international context with a *'konsensuales, international akzeptiertes Begriffsverständnis'* was unlikely to succeed. But, in addition to such difficulties, there are a number of other aspects to this question of 'internationally shared' meanings:

'Leaking Discourses'

We must not forget that the tone and substance of internal conflicts impact on the international debate, if only because public and politicians in the various countries may be informed in a variety of ways - via the media, for instance - about discussions in other cultures. Politicians may be less than cautious about this domestically, even though this could clearly damage the cause of international harmony. Taking the prefix *Mittel-* in a set of related concepts as an example it is a Conservative politician who cautions:

> Ich benutze den Begriff der *Mittellage* nicht gern. Das ist immer ein gefährlicher Begriff in der Geschichte gewesen. (Pfennig in Bulletin, 16 February 1994)
> [I don't like using the concept *'at the centre'*. That has always been a dangerous notion in our history.]

Given that a similar sense of the resonance of such a term - or, at least, of related 'ideas' - must surely be assumed to be common among many of Germany's European neighbours, it is perhaps surprising that the same speaker goes on to say:

> Deutschland als *Hauptmotor* unserer *europäischen Vernetzung* und Integration entspricht unseren Interessen, aber auch den Interessen unserer Nachbarn. (ibid)
> [Germany as the *main engine* of our European network and integration is in our interest, but also the interest of our neighbours.]

and to make the potentially risky point that this German role: '[...] ist nicht allein durch die geographische Lage bedingt'. [is not determined by geography alone.] (ibid.). This construction not quite saved by the insistence that what is happening:

> [...] ist in keinem Falle identisch mit *früheren Mitteleuropakonzepten*, die es in Deutschland gegeben hat, die nicht positiv zu bewerten waren. (ibid) (note the similarity of this formulation to *frühere Nationalstaaten*, above)

['[...]isn't at all the same thing as *earlier ideas of central Europe* which there were in Germany and which were not at all positive'.]

Chancellor Kohl elaborated further in:

Was unsere Verantwortung ist, will ich als die *europäische Berufung* der Deutschen bezeichnen. ... Deswegen tragen wir, die Deutschen, in dem Prozess der europäischen Einigung eine besondere *Verantwortung.* (*Das Parlament*, 29 April 1998)
[I would like to call what I see as our responsibility the *European vocation* of the Germans. That's why we, the Germans, bear a particular *responsibility* in the process of European unification.]

A very particular perception is contained in these and other similar lines of argument. Pfennig, whose words introduced this discussion, argues that:

Wir Deutschen sollten mit den Begriffen *Mitteleuropa* und *Mittellage* etwas umsichtiger umgehen. (because, CG) Das hört sich bei unseren Nachbarn etwas anders an, als wir vielleicht meinen. (*Das Parlament*, 18 March 1994)
[We Germans should be a bit more careful in the way we use the concepts *central Europe* and *'at the centre'*, because they tend to mean something a bit different to our neighbours than we possibly intend.]

This seems to point up the reference above to the influence of domestic debate beyond national borders, raising the question of how seriously neighbours who cannot always listen to propositions in context should take what may or may not be 'rhetoric'. It should be borne in mind that the wider context includes British worries about German hegemony on the one hand and a situation, on the other, where Germany has protested to France:

Wir haben doch nur versucht zu helfen, das hat nichts mit einer angeblichen *Führungsrolle* zu tun. (*Das Parlament*, 29 March/1 April 1994)
[We were only trying to help, that has nothing whatsoever to do with an alleged *leadership role.*]

A similar point can be made concerning *federalism*:

Der föderalistische Staatsaufbau in Deutschland ist *ein gutes Modell für ganz Europa*. Es ist natürlich nicht immer einfach für uns, mit dem *föderalen Verständnis* bei unseren Partnern in Europa durchzudringen. (*Bulletin*, 9 June 1998)

[The German federalist structure is *a good model for the whole of Europe.* It's not always easy for us to get a proper understanding of federalist across to our European partners.]

One can only imagine the impact this statement might have, over and above difficulties with the term itself, on Germany's European partners.

Knowledge of Differences?

The idea of a *konsensuales, international akzeptiertes Begriffsverständnis* is both desirable and naive. For the idea that it is only the conceptual differences implied here which impede communication would surely suggest that politicians and others are unaware of them, whilst only linguists and political scientists are privy to the idea. This is simply not the case. There is ample testimony that both sides - in the German-English discussion - are quite conscious of the risks inherent in the fact that words can mean different things in different cultures:

Im einzelnen gibt es darüber - das ist wahr, das ist ganz normal bei einem solchen dramatischen Prozess der Veränderung in Brüssel und in den einzelnen Mitgliedstaaten gibt es noch sehr *unterschiedliche Vorstellungen.* (*Bulletin*, 3 April 1998)
[On particular points there are - that's perfectly normal in the kind of dramatic process of change that's under way in Brussels - still *very different opinions among* the member states]

Elsewhere in our material, other, similar expressions reveal knowledge of the phenomenon: *unterschiedliche gesellschaftliche Modelle und kulturelle Entwicklungen,* for example.

Politicians and others, in other words, are not naive in this sense. So it is barely plausible that intelligent people cannot remain mindful of this essentially simple issue in the attempt to take away from international conferences 'texts' resting on 'internally accepted concepts'! And indeed, we learn, for instance, that:

Die Formulierung zur *Subsidiarität* im Maastrichter Vertrag wurde durch eine ganze Reihe flankierender Selbstverpflichtungen, vereinbarten *Sprachregelungen* und Auslegungen ergänzt. (*Das Parlament*, 18 March 1994)
[The use of *subsidiarity* in the Maastricht treaty was accompanied by a host of precise commitments by the partners and by *agreed definitions* and interpretations.]

This surely is the right beginning: if you are aware of false friends, you won't judge them by appearances! And indeed, here is one politician, Kohl, whose complaint, in the second part of the following extract, seems to confirm that the problem ought not to exist; here is he is speaking to the French:

> Für Franzosen ist das, was wir in der Diskussion um den *Föderalismus* für selbstverständlich halten, ein mühsamer Prozess. Charles de Gaulle ist an diesem Punkt mit einer entsprechender Politik gescheitert. [...] Wir haben noch das zusätzliche Problem der Sprachen. Wenn ich in einem Vortrag in London von Föderalismus spreche, erreiche ich genau das Gegenteil von dem, was ich beabsichtige, weil die Menschen dort zwar auch das wollen, was wir wollen, die Sprache ihnen aber bei der Verwendung dieses Wortes *etwas anders vermittelt*. (*Bulletin*, 29 April 1998)
>
> [What we take for granted in discussions of *federalism* is a difficult business for the French. Charles de Gaulle failed to gain acceptance for his policies on the matter. ... And then there is the added problem of the languages. If I talk about federalism in a lecture in London, I achieve exactly the opposite from what I intend, because, whilst the people there may want what we want, the word in their language *conveys something quite different* .]

In a similar vein a pronouncement of Santer's was reported, following a statement by Tony Blair that Britain did 'not want a centralised federal European *superstate*: 'At his side Mr. Santer said he was a *federalist*, but that the word meant different things in Britain and Europe. To us it means *decentralisation* to nations and regions' (*The Guardian*, 17 June 1998).

Again, we might justifiably ask, why can language not simply be taken out of the equation? The answer is that unbiased objective communication at an international level remains an ideal, which is, for a variety of reasons not usually attained. One reason is that our leaders are not merely sane minds, engaged in rational discourse; they are party politicians, jockeying for position vis-a-vis one another and caught up at home, too, in the power game. Not to mention that politics is carried on - via the media - beyond the politicians, with the home 'publics at large', publics which also have ideas about words and meanings and values, which no Amsterdam supplement will standardise out of existence, people, furthermore, who, like many politicians themselves, have an underdeveloped ability to understand appropriately how *language itself* works (see below). As soon as they step away from the negotiating table, politicians step back into this interest-ridden semantic environment.

We have already heard Kohl manipulating, for party political purposes, the word *Subsidiarität*, in a way that probably no supplement could codify or prevent, in order to legitimise what some were calling his move towards *Renationalisierung*. The will to clarify, which is already problematical in the international arena (see Blair's reaction) certainly does not necessarily exist domestically. This is because *contexts* on a local political level add to the problem of creating an European discourse. Those contexts will include interlocutors who have no interest whatsoever in letting historically acquired meanings and cultural connotations rest, whose political purposes are best served by not doing so. The trust which might allow communication to proceed in the light of known differences is in somewhat short supply in the political game between and within individual nations.

Tacit Views on Language

We can identify an onomasiological and a semasiological aspect to the problem of communicating across cultural divides. The Kohl extract about his experience in London illustrates the first of these: an educational campaign which aimed to persuade a British audience, not so mindful, perhaps, of matters linguistic as the international negotiators, that since they '*auch das wollen, was wir wollen*' (see above) they should put out of their heads that the word '*ihnen etwas anders vermittelt*', involves an attempt to educate people into 'linguistic relativism' which they will usually reject, be their rejection naive or somehow politically motivated. There is, incidentally, evidence that it may be either or both: a British MP, who could be heard putting forward the apparently enlightened view in the House of Commons 1997 debate: 'Let us forget the ridiculous term *superstate*; that can mean anything to anybody' (*Hansard*), then went on to argue, in a way revealing a kind of belief in 'word magic', naively and in terms of a simplistic dichotomy. The choice, he said, is between a *partnership of nations* and a *federal state*. This is, of course, nonsense, logically or institutionally speaking, involving false antonyms.

   We see here utopia slipping further from our grasp, not just because of non-ideal and politically motivated interlocutors, but also because of a more inherently *linguistic* phenomenon; we might call it 'vulgar semantics'. The same speaker went on to provide us with an example of what I have called the onomasiological dimension, when, after saying: 'This treaty (Maastricht, CG) takes us [...] irreversibly into a *federal* structure.[...] We can debate whether this (the move into a federal structure, CG) is right or not' (*Hansard*).

For him the 'real' conditions created by Maastricht *constitute* 'federalism'. The/a pro-Maastricht argument is simply unwinnable against such a semantics; certain structures are willy-nilly 'federal', so we have federalism 'absolutely'. Interestingly enough, although in one sense the speaker following appears on one level to reject the latter's interpretation, he does so with an argument which is remarkably similar in the naiveté of its - onomasiological - semantics: 'We may, or may not want a federal Europe - I personally do not - , but a proposal for a federal Europe is not contained in the draft treaty' (*Hansard*).

That argument will not convince the first speaker; for him, the word may not be there, but the meaning is! 'Looking at the facts', from any angle whatsoever, will not change this conviction; 'form' and 'meaning' cannot be separated.

Another variant of this way of thinking is to be seen in the words of Bill Cash in the same debate:

> On the Amsterdam Treaty the idea that the EU should be given a legal personality is a massive step in the direction of a *federal Europe*. It is pointless to repeat the mantra that we are not, to all intents, in a federal arrangement. I am more interested in identifying the functions that are being transferred as the constitutional criteria for determining the movement towards Europe than in the *general expression, federal or otherwise*. (*Hansard*)

Similarly, he had earlier described how a series of concessions were being made on the Amsterdam Treaty, '*completely ignoring the federal character of what is being created*'.

For some speakers - be it for mischievous or mistaken reasons - the language is there, whether it is expressed or not, as a kind of necessary accompaniment to certain structures in reality. There was assuredly a similar linguistic aspect to the problems de Gaulle apparently had with the French and 'federalism', even though this is not mentioned by Kohl (see above).

The example of *sovereignty* also illustrates the fact that you cannot easily lift words out of context for international purposes and calmly codify, by dusting off the historical and cultural patina which has accreted round them. Again it is worth reminding ourselves that 'the British' are no more a homogenous bunch than 'the Germans', a construct which is inherent in the 'false friends' version of international communication. One British politician, for instance, quoted Bernard Crick: 'I think that *sovereignty* is an outdated eighteenth-century Whig concept and that it's time we moved into the real world' (*Hansard*).

The trouble is that although many and others - the sort for whom *federalism* is *federalism*, call it what you will - may not inhabit Bernard Crick's real world, their world is every bit as real, even when, as in the case of the following speaker, they sound a bit embarrassed about it:

> To some people it is an assertion of that somewhat old-fashioned and much derided concept of *sovereignty*. When we defend those aspects (he has in mind defence and immigration, CG), as I am sure my Right Honourable Friend does vigorously, we are defending the old-fashioned concept of *sovereignty*. (*Hansard*).

For the people who - self-consciously or otherwise - live in this world, any transfer of any function to Brussels is a loss of sovereignty. It seems unlikely that any internationally agreed definitions could remove this difficulty. It is interesting that one speaker in the House of Commons debate raises the question: 'How does the speaker believe the French and German governments talk to their people?' (*Hansard*).

He implies an answer to his own question when he makes the point that it is not a question of *sovereignty*, but of *shared sovereignty*. The impression is, however, that the concept barely figures in German political discourse. Perhaps this is the real reason for the state of affairs described as follows: 'No British or French politician is prepared to share Germany's preparedness to give up *sovereignty* at state level' (*The Independent*, 15 June 1998).

Possibly because of the long-standing federalist structure in the country, German political discourse seems to be such that neither does the politician find him- or herself in the position of having to put the proposition in these terms, nor would the German public expect to hear a message framed in this way. (Certainly, others have said that full national sovereignty began to interest the Germans only after the '4+2' talks!) And, although the word *Souveränität* does not appear in the following, these words of Kinkel nevertheless suggest that the Germans do not ultimately understand 'this old-fashioned Whig concept' (Crick). Kinkel points out that:

Die nordischen Länder und der Osten haben sorgfältig abgewogen. Sie wissen auch, dass sie keinen *Verlust nationaler Einheit* und heimischer Lebenswerte befürchten müssen. (*Das Parlament*, 18 March 1994)
[The nordic countries and those in the East have considered things carefully. They know also that they do not have to fear any *loss of national unity* or national values.]

Kohl's argument in the following seems to point to a similar understanding:

Aber die nationalen Identitäten werden in der Geschichte und in der Tradition, vor allem in der kulturellen Definition der einzelnen Länder bleiben. (*Bulletin*, 29 April 1998)
[But the national identities will retain the definition they have by virtue of the history and tradition, but above all the culture of the individual countries.]

Being British is for some people all of these things and more, the more being the *sovereignty* which seems to carry much less emphasis in other national political discourses in Europe. *Sovereignty* in British political discourse may involve history, tradition and culture, but it is, over and above these components, quintessentially political, and that at the kind of visceral level John Major has referred to as the instincts of the *British* (*our traditions and instincts are different* [*Hansard*]). This version of independence cannot be by-passed by appealing to history and culture!

The point of this second section has been that the task of achieving a common *Begriffsverständnis* is infinitely more problematic than might seem to be the case: politicians know about differences in meaning, but it is sometimes in their interest and that of other politicians, at home and abroad, not to permit the desired clarity to come between them and their party and its voters.

Tony Blair said, after Cardiff:

Wir sprechen die gleiche Sprache: Umsetzung gesunder, makroökonomischer Politik in Verbindung mit Massnahmen zur Verbesserung der Beschäftigungsfähigkeit, Vollendung des Binnenmarktes bei gleichzeitiger Förderung der Fairness am Arbeitsplatz, Einsatz von Marktmechanismen als Fördermassnahmen für Unternehmer zur Schaffung von Arbeitsplätzen. (*Die Welt*, 12 June 1998)
[We're speaking the same language: the implementation of solid, macroeconomic policies in combination with measures to improve employability, completion of the internal market at the same time as we promote fairness in the work- place, putting in place market mechanisms which will encourage employers to create jobs.]

Possibly - but the 'gleiche Sprache' he has in mind involves the lexicon of policy and planning, not the ideologically problematic discourses which have been the subject of the above. And it is the latter which will allow the Europeans to come together ... or not!

Notes

1	All emphases - here and in the following in italics - are mine, as are all translations German to English, in square brackets.
2	The origins of the term are obscure; commentators note its existence in the European debate (cf. e.g. Jung and Wengeler, 1995, p. 124), but offer no further account. Jacques Santer, too, detected a tendency towards 'renationalisation' in the Kohl/Chirac letter.
3	It is difficult to know how to translate the German term, since the connotations of the German and the British expressions are so different and are themselves the subject of some of the following discussion.
4	e.g. for the SPD, Wiczorek-Zeul in the debate reproduced in the Bulletin, 24 June 1998.

References

Bohley, P. (1993), 'Europäische Einheit, föderalistisches Prinzip und Währungsunion: Wurde in Maastricht der richtige Weg beschritten?', Aus Politik und Zeitgeschichte, Beilage zur Wochenzeitung Das Parlament, 1. January, pp. 33-45.

Bulletin, issued by the Presse-und Informationsamt der Bundesregierung, Bonn.

Das Parlament, issued by the Bundeszentrale für Politische Bildung, Bonn.

Good, C. (1996), 'Political communication and political culture in Germany and Great Britain; Some differences and similarities', in A.Musolff, C. Schäffner and M. Townson, M. (eds), *Conceiving of Europe; Diversity in Unity*, Dartmouth Publishers, Aldershot, pp. 109-20.

Hansard, The Parliamentary Debates; Official Report. HMSO.

Jung, M. and Wengeler, M. (1995), 'Nation Europa und Europa der Nationen. Sprachliche Kontroversen in der Europapolitik', in G.Stötzel and M. Wengeler (eds), *Kontroverse Begriffe. Geschichte des öffentlichen Sprachgebrauchs in der Bundesrepublik Deutschland*, Walter de Gruyter, Berlin/New York; pp. 93-128.

Müller-Brandeck-Bocquet, G. (1991), 'Ein föderalistisches Europa', Aus Politik und Zeitgeschichte, Beilage zur Wochenzeitung Das Parlament, 1. November, pp. 13-25.

Santo, S. (1993), *Die Lüge Europas. Ein Kontinent bangt um seine Zukunft*, Rasch und Roehring, Hamburg.

7 The Metaphorisation of European Politics: *Movement* on the *Road* to Europe

ANDREAS MUSOLFF

Paths and *Ways* towards Europe

In 1994, *The Independent* published an article in which the author, Andrew Marshall, analysed what he called 'Euro-babble', i.e. the multitude of metaphors which permeate and, according to Marshall, confuse the political debate over Europe. Marshall grouped the array of verbal Euro-imagery into five themes: 1) 'The options a la carte', 2) 'Variable Geometry', 3) 'The Hard Core', 4) 'Concentric Circles' and 5) 'Multi-track, Multi-speed'. The last category was explained further as being based on an analogy between the Union and 'a giant motorway system'. The analogical argument runs along the lines: just as only a limited set of traffic rules is required for a motorway system, so in the EU everyone 'must share the traffic rules (free trade, open markets, fair competition) but beyond that, anything goes' (*The Independent,* 11 September 1994). Marshall's account of supposed reactions signals his own critical position to the EU-as-a-motorway concept: 'Critics say: it would end progress towards Union, dangerously weaken the European institutions and mean a return to the Europe of power politics and nation states. Supporters say: oh, good' (ibid).

It is this kind of *argumentative* use of metaphors in the public debates about Europe in Britain and Germany which I will investigate in this chapter. To do this, I shall refer to a selection of *path/movement/speed* metaphors drawn from a special corpus of metaphors in Euro-debates, which is part of the ARC-project on 'Attitudes towards Europe'. So far, the corpus, parts of which already are available on the Internet,[1] contains 2132 separate entries (= 550.000 words) of metaphorical passages, which have been drawn from 28 British and German broadsheet newspapers and magazines from between 1989 and 2000.[2] On the basis of lexical recurrence and collocations, the metaphor passages have been grouped into more than 20

179

thematic fields which are more specific than Marshall's metaphor themes. However, they too can be organised into wider thematic groups such as, for instance, *dynamic* vs. *static* images, images of *group membership* and *group control*, of *strength* vs. *weakness*, and of *competition, fighting* and *war*.[3]

The metaphors depicting political development in (and of) the EU as a form of *travel* along *a road or path* form the largest group within the corpus: general *path* and *movement* metaphors alone account for 210 entries; if we count also more specified examples of *train* and *maritime* and other *vehicle*-related imagery, we get 389 examples altogether. The importance of this metaphor theme for public debates on Europe has already been noted and exemplary analyses have been provided (cf. Musolff, 1996, 2000; Schäffner, 1996); however, the present study aims at providing an overview of the main argumentative uses of these metaphors and especially of significant distributional differences between the British and German samples within the corpus.

Path, road or *way* metaphors abound in the public debate on EU politics, as these metaphors in question belong to one of the most basic schemas for the conceptualisation of processes *spanning* any *stretch* of time as well as for abstract social and psychological experience;[4] however, this does not mean that they are devoid of political significance or argumentative function. In British public discourse, for instance, *way* imagery has gained special connotations in the party-political debate since Tony Blair and intellectuals close to the Labour movement successfully launched the slogan of a *Third Way* as a label to characterise New Labour's policy as being different from both conservative/neo-liberal thinking on the one hand and Old Labour politics or orthodox socialist/communist ideology on the other (cf. e.g. Giddens, 1998). The *Third Way* catch phrase also made its way into the Euro-debate: Labour's Chancellor of the Exchequer, Gordon Brown, for instance, announced that 'Britain wanted to create a third way, between rampant free-market economics and stifling over-regulation, combining economic German efficiency and social inclusion' (*The Guardian*, 14 October 1997). The successful party-political slogan was thus promoted to the status of a national policy strategy, defined by reference to a double comparison with competing economic models in Europe. After the election victory of the SPD and the 'Greens' in Germany, *The Observer* (22 November 1998) noted that a joint working group was founded 'to find a means of translating the British Third Way and its

German equivalent *Die Neue Mitte* ('The New Centre') into a practical modernising agenda for Europe'.

However, *third* or *middle ways* are not a prerogative of post-1997/8 social democratic politics: in the corpus we find general political pleas for Europe to 'find a middle way' between fast and slow integration (*The Economist*, 21 January 1995) or for a 'middle way' that is 'neither a federal Europe nor a Europe of the states' (*The Guardian*, 11 September 1995), and - years before Blair's *Third Way* was sketched - his predecessor as Prime Minister, John Major, had already advocated a 'third European path'- however, that *path* was not the *middle road* between free market and planned economy but between 'total integration and a two-speed Europe' (*The Guardian*, 1 June 1994). Irrespective of its specific ideological background, a *third way/path*-policy thus appears to be always the most preferable option. This positive bias is perhaps founded on an assumption that a *third way*, situated *between* other *ways*, is the most sensible one to pursue because it avoids extremes on either side.

Two Speeds on the *Road* towards Integration

At the end of the Amsterdam summit, the then EU Commission president, Jacques Santer, issued the following announcement: 'The road is now open for the European Union to meet its commitment to launch monetary union in January 1999' (*The Guardian*, 17 June 1997). In Santer's statement, the EU is seen as a *traveller on the way towards* the *goal* of EMU; the assertion that the *road is now open* implies that some previously existing *obstacles have been cleared away*. On the non-metaphorical level, the statement *that the road is now open* can be understood as a reassurance that problems which existed before have now been solved. The German daily *Die Welt* (19 June 1997) quoted Santer's use of the *road* metaphor in a slightly different version; according to this paper, he had praised the Amsterdam Treaty as being the 'Königsweg zum Euro' (*royal road to EMU*). In the same article, the editor also used the image of the EU's *path* being *open*; in this case, however, it was not the *path* leading to EMU but to EU enlargement:

> Nach äußerst zähen Verhandlungen [...] ist der Weg frei für die Erweiterung der Gemeinschaft um beitrittswillige Staaten Mittel- und Osteuropas'. (ibid)

[After the completion of extremely difficult negotiations [...] the road is now open for the enlargement of the EU by those central and eastern European countries willing to join].

Apart from references to the processes of economic and political integration of the EU as progress on *one road*, there are also alternative concepts, such as that of progress on *two different tracks*, which a *Guardian* leading article mooted at the time of the preparations for the Maastricht Treaty in 1991:

One road to Maastricht - the economic motorway - suddenly looks pretty clear. The Dutch [...] have produced a draft treaty that everyone can sign. [...] It is the other road - the one marked political union - which remains littered with potholes. [...] Patently, Europe can't plough down the road of economic union without providing some democratic checks and balances. (*The Guardian*, 30 October 1991)

Here, the *road* image is used to distinguish different strands of the EU integration: the one leading to EMU is supposed to be without any problems, open as a motorway when there is no traffic congestion, the other one, i.e. the road to political union, is full of 'potholes', more like a little used country lane. However, the main point of the argument indicated in the last sentence of the quotation is that these two integration strands should *not* be treated as if they were distinct tracks, because they are in fact one and the same road - or at least that they are so closely connected that progress on one of them must not be allowed to 'get out of step' with progress on the other. In the German press, the magazine *Der Spiegel* echoed the *Guardian's* warning about the EC's *two roads*:

Auf dem Weg zur ökonomischen Einheit ist die EG vorangekommen, von der politischen Union ist sie weit entfernt'. (*Der Spiegel*, 16 December 1991)
[The EC had made progress on the path leading to economic union but is still far away from political union].

The most prominent distinction between degrees of commitment to EU integration was expressed by the slogan of the *two-speed Europe*. The earliest examples of this phrase in the Euro-debate corpus date from December 1991, i.e. from the time of the Maastricht summit. Will Hutton in *The Guardian* (11 December 1991) interpreted its outcome - in particular, the opt-out clause from the third stage of Economic and Monetary Union (EMU) for Britain - as leading to the 'two speed Europe that EC leaders have continually said they are against'. In Germany, the daily *Frankfurter Rundschau* (12 December 1991) asked (rhetorically) whether the Treaty was 'not' - despite contrary statements from Kohl and Major - constituting a *two-speed Europe* - this time, however it was not Britain's opt-out from EMU but the one from the social chapter of the Maastricht Treaty which motivated the *two-speed* diagnosis ('Die Sozial-politik der Europäischen Union wird [...] zur kontinentalen Elfer-Veranstal-tung, [...] Und das soll, wie Kohl und Major unisono beteuern, kein Europa der zwei Geschwindigkeiten sein?').

Nine months later, after the dramatic withdrawal of the British Pound Sterling and the Italian Lira from the Exchange Rate Mechanism (ERM) on 16 September 1992, the *different speeds* of member states' *movements* towards currency union were again on the agenda. *Die Welt* (28 September 1992) reported that 'nobody spoke about anything else' ['niemand redet über anderes als das Europa der zwei Geschwindigkeiten']. However, the concept was still too controversial for heads of government to endorse it. *The Guardian* (30 September 1992) quoted Chancellor Kohl as insisting that his government definitely did 'not want a two-speed Europe' to come about. The problem with the *two speed* notion was that it introduced an overtly hierarchical element into the picture of the EU. If some countries went *faster* than others, they would form an elite group, which would prob-ably *arrive first at the goal*. This hierarchical perspective left politicians of supposed *slow-speed* countries in an awkward position: on the one hand, any assertion of their will to *catch up* could be seen as an admission that their country had indeed *fallen behind*, but a total refusal *to move forward* together with the other member states would not look too good either. To get out of this dilemma, John Major tried to make stake the sting out of the concept of a differentiation of *speeds*:

> The Prime Minister last night indicated that a Conservative government would refuse to join the next phase of European integration, and held out a vision of a multi-speed Europe in which all member states would proceed at a speed of their own choosing. [...] Mr Major, insisted: 'I don't happen to think it threatens Europe if member states are free to do some things in their own way and at their own speed'. A multi-speed, multi-track, multi-layered Europe was a Conservative idea in line with the mood of the people everywhere. (*The Guardian,* 1 June 1994)

It was a brave attempt at reversing the hierarchical bias of the *two-/multi-speed* image but Major's proposition, supposedly 'in line' with

184 Attitudes Towards Europe

everyone's mood, did not find great favour with the partner governments in France and Germany. Just three months later, both the French Prime Minister Edouard Balladur and the ruling German Christian Democrats suggested a division of the Community into several *tiers* or *circles* or a *hard core* and a *periphery* respectively (*The Times*, 31 August 1994; *The Guardian*, 2 September 1994). The German proposals, which were published as a discussion paper by the parliamentary group of CDU and CSU in the Bundestag, also made use of the *multi-speed* phrase: the *multiple speed-Europe* was now presented as a feasible and plausible policy option rather than a worst-case scenario that should be avoided:

> Die institutionelle Weiterentwicklung muß Kohärenz und Konsistenz mit Elastizität und Flexibilität verbinden. [...] Hierfür sollte die Methode 'variable Geometrie' oder 'mehrere Geschwindigkeiten' trotz erheblicher rechtlicher und praktischer Schwierigkeiten soweit wie möglich durch den Unionsvertrag bzw. das neue verfassungsähnliche Dokument sanktioniert und institutionalisiert werden [...]. (CDU/CSU, 1994)
> [The institutional development must combine cohesion and consistency with elasticity and flexibility. [...] To achieve these aims, the method of 'variable geometry' or 'several speeds' should be sanctioned and enshrined in a new treaty or constitution for the Union, despite considerable legal and practical problems of its implementation [...].][5]

Ironically, in the light of later developments, the first British press reaction interpreted the French and German statements as 'giving their open blessing to [Major's] concept of a multi-speed Community' (*Financial Times*, 1 September 1994). This might indeed have been the reading which French and German politicians had hoped for, but it was not how the recipient of the 'blessing' saw it. Within a week, Major took the opportunity of a lecture at Leiden University in the Netherlands to object to the CDU/CSU discussion paper because in his view, it insinuated the idea of a Europe in which, according to the undemocratic principle of George Orwell's *Animal Farm*, 'some would be more equal than others'; on the other hand, he still clung to the idea that it was 'perfectly healthy for all member states to agree that some should integrate more closely and more quickly in certain areas' (*The Daily Telegraph*, 8 September 1994). If Major had hoped his compromise solution might stop further German suggestions of a *multi-speed Europe*, he was wrong. German commentators denounced his protest against the CDU/CSU's ideas as a U-turn on his previous endorsement of a *multi*-structured Union and stated that the *variable geometry/multi-speed* Europe had been a political reality since the Maastricht Treaty (cf. e.g. *Die Zeit,* 9 September and 16 September 1994).

This Anglo-German row over the interpretation of *multi-speed* metaphors from September 1994 marks the peak occurrence, with 21 out of altogether 88 quotations that refer to the *speed* of EU member states' *movement* towards the *goal* of economic and/or political integration, either in the form of the *two-/multi-speed* phrase itself or by way of references to some member states *going faster* or *slower* than the rest. Except for 1994, the occurrence of *two-speed* imagery is evenly spread over the period from 1991 up to 1999; the first quotes from 1991 refer back to an already well-established use of the *two-speed Europe* formula; after Labour's victory in May 1997, the occurrence seems to drop off slightly. 28 passages (16 from British, 12 from German sources) identify Britain as the country *going at a slower* - or *at the slowest - speed in a two-speed Europe* or as *being in the slow lane/track* or *on the sidelines.* By comparison, there are only two instances of Britain being portrayed as being *in the vanguard* of or *setting the pace* for the EU: one criticising Major for not taking advantage of Britain's *leading* position in military expertise and technology (*The Independent,* 8 September 1994); and a 1997 quote from Gerhard Schröder, then the emerging Social Democrat contender for Germany's Chancellorship, praising Britain under the Labour government as becoming 'the driving force behind the 'renaissance' of European politics' (*The Independent,* 17 June 1997). On the other hand, there are 12 instances of the EU as a whole or a *core* group of Germany plus France and Benelux being depicted in British texts as going *too fast,* starting in 1991 with reports on Major's rejection of Kohl's *timetable* for EU integration during the negotiations for the Maastricht Treaty. On the German side, there are just three instances of criticism of EU integration being pursued *too fast,* but eight criticisms of the EU as a whole going *too slow.* Only twice are Germany and Belgium criticised for being *too slow* for the rest of the EU - against the aforementioned 28 instances of blaming Britain for *travelling at slow speed.* Even though these figures cannot be regarded as statistically valid, a pattern emerges from the data in the sample. Britain is perceived - by British and German media and politicians alike - as *holding up* the *fast progress* towards economic and political integration that other EU countries (especially, Germany) want, and consequently as being in danger of relegation to a *second track* or a *slow lane* of its own.

This *slow-lane/slow-speed* image of Britain proved hard to overcome - as late as December 1998, after plans for EU-wide tax harmonisation mooted by the German and French governments were greeted with scepticism by Tony Blair, *The Guardian*'s political editor Michael White felt reminded of 'the familiar impression that London [was] again being sidelined by the Bonn-Paris axis' and that 'France and Germany raced ahead towards yet another distant Euro-goal' (*The Guardian*, 2 December 1998). Not that this was the first time that British commentators highlighted that Britain was typecast as the *slowest* EU state: in 1992, after the first, negative referendum in Denmark on the ratification of the Maastricht Treaty, a *Guardian* article facetiously lamented the 'loss' of Britain's 'familiar role' as the community's 'slowest and the grouchiest member' (*The Guardian*, 4 June 1992). Similar references to the well-established status of the *slow-speed* image of Britain were also made in the German press, sometimes on the occasion of British attempts to take a *lead* in some strand of the EU's integration process, which were perceived as being so untypical that they were contrasted with Britain's usual role of *applying the brakes* (e.g. *Die Zeit*, 22 May 1992: '[Britannien] will nicht länger nur Bremser, sondern auch Gestalter der europäischen Politik sein').

The study of general *path/movement/speed* metaphors thus reveals one stereotypical perception pattern concerning Britain's role in the EU: among the 15 EU states that are *on the way towards* economic, social and political integration Britain is predominantly perceived to be a or the *slow(est)* member state, the *latecomer* that may even endanger the *progress* of the whole group. The interesting aspect is that this perception of Britain as a *laggard* is similar across the British and German press, irrespective of the differing political evaluation of this state of affairs. The political function of this perception pattern is, of course, different in the two samples: in the case of the British texts, we are dealing with *self*-perception or -criticism, whereas the German texts criticising Britain's alleged *slow progress*, express an evaluation from a side that implicitly assumes itself to be among the *fast-moving* EU states (if not even *the fastest* one). However, among the texts employing general *path/movement* metaphors there are no explicit claims to such a *leader*-position. In the following paragraphs we shall look at metaphorical passages that provide detailed scenarios of the EU as a *vehicle travelling towards integration* to test if these hypotheses can be corroborated, or corrected and complemented by further corpus data.

The EU Train

Train metaphors have 79 occurrences in the Euro debate corpus, roughly equally distributed across the English and German side (38:41). Typically, the process of economic and political integration of the European Union, with EMU as its central aspect, is presented as a *railway journey*; the *train* - or the *locomotive* as *pars pro toto* - *stopping* at and *departing* from certain *stations*, which are used to signify important EU summit meetings:

> Will future historians look back on Maastricht as the moment when the loco-motive of European monetary unity opened the throttle, not to halt again until it reached the terminus, or will they note with mild amusement how it ground to a halt at the next red light? (*The Guardian*, 16 December 1995)

Individual nations are identified as *carriages of the train*, as in this comment on the withdrawal of the Pound Sterling and the Lira from the European Exchange Rate Mechanism in 1992:

> The locomotive may have a defective valve and at least two of its carriages appear to have become unhooked, but the European Union train - a little be-hind schedule - is about to resume its journey. As the British government de-cides for just how long it dares hold up ratification of the Maastricht treaty, plans are being laid for a two speed track to European union, which risk it being left behind. Since the narrow French referendum majority for treaty ratification, Britain has emerged, once again, in its role as principal obstacle to European integration. (*The Guardian*, 26 September 1992)

Here, Britain and Italy are seen as having become detached for the moment from the *EU train* that is being pulled by the ERM-to-become-EMU *locomotive*; furthermore, Britain is not only again deemed to be the *main obstacle* but to be so obstructive that the EU even considers *building a two speed track*: the rest of the EU would run *on the fast track*, Britain's *train* would run in the *slower lane*. There is even less chance here for Britain *catching up* than in the general *two-speed* schema, which is probably why Conservative British Prime Ministers took a special dislike to the *train* metaphor:

> [M. Thatcher] issues one of her strongest warnings to date about Maastricht. [...] Misleading analogies such as the European train leaving the station have been used in the debate she says. 'If that train is going in the wrong direction it is better not to be on it at all'. (*The Times*, 31 October 1992)[6]

[ich (= John Major) habe] stets darauf bestanden, daß wir uns nicht dem Druck beugen werden, Europa als einen Zug zu entwickeln, dessen Wagen alle mit gleicher Geschwindigkeit vorankommen. (John Major, in *Die Zeit*, 12 December 1996)
['I have always insisted that we must not bow to any pressure to develop Europe as a train, whose carriages all move along at the same speed'.]

In the first of these examples, Thatcher manages to have her metaphorical cake and eat it by rejecting and utilising the *train* image at the same time. First, she disqualifies the *EU - train* analogy as 'misleading', only to recycle it then in her warning that *the train might be going in the wrong direction*. Major simply rejects the whole image because he does not want the normal operation of a train -   *all carriages* coupled to a *locomotive* moving at the *same speed* and going in the *same direction* - to become a model of EU policy. In both cases, the metaphor is used to not only convey a special vision of the EU but also to criticise uses of this image by other participants in the Euro-debate about EU-politics. Who might these champions of the *EU-as-a-train* model be? The following examples speak for themselves:

Wir können also mit voller Berechtigung sagen, daß Deutschland dank des Vereinigungsprozesses die europäische Konjunkturlokomotive ist, die verhindert, daß der europäische Zug nicht [sic!] allzu stark abgebremst wird. (Helmut Kohl, 13 March 1991; documentation: Presse- und Informationsamt der Bundesregierung)
['We are therefore fully justified in claiming that, thanks to the unification process, Germany is the European economic locomotive which will prevent the European train from slowing down too much'.]

Interview with the Bavarian Minister-President Edmund Stoiber (CSU):
Stoiber: [...] Wir müssen uns auch nach 1997 anstrengen. Da gibt es einige, die sagen, dann haben wir wieder ein bißchen Luft für höhere Staatsschulden. Die deutsche Seite kann so etwas nicht akzeptieren.
SZ: Also müssen wir den Zug anhalten?
Stoiber: Nicht anhalten. Wir müssen den Zug auf das richtige Gleis setzen. [....]
Stoiber: [...] Wenn man sich hinterher nicht mehr an die Kriterien halten müßte, wäre die europäische Zentralbank nicht in der Lage, wie die Bundesbank Hüter der Währung zu sein.
SZ: Müssen wir in einem solchen Fall den Zug anhalten, ja oder nein?
Stoiber: Wir müssen ihn nicht anhalten. Ohne uns fährt er nicht.
(*Süddeutsche Zeitung*, 9 December 1996)

[*Stoiber*: We are telling our friends absolutely clearly: We must work hard also after 1997. There are some who say: by then there'll be a bit of slack in the budget, so we can risk higher deficits again. The German side can't accept that.
SZ: So we must stop the train?
Stoiber: No, not stop it. We must put the train on the right track. [...]
Stoiber: [...] If after that year member states would no longer have to meet the criteria the European Central Bank would not be able to guard the strength of the currency as well as the Bundesbank is doing now for the Deutschmark.
SZ: Must we stop the train in such circumstances, yes or no?
Stoiber: We don't have to stop it. It won't go anywhere without us.]

Both Kohl and Stoiber spell out 'absolutely clearly' that they deem the *EU-train* to be incapable of *going anywhere* without Germany being *in charge of the locomotive*. These are by no means isolated examples: out of the 41 German *train* metaphor passages, fifteen identify Germany as being *in charge of or driving the EU train* and/or criticise other states (mainly Britain) *for not being on the train*. This compares with only singular occurrences of other countries being mentioned as being *in charge of the train* (i.e. France and Britain).

The pattern is repeated on the side of the British press as regards Britain's role of *being not (yet) on the train*, *trying to get off the train* or *trying to stop it*. The main difference to German uses of the Britain-*as-a-problem-passenger* version of the *train journey* scenario is the political evaluation, which is sharply divided between Euro-sceptic and pro-European positions. To British Euro-sceptics, *missing* or *leaving the EU train* has been the ideal solution throughout the 1990s. Jonathan Aitken, then Conservative MP and for a time Chief Secretary to the Chancellor of the Exchequer, later disgraced in a corruption scandal, hailed the Major Government's opt-outs at Maastricht as a sign 'that the Delors train may have been slowed' and that 'alternative routes and destinations' might become available (*The Times*, 19 December 1991). Seven years later, with the introduction of the euro-currency imminent, Europe still seemed to *The Times* (5 December 1998) 'like a high-speed train, hurtling its reluctant passengers into a new millennium of continental government'.

From a Europhile view, any wishes to *slow down* or *not to be on the Euro train* are nothing to be proud of. As early as 1991, Hugo Young, one of the most prolific opponents of Euro-scepticism, warned that the decision to go ahead with EMU, which was then still under negotiation, was an 'inescapable conclusion' also for Britain and that 'once you've decided to stay on the train, you cannot alone control the speed' (*The Guardian*, 13 June 1991; cf. also Young 1998, p. 391). Likewise, the *Guardian's* then economic editor, Will Hutton, tried to alert the readers to the imminent *departure* of the 'European train we must not miss' (*The Guardian*, 1 November 1993), in order to criticise the Major government's opting-out policy. *Missing the Euro train* became the catch phrase of Europhiles in their attempts to plead the urgency of the situation and warn of the consequences of Euro-sceptic resistance against EU integration. Four years later, again in *The Guardian* (5 December 1997), Ian Black reissued the same warning, this time to a Britain under a Labour government: 'the train heading to the heart of the continent is now leaving, on time, without Britain, cool or not'.

EU Politics as a *Sea Voyage*

Another field of vehicle-specific transport imagery is that of a *ship* or *group of ships travelling* from one *port* to another. The corpus contains 54 passages referring to the EU and its member states as *sea-faring vessels*, most of which, like the *train* metaphor, are used to highlight problems of hidden hierarchies among the EU member states or of policy co-ordination within the EU institutions. Thus, the resignation of Santer's EU Commission in the wake of a fraud and nepotism scandal provided a good occasion for *The Economist* (20 March 1999) to dispense advice on *how to run the EU ship*: 'if, as president of the European Commission, you have a choice between dumping overboard someone like Mrs Cresson on the one hand, and risking the shipwreck of your whole commission on the other, you will do better to choose the first of those options'. Likewise, *The Guardian* (17 March 1999) pictured Santer as clinging 'to the wreckage' of his Commission. The Commission president thus appeared as a hapless *captain* who was not decisive enough to dump a *sailor* that was not able or willing to work properly.

Whilst the notions of authority and hierarchy that come with the role of *captain* can easily be applied to identifiable top functionaries 'in command' of an organisation such as the EU Commission, they are controversial when it comes to the EU itself, understood as a union of sovereign states, in principle equal with one another. As with *train* metaphors, the scenario of the EU states taken together as *one single vehicle*, lends itself to raising the problem of *who is in control*:

Weil der Tanker EG keinen Kurs ändert, ohne daß alle Hände das Ruder in dieselbe Richtung drehen, umgibt Maastricht als Anlaufhafen die Aura der

Unabänderlichkeit. Der Vertrag wird jedoch längst milder interpretiert. [...] Die Erweiterung um vier neue Mitglieder [...] wird nicht nur jede europäische Übereilung verhindern, sondern eher das durchaus nötige Einigungstempo zusätzlich bremsen. (*Die Zeit,* 15 October 1993)
[As the EC steamer won't change its course unless all hands turn the steering wheel in the same direction, it appears that Maastricht has to be its one and only port of destination. But the Treaty has already been interpreted loosely for a long time. [...] The enlargement by four new members will not only prevent any excessive acceleration of the speed of European integration, it will also lower the necessary minimum speed even further.]

The EU's principle that any major policy change - in terms of the *maritime journey* metaphor this means: any *change of the ship's destination and/or speed* - has to be agreed by all member states, is expressed here by the proposition that *all hands turn the steering wheel*. However, this arrangement is said to result in inflexibility, and furthermore, the *ship's speed* is predicted to fall below *the necessary minimum* soon because of new *crew members coming aboard*. Thus, although the image of *manoeuvring* and *smooth progress of a ship* is used first of all just to illustrate a political development, in the context of the article's specific discussion of the EU integration process, it also fulfils the function of highlighting the alleged problems of *delay* and indecision.

Whilst *Die Zeit's* criticism focuses on a potential *decrease* of the *EU steamer's speed*, the scenario presented by the former Conservative party chairman Lord Tebbit in the following example is one of impending disaster. It shows the *EU ship* as the *Titanic*, i.e. as *doomed to go under*, on account of the 'bankers' (hypothetical) decision in Germany's favour. One 'other country' (= Britain?) is the helpless *victim, going down with the ship* through no fault of its own:

Welcome aboard the Euro Titanic.
Everyone knows that within a monetary union there can be only one bank rate. [...] Suppose then that one country [...] needs lower interest rates to avoid sliding into a recession or slump, but the bankers decide that Germany needs higher rates to cool down a boom. [...]. Suppose, then, at an election the people elected a parliament committed to lower interest rates and taxes. What then? Tough luck. That is what I described as the Euro *Titanic* — with no lifeboats. (Lord Tebbit, quoted in *The Times*, 18 June 1998)

Individual member states can be portrayed not only as crew members but also as *passengers* of the *EU ship*, especially when they are in danger of being excluded from the *voyage*:

Fears grow that Germany may miss the EMU boat. German economic performance may not be able to deliver the Maastricht criteria [...]. (*The Guardian*, 13 January 1996)

Die Engländer hängen außenbords an der Reling des Eurodampfers und wagen weder loszulassen noch sich ganz an Bord zu schwingen - ein kläglicher Anblick; dabei könnten sie mit auf der Brücke stehen. (*Die Zeit*, 16 September 1992)
[The British are hanging over the ship's railings and dare neither to let go nor to jump fully aboard. It's a pitiful sight, considering they could be standing among the officers on the bridge instead.]

[...] die britische Maastricht-Debatte [steuert] in gefährliche Gewässer. Die Briten, die derzeit die Präsidentschaft innehaben und deren Aufgabe es eigentlich wäre, das leckgeschlagene Schiff abzudichten, sind tief zerstritten. (*Die Zeit*, 25 September 1992)
[The British Maastricht-debate is sailing into dangerous waters. The British, who currently hold the [EU-] Presidency and whose job would normally be to repair the leaks in the ship, are deeply divided among themselves.]

As with *train* metaphors, the ratio of references to Germany vs. those to Britain as the *'problem passenger' on the EU ship* is 1:4 across the British and German samples. This pattern is repeated also in the second main type of *maritime journey* metaphors, i.e. statements that *the speed of the European convoy must not be dictated by that of the slowest ship(s)*. Although sometimes Britain is not explicitly 'named and shamed' as *the slowest ship*, the context of the *two-speed-Europe* debate makes it clear that it is the chief addressee. All 'original' occurrences of this variant are on the German side of the corpus; British media and politicians use it only to comment on the Germans' views. The first such comment in the corpus dates from 1992, when the *Guardian's* correspondent David Gow quoted Chancellor Kohl's as stating that he neither 'wanted a two-or-three-speed Europe [...] nor a Europe in which the speed of the slower ship determines the pace of the entire convoy' (*The Guardian*, 28 October 1992). Gow highlighted this passage as 'a pointed intervention in the British debate over ratification' and reported that Kohl's aides afterwards stressed that 'this was not meant as a specific threat to John Major' (ibid.). Notwithstanding this dementi, the *Guardian* journalist read Kohl's speech as proof that the Chancellor 'laid claim to the supreme role of leading the European Community in ratifying the Maastricht treaty' (ibid).

His aides' awareness of British sensitivities — perhaps also connected to memories of World War I and II convoys being attacked by German submarines — did not deter the Chancellor from continuing to use the *convoy* scenario. In the next big Anglo-German dispute on EU-policy in September 1994, which was triggered by the CDU/CSU discussion paper referred to earlier, British newspapers found ample occasion to comment on his *convoy* statements:

> A plan put forward by German Christian Democrats for a two-tier reconstruction of the EU has destabilised European diplomacy because it dares to suggest that Europe cannot expect to achieve 'ever closer union' if it steams at the speed of the slowest ships in the convoy. (*The Guardian*, 7 September 1994)
> While restating Bonn's commitment to integration, Mr Kohl insisted that Germany did not want the 'convoy's speed dictated by the slowest vessel'. (*The Daily Telegraph*, 8 September 1994)

As these quotes show, British commentators continued to read Kohl's use of the *convoy* image as a warning or even as a threat, i.e. as a suggestion with 'destabilising' results or as a condition for Germany's continuing 'commitment to integration'. The *convoy* metaphor was seen as summarising the German government's perception of Britain as the *problem ship in the EU convoy*. In the German press, too, the predominant perception was that of Britain as *the last ship in the convoy*, but the responsibility for its *falling behind* was not seen as lying with the *fast ships racing on* but with Major's government being *too slow*, thus causing the EU *convoy's* division:

> Es war ja doch John Major, der bei den Verhandlungen über den Maastrichter Vertrag für Großbritannien das Recht durchsetzte, bei dem Projekt Währungsunion und Sozialpolitik aus dem europäischen Konvoi auszuscheren. (*Die Zeit*, 16 September 1994)
> [It was, after all, John Major who, during the Maastricht negotiations, secured the right for Britain to leave the European convoy, with respect to the projects of EMU and common social policy.]

In the following years leading up to the change of government in Britain, the *convoy* image gained some notoriety for exposing all too clearly the widening Anglo-German rift on European policy. The Tories' Defence Secretary, Michael Portillo, publicly protested against the 'slow boat taunt' (*The Times*, 5 February 1996), and in the run-up to the general election in 1997, the Foreign Secretary, Malcolm Rifkind, carried his government's protest at Kohl's metaphor into the lion's den, i.e. the CDU's

Konrad Adenauer Institute in Bonn, arguing that there 'was no point in talking about a faster integration which left behind the "slowest boats" in the convoy: "We are not talking about convoys, we are talking about democracy"' (*The Times*, 20 February 1997).

Soon afterwards, the Conservative government ship in Britain was sunk, so to speak, by the election results of May 1997. The German Christian Democrats' crew also sailed into troubled waters when a severe recession threatened its capability to meet the convergence criteria for EMU. Shortly before the EU commission deemed Germany and France to have met the EMU criteria after all, the *Süddeutsche Zeitung* (15 April 1998) warned that both nations might be viewed *by the other members of the European convoy* as hindering its progress ('[es] könnte [...] leicht passieren, daß [Frankreich und Deutschland] von den anderen Mitgliedern des europäischen Geleitzugs als Hemmschuh empfunden werden'). In March 1999, after his first finance minister, Oskar Lafontaine, had re-signed, the Social Democratic Chancellor, Gerhard Schröder, even had to reassure the other EU member states that his government would in future *stay within the European convoy* in matters of finance policy (*Süddeutsche Zeitung*, 16 March 1999: 'Schröder [hat] erklärt, Deutschland werde sich auf dem Gebiet der Finanzpolitik künftig "im europäischen Geleitzug bewegen"'). Little had remained of the self-confident assumption that Germany had a guaranteed place at the *head of the convoy* and could admonish other states to *catch up*. Now its own government had to make excuses for *lagging behind*.

Like the *train journey* scenario, *maritime journey* metaphors in British and German debates lend themselves to comparisons of member states' performance in the integration process. When the EU is pictured as a *single ship,* its *crew members* or *the passengers who are already on board* are distinguished from those *who are in danger of missing the boat* or *falling overboard*. In the *convoy* variant, the EU member nations are seen as *ships travelling at different speeds*. In both British and German public discourse, the emphasis is on Britain's role as the *problem passenger* or *slow convoy ship*. However, British pro-European media tend to lament this stereotype, whilst Euro-sceptics, such as Tebbit or Portillo, either try to make a virtue out of not being on the *Euro Titanic* or plainly reject any *slow ship* allegations. On the German side, the media and the government's criticism of supposedly *slow ship(s)* rested on the assumption that Germany was one of the *leaders of the convoy*. Following the reassessment of Germany's position in the EU as a consequence of its struggle to meet the Maastricht convergence criteria and its change of government, the *convoy* scenario has been turned around to cast Germany in the role of *a slow ship that must catch up with the others*.

Modern Transport for the EU: Cars, Bicycles and Aeroplanes

Whilst the images of the EU as a *train* or *ship/convoy* dominate the *vehicle*-specific transport imagery in the Euro-debate, the corpus also contains smaller samples of *bicycle* metaphors (fifteen examples), *car* metaphors (thirty-one) and passages that refer to *air* or *space travel* (eleven).

The *bicycle* metaphor has three main variants. The first type concentrates on a characteristic aspect of *bicycle motion*: unlike other means of transport, a bicycle falls down if it stops moving. This special manner of locomotion is used for the analogical argument that the EU integration project must proceed or else the community will *fall down*. The image seems to be particularly popular with advocates of deepened EU integration: the *Süddeutsche Zeitung* (5 May 1998) quoted it from the French conservative-leaning newspaper *Le Figaro* ('Europa ist ein Fahrrad. Wenn man aufhört zu treten, fällt es um'), W. Hutton attributed the conclusion to Jacques Delors: 'Europe [...] is like a bicycle: allow it to stop moving and it falls' (*The Guardian,* 11 September 1995) and A. Marshall named Walter Hallstein, the first German EEC Commission president, as the source (*The Independent*, 11 September 1994). From the Euro-sceptic viewpoint of *The Times*, however, the *bicycle-that-falls-down-if-it-does-not-go-forward* simile belonged to those 'trivial travel metaphors, used to drive an argument to a conclusion before a consensus can be reached' (*The Times*, 10 February 1996).

In the German sample, the most popular variant of the *bicycle* metaphor is the image of a *tandem, ridden by partners* France and Germany. After the 1998 row over the ECB presidency (the main candidate W. Duisenberg being challenged by the French government's demand for a French banker), the *Süddeutsche Zeitung* (8 May 1998) complained that France put its partnership with Germany as well as the success of Europe at risk by claiming the privilege *of steering the tandem* ('Wenn Frankreich auf dem Tandem den vorderen Platz für sich reklamiert, wird es zum Schluß sowohl seine Macht als auch Europa verspielen'). In all cases but one the other EU partner states remain anonymous - perhaps they are supposed to form the *bicycle*. The exception is the eccentric version of a *tandem à trois*, promoted again by the *Süddeutsche Zeitung* (6 May 1997). Observing that until then, Kohl and Chirac had been able to *steer* the EU-bicycle comfortably 'à deux', the editor Josef Joffe pointed out that Tony Blair would want his share of the action. Drawing on the German idiomatic expression 'ein fünftes Rad am Wagen sein' (literally: 'to be the fifth wheel on a car', i.e. 'to be superfluous'/'in the way'), Joffe insisted that Britain under Blair would not be content to be *the third wheel on the Kohl-Chirac tandem* ('Mit der Rolle des dritten Rades am Tandem Kohl-Chirac wird es [= Großbritannien] sich nicht begnügen').

Moving up a gear to higher-powered vehicles, we find metaphors of the EU or its member states as *cars*, or as *car parts* or *car drivers*. The distribution is lop-sided: there are 26 occurrences in the British press against five occurrences on the German side. Most of the German examples are focused on *accidents of the EU's drive* towards integration. In 1998, the Green Party leader Joschka Fischer used the image of a *car crash* to criticise Kohl for delaying the urgently needed integration of social, economic and financial policies to supplement EMU ('Wenn es nicht gelinge, auch zu einer gemeinschaftlichen Wirtschafts-, Sozial und Finanzpolitik zu kommen, fahre die Währungsunion "krachend gegen die Wand"') (quoted after *Süddeutsche Zeitung*, 3 April 1998). In 1990, *The Guardian* declared its gratitude about any 'hold-ups' in the 'dash' towards EMU *driven* by the then Commission President Jacques Delors: 'Having had his own way for much of this year on the drive toward European Monetary Union, the EC president Jacques Delors is becoming tetchy now that his Mercedes is slowing' (*The Guardian*, 13 September 1990). The choice of the brand name *Mercedes* for Delors' *car* in this passage is no accident: as the most famous top-of-the-range German *car* model it represents Germany as the *main vehicle* in Delors' *drive* towards EMU, which - it is alleged - is beginning to falter.

The British sample has a number of reported statements by French politicians using references to *top-of-the-range car models* as metaphors for the EU or for EMU. *The Guardian* (15 November 1995) quoted the then French foreign minister, Hervé de Charette, reassuring Germany that his government still regarded the Franco-German *car* as the European 'Formula One engine [...] in full action'. In 1997, the French EU Commissioner for financial policy, Yves-Thibault de Silguy was quoted praising the euro as a *Jaguar* car, which the British had helped to build, only 'to have it driven by the Germans and French and others' (*The Times*, 5 February 1997).

From a Euro-sceptical British viewpoint, however, a similar appreciation of the EU or the euro as *high-performance vehicles* would be untypical. Here the emphasis is on downplaying new political initiatives by characterising them as *maintenance service stops* rather than substantial progress. The metaphor was used so often that it became the object of critical comments in the press:

> If the Maastricht treaty was the juggernaut that pushed Europe off towards full union, then the 'Maastricht 2' conference, beginning in Turin on Friday, is merely 'a 5,000-mile service'. Or so British ministers, wishing to prevent a fast gear change towards a federal Europe, would have us believe. But then, lowering expectations has become the government's natural defence mechanism in its fraught dealings with Europe. (*The Sunday Times*, 24 March 1996)

This *Sunday Times* quote includes a further variant of the *car* image expressing Euro-sceptics' fears: progress towards further EU-integration looks to them like a *juggernaut that crushes everything in its path*. Based on a lexicalised, dead metaphor (derived from the Hindi word *Jagannath* for an idol of Krishna that was dragged on a huge car in processions; cf. COD 1979, p. 585), the *juggernaut* image is the equivalent of the *runaway train*, but the emphasis is mainly on the *blind force* of the vehicle rather than on a specific impending catastrophe, such as the *derailment of a train*.

The risks of future EU integration also form the target domain of the few metaphors of *air* or *space travel* in the corpus. In 1997, the *Guardian* editors Ewen MacAskill and Larry Elliott warned of the consequences, if EMU, 'as many suspect, [...] aborts on takeoff' (*The Guardian*, 15 October 1997). Elliott also constructed an ambivalent analogy between EMU and an *aeroplane,* which it would be a *pity to miss* but which might be *unfit for travel*:

> The danger of not getting on board is that all the best seats in the club class will be taken and that, when Britain does decide to take the plunge, there will be only seats in steerage left. On the other hand, the plane has been on the Tarmac for some time now and [...] the suspicion is that one of the engines is a bit dodgy. The question is: would you get on board? Well, would you? (*The Guardian*, 10 February 1997)

On the German side of the corpus, the only image related to *air travel* is that of a *precise landing* [*Punktlandung*] on the *spot* defined by the convergence criteria agreed in the Maastricht treaty, especially the 3 per cent budget deficit criterion. The metaphor conjures up the image of a *parachutist* or a *sports pilot* trying to *hit the target*. After having fixed the *target spot* by reiterating publicly that every country had to obey the principle that '3.0% was 3.0%', the German finance minister Waigel found himself put on the spot by economic statistics published in spring and summer 1997, which indicated that the German budget might miss the target by a few decimal points.

> Waigels Ziel bleibt die Punktlandung. [...] 'Wenn wir in Deutschland anfangen, über 3,3 oder 3,4 zu sprechen, wird man in anderen Ländern über 3,8 oder 3,9 diskutieren'. (*Die Welt*, 14 June 1997)
> [Waigel's objective is the precise landing. [...] 'If we start to discuss 3.3 or 3.4% in Germany, other countries will be considering 3.8 or 3.9%'.]

The overall distribution of *bicycle, car and aeroplane* metaphors in the sample, though not statistically conclusive, indicates that they play a bigger role in British than in German public discourse. A further aspect, which calls for an extension of the analysis of Euro-imagery to other national debates is the apparent influence of French politicians' use of *car-* and *car-technology* metaphors. Again, the sample makes it difficult to draw any definite conclusions; a speculative interpretation might be that technology-related imagery in general could be particularly prominent in French public discourse.

Conclusion

The distribution of the different variants of vehicle-specific *transport* imagery shows similar patterns of public perception of the EU policies in Britain and Germany. Overall, across both samples, some 30-50% show a stereotyping division of roles between Germany as the *driver/locomotive/fast ship* vs. Britain as the *late passenger*, as a *passenger* or *crew member trying to get off the train* or *ship*, or *missing* the *aeroplane*. Among German sources there is no significant difference in the political evaluation, whereas on the British side, pro-European and Euro-sceptic evaluations are clearly divided: Britain's *lateness* is either lamented or praised. Germany's supposed or assumed role as the *driving force* is almost uniformly resented in British sources. In general, Euro-sceptical uses of the various metaphors seem to be particularly colourful and dramatic (EU-*runaway train/-Titanic/-juggernaut*) and they appear to dominate the British sample by a ratio of 4:1. A more comprehensive corpus-study could provide statistical evidence that this distribution is indeed characteristic. If proven to be correct such a finding could go some way in explaining the strength of the Euro-sceptical bias of British Euro-debates in comparison with German debates, especially at the level of emotive language use and political stereotyping.

Notes

1 Cf. the web-site: 'www.dur.ac.uk/SMEL/depts/german/euro-arc/eurometa.htm'.
2 Tabloids have been almost completely excluded, as they showed little variation or innovation in metaphor use. For comparisons of British broadsheet and tabloid coverage of European politics cf. Mautner, 1995, 1997.
3 For the analysis of the whole euro-metaphor corpus cf. Musolff, forthcoming; for general aspects of corpus-based metaphor analysis cf. Deignan 1999.
4 Cf. e.g. Paul 1920, pp. 96-8; Lakoff 1993, pp. 220-4; Lakoff/Johnson 1980, pp. 41-5.
5 For the specific translation problems connected with the CDU/CSU proposals cf. Schäffner (this volume).
6 For the development of Thatcher's Euro-sceptical stance in the context of her resistance against German unification cf. Wittlinger (this volume).

References

CDU/CSU-Fraktion des Deutschen Bundestages (1994), *Überlegungen zur europäischen Politik*. CDU/CSU, Bonn.
COD [*Concise Oxford Dictionary of Current English*] (1979), Sixth edition, edited by J.B. Sykes. Oxford University Press, Oxford.
Deignan, Alice 1999, 'Corpus-based research into metaphor', in L. Cameron and G. Low (eds), *Researching and Applying Metaphor*, Cambridge University Press: Cambridge, pp. 177-199.
Giddens, A. (1998), *The Third Way. The Renewal of Social Democracy*, Polity Press, Cambridge.
Lakoff, G, and Johnson, M. (1980), *Metaphors we live by*, University of Chicago Press, Chicago.
Mautner, G. (1995), 'How does one become a good European? - The British Press and European Integration', *Discourse & Society*, vol. 6/2, pp. 177-205.
Mautner, G. (1997), *Der britische Europa-Diskurs: Reflexion und Gestaltung in der Tagespresse*, unpublished *Habilitationsschrift*. Wirtschaftsuniversität, Vienna.
Musolff, A. (1996), 'False Friends borrowing the Right Words? Common Terms and Metaphors in European Communication', in A. Musolff, C. Schäffner and M. Townson 1996, pp. 15-30.
Musolff, A. (2000), 'Metaphors and Trains of Thought: spotting journey imagery in British and German political discourse', in S. Wright, L. Hantrais and J. Howorth, J. (eds),

Language, Politics and Society. The New Languages Department. Festschrift in honour of Dennis Ager, Multilingual Matters, Clevedon, pp. 100-109.

Musolff, A. (forthcoming), *Mirror-Images of Europe. Metaphors in the public debates about Europe in Britain and Germany,* iudicium, Munich.

Musolff, A., Schäffner, C. and Townson, M. (eds) (1996), *Conceiving of Europe — Unity in Diversity.* Dartmouth Publishers, Aldershot.

Paul, H. (1995[1920]), *Prinzipien der Sprachgeschichte,* Fifth edition, Niemeyer, Tübingen.

Schäffner, C. (1996), 'Building a European House? Or at Two Speeds into a Dead End? Metaphors in the Debate on the United Europe', in A. Musolff, C. Schäffner and M. Townson 1996, pp. 31-59.

Schäffner, C., 'Attitudes to Europe — Mediated by Translation', (in this volume).

Young, H. (1998), *This Blessed Plot. Britain and Europe from Churchill to Blair,* Macmillan, London.

8 Attitudes to Europe - Mediated by Translation

CHRISTINA SCHÄFFNER

Introduction: The Need for Translation

The project of European integration is not only a multinational project but also a multilingual project. The European Union has a declared policy of democratic multilingualism, i.e. in the EU's language charter it is stated that all official languages have equal status. Currently, there are 11 official languages (Danish, Dutch, English, Finnish, French, German, Greek, Italian, Portuguese, Spanish and Swedish), and this number will increase with new members joining the EU. Documents submitted by a member state or also by a citizen of the Union may be written in any of the official languages, and the institutions of the EU are obliged to send their replies in the language of the original sender.

For obvious reasons, multilingualism at the level of the individual citizen, allowing for unlimited direct communication, is not a realistic objective. That is why mediated communication via translation and interpreting plays an ever increasing role for European integration. The European Commission's Translation Service is the largest in the world, translating a variety of documents from and into the individual languages of the member states. Those documents include legislation, international agreements, speeches, policy statements, minutes, promotional material, etc. But reaching consensus on EU-wide legislation is a lengthy process, involving a number of stages of proposals, drafts, debates at local, national and European level. Translation is decisive during these stages too, and debates about content are often intimately linked to debates about language. In fact, the whole process of European integration is accompanied by linguistic developments, concerning semantics, genre conventions, and discourse. The reason for that development is that EU texts reflect a drive towards full equivalence and immediate transparence.

Terminology development is usually monitored and often planned with the aim of 'harmonising' terminology (cf. the role of the Terminology unit of the Translation Service in providing linguistic support, such as setting up subject glossaries or multilingual data banks, e.g. *Eurodicautom*). With every new concept introduced, or whenever a new meaning is attached to an existing term, equivalent expressions in the other languages are required, which often come about in the process of linguistic negotiation.

Apart from lexical harmonisation, genres too become more and more similar, displaying certain textual features (vocabulary, syntax, style, etc.) which may clash with the conventions of the home culture. Such 'Eurotexts' (Born and Schütte, 1995) reflect a Eurojargon, i.e. a reduced vocabulary, meanings that tend to be universal, and a reduced inventory of grammatical forms. Such developments are increasingly analysed also from the perspective of the discipline of Translation Studies (e.g. Dollerup, 1996, Schäffner, 1997a; Koskinen, 2000). 'Eurotexts' are predominantly texts and genres intended for internal use by EU institutions and bodies. But debates about European integration, EU policies and European affairs are not only conducted within EU institutions themselves. National governments, national parties, organisations, groups and individuals produce written or oral texts on the topic of European integration. These texts can also be intended for internal use only (e.g. a food chain in Britain discussing consequences of EU regulations on banana imports for their sales strategies), but more often than not texts on European topics, i.e. topics which by their very nature are of supra-national relevance, will also be addressed to an audience in other EU member states, even if only implicitly or potentially.

If such texts are produced by political actors, it can generally be assumed that although they were produced within one country primarily for the home public (e.g. members of parliament), they also explicitly aim at an audience outside. These may be texts in which one political party or government outlines specific ideas as to the future development of the EU, position papers as to specific decisions or proposals, statements about upcoming EU meetings or Intergovernmental Conferences (IGC), and subsequent statements about their outcomes. In order to reach addressees outside the boundaries of the home state and the national language, these texts need to be translated. National governments usually employ professional translators to do this job, for example, political texts are translated in-house and then sent to the respective addressees abroad (i.e. a source text is translated within the source culture and sent to addressees in the target culture). Alternatively, a national government may be interested in being informed of the content of a speech by a head of government of another country and therefore commissions a translation (i.e. a source text is translated within the target culture).

In the field of politics, translations are both highly common and politically relevant. In this process of translation as interlingual and intercultural communication target texts are produced which are normally intended to be reproductions of the source texts. But if we look at authentic translations we often discover that they are not mirror-images of the source text, as generally assumed (cf. Hönig, 1995 on the problematic status of some of the traditional assumptions about translation). Questions which can be asked in this respect are, among others, how are target texts received in the target culture(s)? If target text readers interpret a text in a different way than was intended by the source text producers, what are the reasons? In this chapter, I will discuss these questions on the basis of two authentic examples. The empirical data are English and German original texts as well as translations on topics of European integration. These texts are statements and documents by politicians, press releases, and newspaper texts. One issue concerns the debate in 1994/95 on the metaphorical concept of a 'Kerneuropa - core Europe', and the other one the 1999 debate on tax harmonisation in the European Union. These issues will be illustrated by means of the concepts and method of Translation Studies. Before discussing these two sample cases, I will give a short overview of the discipline of Translation Studies, of its main concepts, approaches, and research methods.

The Discipline of Translation Studies

Although Translation Studies is still a relatively young, and also not a homogeneous discipline, it has become more and more recognised as an academic discipline in its own right. With the development of the discipline in the second half of this century, theoretical principles have been formulated which are the basis for the description, observation, and teaching of translation.

When translation studies came on the scene after the second World War it was conceived as a subdiscipline of (applied) linguistics. Dominant definitions saw translation as a transfer of meaning, as a process in which signs of the source language (lexical units and syntactic structures) were replaced by equivalent signs in the target language. Translation scholars saw their task as describing language pairs and establishing the potential equivalence relations (e.g. Kade, 1968), based on which guidelines and/or rules for translators could be produced (e.g. Vinay and Darbelnet 1958)

In the course of its development, Translation Studies has taken on concepts and methods of other disciplines, notably textlinguistics, sociolinguistics, psycholinguistics, pragmatics, and, recently, cultural studies (cf. Gentzler, 1993; Stolze, 1994). Textlinguistic approaches to translation define translation as source text induced target text production (Neubert, 1985) and treat the text itself as the unit of translation. It is stressed that a text is always a text in a situation and in a culture. Therefore, consideration needs to be given to situational factors, genre or text-typological conventions, addressees' knowledge and expectations, and text functions. Functionalist approaches emphasize that the actual linguistic form of the target text is dependent on its intended purpose, and not primarily and exclusively on the structure of the source text. They define translation as purposeful activity (cf. Nord, 1997), as production of a target text which is appropriate for its specified purpose (its *skopos*) for target addressees in target circumstances (cf. Vermeer's 'Skopos theory', e.g. Vermeer, 1996).

The socio-historical constraints are even more emphasised by scholars within the strand of descriptive translation studies. Translation is seen as the result of a socially contexted behavioural type of activity (e.g. Toury, 1995). Descriptive translation studies describe translations as facts of target systems, and they examine, for example, decision-making in translation, translational norms, and effects of translated texts within the target national literature. In common with descriptive approaches, more recent approaches to translation that are inspired by Cultural Studies argue that texts do not have any intrinsically stable meaning that could be repeated elsewhere. Since there is always some interference of the subjective translator, as well as constraints from cultural, historical, ideological or political circumstances, the discipline of linguistics is dismissed as too narrow for describing and explaining translations. Translation is defined as a form of regulated transformation, and a translation method is recommended which signifies the 'linguistic and cultural difference of the foreign text' (Venuti 1995, p. 23) and which allows the reader to discover the cultural other (Venuti calls this strategy 'foreignization').

Within the discipline of Translation Studies, we are currently experiencing that scholars debate the validity of linguistic versus cultural studies approaches, sometimes even asserting the exclusive validity of either approach. But these approaches are not all exclusive, but rather complimentary, as is also stressed by Baker (1996). This ties in with the view that translation studies, applying insights and methods from various disciplines, can be characterised as an interdiscipline (cf. Snell-Hornby et al., 1992). Translations, i.e. target texts, can be described as to their linguistic profile, segmenting the text into smaller and smaller units, applying concepts and methods of linguistics, textlinguistics, pragmatics. Target texts can also be studied by linking them to the social context, discovering causes and effects of translations (cf. Chesterman, 1998). A causal model of translation allows for questions such as: What causal conditions seem to give rise to particular kinds of translations and translation profile features? What effects do given profile features seem to have, on readers, clients, cultures? Can we explain effects that we find by relating them to profile features and to causal conditions?

It is in this framework of linking textual features and translation effects that I will discuss my empirical data. In particular, I shall analyse examples where due to translation problems (i.e. textual peculiarities, translation choices) German and British politicians clashed over issues related to the further development of the European Union (i.e. translation effects).

Example 1: Lexical Choice and Political Effects

The first case concerns the effects of a specific translation solution: 'fester Kern' - 'hard core'. As said in the introductory comments, proposals concerning EU-policies often originate in one member state, and they are adopted, modified, or rejected in a lengthy process, which involves debates both in the other members states and in the EU institutions. Such debates at local, national and European level are to a large extent accompanied, and indeed facilitated, by translations.

One such proposal about future EU policies was put forward in the autumn of 1994 in a German document produced by the parliamentary group of the German Christian Democratic Union / Christian Social Union (CDU/CSU), with Wolfgang Schäuble, the then CDU parliamentary floor leader, and Karl Lamers as the main co-authors. In this document, the CDU/CSU stated that there was a danger that the EU could become just a loose federation. Therefore, the document argued for the formation of an inner group of closely integrated EU member states which would lead the way to further EU integration. This inner group is referred to in the German original as 'ein fester Kern'. The document was translated by in-house translators in Germany (i.e. in the source culture) and sent abroad. Thus, it was through the English target text that addressees in the UK (in the target culture) learnt of the arguments and proposals put forward in this paper. In fact, one day after its publication in Germany, an extract of the document was published in *The Guardian*, using the translation that had been produced in Germany. The highly controversial political debates that followed, centred around the notion of the 'fester Kern', which had been rendered as 'hard core' in the target text, cf. the relevant shortened parts from the German original text and the authentic English translation (italics are mine):

> Den festen Kern weiter festigen
> Daher muß sich [...] der feste Kern von integrationsorientierten und kooperationswilligen Ländern [...] weiter festigen. Zu ihm gehören z. Zt. fünf bis sechs Länder. Der Kern darf nicht abgeschlossen, muß hingegen für jedes Mitglied offen sein,
> Der feste Kern hat die Aufgabe, den zentrifugalen Kräften in der immer größer werdenden Union ein starkes Zentrum entgegenzustellen und damit die Auseinanderentwicklung [...]zu verhindern. [...]
> Die Vorschläge zur Herausbildung eines Kerneuropa [...] bedeuten nicht, daß die Hoffnung aufgegeben wird, daß Großbritannien seine Rolle "im Herzen Europas" und damit in seinem Kern übernimmt.
> (CDU/CSU Fraktion, Überlegungen zur Europäischen Politik, 1 September 1994, p.7)

> Further strengthening the EU's hard core
> [...] that existing hard core of countries oriented to greater integration and closer co-operation must be further strengthened. At present, the core comprises five or six countries. This core must not be closed to other member states; rather, it must be open [...]
> The task of the hard core is, by giving the Union a strong centre, to counteract the centrifugal forces generated by constant enlargement and, thereby, to prevent a [...] drifting apart [...]
> To propose the formation of a hard core in Europe [...] does not, however, imply the abandoning of hopes that Great Britain will assume its role "in the heart of Europe" and thus in its core.
> (CDU/CSU Fraktion des deutschen Bundestages, Reflections on European Policy, 1 September 1994, p. 7).

'Fester Kern' was meant to be interpreted in a positive way in German, suggesting sincerity, a firm commitment to European integration. This German proposal, however, was received in a negative light by the British government and the media, caused by the - unfortunate - choice of the phrase 'hard core' which significantly shifted the tone of the document. 'Hard core' is frequently associated with people and things that are tough, immoral and incorrigible. The reactions in the UK thus typically reflect an interpretation of the core countries (and in particular Germany) trying to impose their ideas on all members states. As a result of such attempts, it was argued, the EU would be divided into first and second class members, cf.:

> But the CDU proposal took the logic to an extreme by calling for *a hard core* of five member states - Germany, France and the Benelux countries - to press ahead with rapid integration, leaving the rest to catch up as best they can. [...] The CDU plan would divide the community into *first-class and second-class* members, destroying any claim that Britain remained *at the heart of Europe*, [...] (*The Guardian*, 7 September 1994)

> John Major warned his European partners last night that French and German proposals for an elite grouping within the European Union were a recipe for disaster. [...] 'I recoil from ideas for a Union in which some would be more equal than others. There is not, and should never be, an *exclusive hard core* either of countries or of policies. [...] 'I see a real danger in talk of a "*hard core*", inner and outer circles, a two-tier Europe,' [...] 'But no member state should be excluded from an area of policy in which it wants and is qualified to participate. To choose not to participate is one thing. To be prevented from doing so is quite another'. (*The Times*, 8 September 1994)

The 'core' is an example of a conceptual metaphor (for a cognitive approach to metaphor cf. Lakoff and Johnson, 1980). In political discourse, metaphors are fairly common (cf. Chilton, 1996) and they contribute decisively to shaping and directing political processes (in the context of European integration, cf. such prominent metaphors as 'the European house, a two speed Europe, Europe à la carte'). In the original German source text, the base schema for 'fester Kern' was not made absolutely clear. There are expressions in the source text that allow for an interpretation as a container (conceptual metaphor: THE CORE IS A CONTAINER, e.g. 'abgeschlossen, offen - closed, open'), but also as a centrifuge (THE EU IS A CENTRIFUGE, e.g. 'zentrifugale Kräfte, Auseinanderentwicklung - centrifugal forces, drifting apart') or as an orientational metaphor (HAVING CONTROL IS BEING AT THE CENTRE, e.g. 'ein starkes Zentrum entgegenstellen - a strong centre, to counteract'). It is mainly this last metaphor, the orientational one, which was the basis for the debate in the UK, i.e. resisting (presumed) attempts at setting up a centre and a periphery, and deciding on inclusion or exclusion from the core.

The idea of establishing a 'fester Kern' was not unanimously supported within Germany either. In German political discourse, consequently, the metaphor of the 'core' was discursively elaborated (building on the polysemy of 'Kern'), thus also introducing new conceptualisations, new conceptual metaphors. For example, critics argued that speaking of core countries will lead to a 'Kernspaltung'[nuclear fission] of the EU (cf. Schäffner, 1997b). When challenged that his idea of a 'Kerneuropa' would mean that a few take the initiative in decision-making processes, thus leaving others outside, Schäuble linked it to another metaphor, the magnet, cf.:

> Wir haben immer das Bild des Magnetfelds gebraucht: Der Kern zieht an und stößt nicht ab. (*Der Spiegel*, 12 February 1996)
> [We have always used the image of the magnetic field: the magnetic core attracts, it does not repel.]

Although this argumentation cannot be justified by reference to the document itself, the 'magnet' has now become the dominant metaphor in the CDU discourse. This can be seen in a more recent new paper about the future of the EU in view of its enlargement, again jointly produced by Schäuble and Lamers. In arguing about problems in unanimous decision making within an enlarged EU, they refer to their original concept as that 'was wir einen festen, magnetischen Kern genannt haben' [what we called a firm, magnetic core] (*Frankfurter Allgemeine Zeitung*, 7 December 1999).

From the translational point of view it can be said that the translator only accounted for the metaphorical expression (translation strategy: metaphorical expression into same metaphorical expression, 'Kern - core'), without reflecting about underlying conceptual metaphors. The consequence was a - politically motivated - heated debate in Great Britain and in Germany, which ultimately resulted in a shift from an orientational metaphor (HAVING CONTROL IS BEING AT THE CENTRE) to a structural metaphor (THE EU IS A MAGNET). The most interesting point for translation studies in this respect is that the whole debate and the conceptual shift was initiated by a specific translation solution. Elsewhere I have used the term intercultural intertextuality to characterise such cases, where a metaphor is further elaborated as a result of intercultural communication and/or of translation (Schäffner, in press).

As this example shows, the pragmatic success or failure of a particular translation solution will become obvious in international political discourse. But political conflicts can also be caused or kindled by other strategies that involve language and translation, which will be illustrated by the following example.

Example 2: Information Selection

In 1994, at the time of the 'hard core' debate, there were conservative governments in power in both Great Britain and Germany, but with different attitudes towards European integration. Whereas in Germany, all major political parties have always been principally in favour of European integration, the British governments under Margaret Thatcher and John Major were rather critical and sceptical of all developments that would result in ever closer co-ordination of policies. Since 1998, there are Labour and Social-Democratic led governments, respectively, with New Labour openly propagating a more EU-friendly attitude. Tony Blair's policy is that Britain should actively engage in EU policies in order to influence the direction of the future development. But in the discourse of New Labour (cf. Fairclough, 2000) this positive attitude is regularly 'balanced' by more critical or cautious statements, particularly concerning the single currency, in order to account for reservations in large parts of the public (fuelled by some media) and by a still strong Euro-sceptic policy of the Tories. The pledge to pursue policies that are in the British interest and to stand up for sovereignty is repeated again and again. This pledge is also made with reference to taxation and tax co-ordination in the EU.

Tax co-ordination in the EU has been on the agenda of the European Commission for a while. In the autumn of 1997 a document 'Towards Tax Co-ordination in the EU' was prepared by EU-commissioner Mario Monti, intended as a package to tackle harmful tax competition. One of Blair's election pledges was that he would not surrender tax powers to Brussels. The German government, on the other hand, was very much in favour of EU-wide tax harmonisation. In November 1998, the eleven Socialist finance ministers of the EU met in Brussels and issued a common statement, setting objectives for co-operation on economic policies after the launch of the euro on 1 January 1999. The then German finance minister Oscar Lafontaine declared that the German government would make tax harmonisation a top priority of its EU presidency (January till June 1999). He was arguing for similar tax conditions in all EU countries to prevent member states from competing with one another by offering lower rates to attract investors. The British Chancellor Gordon Brown immediately announced that he would be prepared to veto tax harmonisation should any such proposal come forward. Tax harmonisation was thought to destroy business competitiveness because it would mean losing the possibility to use low taxes to create jobs. This argument between Lafontaine and Brown led *The Sun* to describe Lafontaine as the 'most dangerous man in Europe' (25 November 1998), interpreting the plea for tax harmonisation as Germany wanting to dictate the conditions for Britain's entry into the Euro.

The issue of tax harmonisation was again on the agenda of the Helsinki summit meeting in December 1999. But no agreement could be achieved on all points of the tax package, with Germany's proposal to introduce a EU-wide withholding tax in particular meeting with Britain's resistance. The passage under the heading 'The tax package' in the Helsinki communiqué mentions only a general agreement that 'all citizens resident in a Member State of the European Union should pay the tax due on all their savings income', and then refers to a high level working group that will consider how this principle can be implemented. In order to understand this result, described as a 'feeble outcome' by Romano Prodi, it is necessary to look at the debates in preparation of the Helsinki summit, and here again aspects of language and translation seem to have played a role.

Before the Helsinki summit, statements were made by governments in the national parliaments, outlining the positions they were going to take. In the debate in the House of Commons on 1 December 1999 the Foreign Secretary, Robin Cook, reconfirmed that Great Britain had 'no intention of agreeing to a taxation on savings' (cf. web-site http://www.fco.gov.uk/news/speechtext.asp?3168). A number of British newspapers reported on the policy statement [*Regierungserklärung*] that the German Chancellor Gerhard Schröder had given on 3 December 1999 in the Bundestag, the lower house of parliament, in preparation of the Helsinki summit. In *The Guardian* and the *The Daily Telegraph*, the same passages from Schröder's speech were quoted, with the tone of the reports being rather critical. For example:

Schröder says he will act alone on savings tax.
Chancellor Gerhard Schröder gave a fresh twist to the row with Britain over plans for a cross-border savings tax by threatening unilateral action if a European Union agreement cannot be reached.
The German chancellor accused Britain of 'intransigent behaviour' and claimed there was 'an unacceptable lack of fairness in capital taxation'. [...]
According to the German chancellor: 'We will exert pressure at all levels to find an EU-wide solution. If that doesn't work then if necessary we should consider a national solution'. (*The Guardian*, 4 December 1999)

German fury at Blair over tax 'intransigence'.
Gerhard Schroder [sic!], the German Chancellor, lashed out at Britain yesterday for blocking the proposed withholding tax, saying Germany would embark on a 'national solution' if Tony Blair failed to co-operate. [...]
Mr Schroder said London's 'intransigence' was damaging to Europe. He told the German parliament: 'I make no secret of the fact that I have little understanding for such blockade tactics that place national interest above necessary European solidarity. This policy is damaging to Europe and, over the long term, their own interests'.
[...] Mr Schroder added: 'If necessary we should consider a national solution'. (*The Daily Telegraph*, 4 December 1999)

And in another text on the same day:

Tony Blair's dream of exporting his New Labour vision across Europe suffered a serious setback yesterday when Gerhard Schröder, the German Chancellor, blamed him for the collapse in the value of the euro [...]
[...]Mr Schröder was blaming Britain's decision to veto an EU-wide tax on savings, known as the withholding tax. He told the German Parliament: 'I make no secret of the fact that I have little understanding for such blockade tactics that place national interest above the necessary European solidarity. This policy is damaging to Europe and, over the longer term, its [Britain's] own interests'[...]
He said the tax issue would be the subject of intense discussions at the EU summit in Helsinki next week and he hoped Britain would make a 'decisive move'. His comments set the scene for what could be a highly confrontational gathering in Finland. (*The Daily Telegraph*, 4 December 1999)

In these extracts we can see direct quotes from Schröder's statement, which were obviously translated from German into English. Here are the relevant extracts on the tax issue from the German text:

Während die Beratungen zum Verhaltenskodex und zur Lizenzrichtlinie weit vorangebracht werden konnten, sind die Verhandlungen zur Besteuerung von Zinserträgen wegen der unnachgiebigen Haltung eines Mitgliedsstaates blockiert. Ich mache keinen Hehl daraus, dass ich für eine solche Blockadehaltung, die nationale Eigeninteressen über die notwendige europäische Solidarität stellt, wenig Verständnis habe. Diese Politik schadet Europa und längerfristig auch den eigenen nationalen Zielen.
[...] Wir müssen und werden aus diesem Grunde hierüber in Helsinki einen intensiven Meinungsaustausch führen. Ich hoffe, dass sich Großbritannien in dieser Frage entscheidend bewegt.
(Regierungserklärung von Bundeskanzler Gerhard Schröder zum bevorstehenden Europäischen Rat in Helsinki am 10./11. Dezember 1999 vor dem Deutschen Bundestag am 3. Dezember 1999, *Bulletin* vom 8. Dezember 1999, http://www.bundesregierung.de)

This speech was translated into English by the translation service of the German government and handed out to journalists who were present at the Bundestag session shortly before the speech was delivered (as is common practice in the case of policy statements - personal communication with staff members in the translation service). The respective passages quoted above read as follows in the official translation produced in Germany:

Considerable progress has been made with our consultations on a code of conduct and on the license directive. However, the intransigent stance of one member state has blocked negotiations on the taxation of interest income. I make no secret of the fact that I have little understanding for this type of stance which gives priority to national interests over necessary European solidarity. This policy hurts Europe and - in the long term - that country's own interests. [...]
For this reason, we must and we will conduct an intensive exchange of views on this subject in Helsinki. (Press release 7 December 1999, http:/www.bundesregierung.de/english)

When we compare the official translation made in Germany and the quotes in the British media, we notice a few differences, albeit of different degrees of significance. There is no difference between 'intransigent stance' in the authentic translation and 'intransigent behaviour' (*The Guardian*) and 'intransigence' (*The Daily Telegraph*) for 'unnachgiebige Haltung', since these forms are synonymous. The various renderings of the sentence 'Ich mache keinen Hehl daraus, [...] wenig Verständnis habe' can also be considered identical in content despite minor variations in style. In this paragraph it is not explicitly stated which country Schröder is speaking about (cf. 'unnachgiebige Haltung eines Mitgliedsstaates' - i.e. of one state, and '[...] den eigenen nationalen Zielen' - i.e. own national aims). Due to their background knowledge of the political developments, the addressees of this speech can easily identify the implicit referent, i.e. Great Britain. It is a bit further on in Schröder's speech that he explicitly mentions Great Britain (cf. 'Ich hoffe, dass sich Großbritannien in dieser Frage entscheidend bewegt'. - I hope that Great Britain will make a decisive move in this respect). The official translation keeps the implicitness ('intransigent stance of one member state [...] This policy hurts [...] that country's own interests'). The sentence mentioning Great Britain has not been rendered in the official translation. As can be seen in the newspaper quotes, there was no problem identifying the intended referent, with the newspapers adding the specification (cf. 'accused Britain of intransigent behaviour', 'London's intransigence', 'damaging to [...] its [Britain's] own interests'). *The Daily Telegraph* even quoted Schröder's statement regarding his 'hope that Britain would make a decisive move', although this sentence is missing in the official translation.

In the cases discussed so far, the differences between the official translation produced in Germany and the quotes in the English newspapers are mainly stylistic ones. But both papers also refer to another statement by Schröder, i.e. they quote him as saying that he will act alone, that Germany will 'exert pressure' and, if necessary, embark on a 'national solution'. In the official German text, however, there is no statement whatsoever to this effect. This raises the question, how this interpretation has come about. In the case of policy statements, delivered in the German Parliament and also intended for distribution to representatives from other countries (this is the reason for these texts being translated), the wording is highly important. Therefore, these statements are read out verbatim, with no (or only minor) changes to the text, and sometimes spontaneous reactions to interruptions from other members of Parliament. The stenographic records of that particular session of the Bundestag are evidence that the statement that was given by Chancellor Schröder was exactly the same as the written version of the document. There is no additional reference to embarking on a national solution. Interestingly, the stenographic records also show that the audience was well aware who was meant by the implicit reference to 'unnachgiebige Haltung eine Mitgliedsstaates'. The records note two interruptions here, both from CDU/CSU members. Wolfgang Schäuble asks 'Wer ist denn das?' [Who is this?], and Michael Glos 'Sind Sie nicht

mit dem Premier befreundet?' [Are you not a friend of the Prime Minister?]
- but Schröder does not give an answer.

Further on in the stenographic records there is indeed a reference to a
national solution, but this time it is not Chancellor Schröder or any other
member of the German government who is being quoted, but Wolfgang
Schäuble, presenting the CDU's comments on the policy statement.
Schäuble said:

> Ich stimme Ihnen ja zu, daß wir dringend die Harmonisierung der
> Besteuerung von Kapitaleinkünften brauchen. [...] Ich möchte zu erwägen
> geben, ob wir unseren britischen Freunden nicht sagen sollten: Wenn sie
> partout nicht wollen, daß wir in der Europäischen Union zu einer
> Harmonisierung der Besteuerung der Kapitaleinkünfte kommen, dann gehen
> wir diesen ersten Schritt im Rahmen der Eurozone - das ist flexibles
> Vorgehen -, dann harmonisieren wir die Besteuerung der Kapitaleinkünfte in
> der Eurozone.
> [I agree with you that we urgently need harmonisation in the taxation of capital gains.
> [...] I would like to suggest that we tell our British friends: If they do resist achieving
> harmonisation in capital taxation within the European Union, then we will take this
> first step within the Euro-zone - this is flexibility - then we will harmonize capital
> taxation in the Euro-zone.]

So even Schäuble did not suggest a national solution, but one for the
Euro-zone. The fact remains, however, that the readers of British
newspapers were given information which was inaccurate. The choice of
words such as 'row, accuse, fury, lash out, blame' in the articles quoted
contributed to the impression that Germany - once more - wanted to impose
a decision on EU member states, thus setting the scene for a British-
German clash at the Helsinki summit. For the articles quoted from *The
Guardian* and the *The Daily Telegraph*, names of journalists are given as
authors of the news reports. But it is not clear from the texts whether those
journalists were themselves present during the Bundestag session in Berlin,
or whether they relied on reports from others. Due to the examples which
showed minor differences in the wording of the official translation and the
newspaper articles, as discussed above, it could be possible that the
journalists were indeed present in person. Following the complete debate,
however, requires a knowledge of the German language, since
simultaneous interpreting is normally not provided at Bundestag sessions
(personal communication with staff members of the Bundestag translation
service). It might therefore also be possible that the journalists

misinterpreted statements, maybe because they lacked competence in German.

As mentioned above, the Helsinki summit did not reach an agreement on the tax package. It may well be that the style of reporting in Britain had contributed to Blair's tough negotiating position. In a Debate in the House of Commons after the summit, Blair characterised the outcome on the withholding tax as a sensible way forward, whereas Schröder stressed his disappointment, once more in an implicit way:

> Leider erfolglos blieben die Beratungen zum Steuerpaket, weil sich ein Mitgliedstaat nicht kompromissbereit gezeigt hat. (Policy statement on the results of the European Council in Helsinki on 10/11 December 1999 delivered to the German Bundestag on 16 December 1999)
> [Unfortunately, our consultations on the tax package were not successful, as a result of the fact that one member state was not willing to compromise.]

What this example reveals is that the selection of information, whether due to lack of linguistic competence or to carelessness, nevertheless fits into a traditional way of reporting about Germany and seems to reveal deep-seated perceptions and stereotypes about the Germans. As Kielinger (1999, p. 23) argues, the more Europe-friendly discourse of New Labour does not mean an end to the wide-spread view of the typically German obsession with pushing through supranational concepts and policies at all costs. In an article in *Die Welt* (22 March 2000), the same author argues that such stereotypical views about Germany are deeply ingrained in the English psyche and can and will easily be put to use whenever an occasion arises, i.e. when British and German interests diverge (e.g. different taxation policies). Thus, stereotypes can become explosive the moment they leave the intimacy of the mind and find their way into public life through discourse (Kielinger, 1999, p. 20).

Conclusion

Very often, cultures learn about each other by means of translations. When one culture reports about another culture, it often quotes members of that other culture, either by taking over the translations that were produced in the source culture itself, or by producing its own translations. Preconceived notions about each other can have an impact on the linguistic structure of a text. In other words, particular choices of linguistic expressions serve to express ideological and socio-cultural values, decisions by translators at the linguistic micro-level can have large effects for society and politics. Translations themselves can thus highlight sociocultural and political differences, and can serve as a window onto something else, such as cultural history and power relations in the contemporary world. A translation perspective to political discourse, combining concepts and methods of modern linguistics, (critical) discourse analysis and of cultural studies, can make a substantial contribution to the study of cultures in contact.

References

Baker, M. (1996), 'Linguistics and Cultural Studies', in A. Lauer, et al (eds), *Übersetzungswissenschaft in Umbruch: Festschrift für Wolfram Wilss*, Narr,Tübingen, pp. 9-19.

Born, J. and Schütte, W. (eds) (1995), *Eurotexte. Textarbeit in einer Institution der EG*, Narr, Tübingen.

Chesterman, A. (1998), 'Causes, Translations, Effects', *Target*, vol. 10, pp. 201-30.

Chilton, P. (1996) *Security Metaphors. Cold War Discourse from Containment to Common House*, Lang, New York.

Dollerup, C. (1996), 'Language Work at the European Union', in M. Gaddis Rose (ed.), *Translation Horizons Beyond the Boundaries of Translation Spectrum*, State University of New York, Binghamton, pp. 297-314.

Fairclough, N. (2000), *New Labour, new language?* Routledge, London.

Gentzler, E. (1993), *Contemporary Translation Theories*, Routledge, London.

Hönig, H.G. (1995), *Konstruktives Übersetzen*, Stauffenburg, Tübingen.

Kade, O. (1968), *Zufall und Gesetzmäßigkeit in der Übersetzung* (Beiheft I zur Zeitschrift *Fremdsprachen*), Enzyklopädie, Leipzig.

Kielinger, T. (1999), 'Zwei Jahrhunderte deutsch-britischer Begegnungen', W. J. Mommsen, (ed.), *Die ungleichen Partner. Deutsch-britische Beziehungen im 19. und 20. Jahrhundert*, Deutsche Verlagsanstalt, Stuttgart, pp. 18-30.

Koskinen, K. (2000), 'Institutional Illusions: Translating in the EU Commission', *The Translator*, vol. 6, pp. 49-65.

Lakoff, G. and Johnson, M. (1980), *Metaphors We Live By*, University of Chicago Press, Chicago.

Neubert, A. (1985), *Text and translation* (Übersetzungswissenschaftliche Beiträge 8), Enzyklopädie, Leipzig.

Nord, C. (1997), *Translating as a purposeful activity. Functionalist approaches explained*, St. Jerome, Manchester.

Schäffner, C. (1997a), 'Where is the source text?' in H. Schmidt and G. Wotjak (eds), *Modelle der Translation. Models of Translation. Festschrift für Albrecht Neubert*, Vervuert, Frankfurt, pp. 193-211.

Schäffner, C. (1997b), 'Metaphor and Interdisciplinary Analysis', *Journal of Area Studies*, no. 11, pp. 57-72.

Schäffner, C. (in press) 'Metaphor and Translation', *Journal of Pragmatics*.

Snell-Hornby, M., et al. (eds.) (1992), *Translation studies. An interdiscipline*, Benjamins, Amsterdam/Philadelphia.

Stolze, R. (1994), *Übersetzungstheorien. Eine Einführung*, Narr, Tübingen.

Toury, G. (1995), *Descriptive Translation Studies and Beyond*, Benjamins, Amsterdam/Philadelphia.

Venuti, L. (1995), *The translator's invisibility*, Routledge, London.

Vermeer, H.J. (1996), *A skopos theory of translation (Some arguments for and against)*, TEXTconTEXT, Heidelberg.

Vinay, J.-P. and Darbelnet, J. (1958), *Stylistique comparée du français et de l'anglais. Méthode de traduction*, Didier, Paris.

9 Der Ton wird schärfer. Stereotypes in Media Translation

ARACHNE VAN DER EIJK-SPAAN

In November 1996, the German weekly newspaper *Die Zeit* published an article 'Der Ton wird schärfer', written by Fredy Gsteiger. Its English translation was published in *The Guardian* of 4 December 1996 under the title 'Nerves fray in the Elysée'. The translation is a good example of the subtle but profound impact that choices made by a translator to accommodate the specific readership in a foreign public discourse community can have on the transferral of the author's ideas. In this chapter I will discuss the specific translation difficulties and the ways in which the translator addresses these problems.

The German Article

Fredy Gsteiger's original text contains both informative and persuasive elements and has a strong vocative aspect in the sense in which Newmark (1998, pp. 40-2) uses this term, i.e. as an appeal by the author to his readership to react to the text in a specific way. Gsteiger's style is characterised by rhetorical questions, contrastive expressions, and short sentences to focus the argument, which concerns the role of Germany in the Franco-German relationship (especially in the preparations for European Monetary Union). Gsteiger expresses firm opinions and strong criticism, exposing the Germans as obsessed with the fear of inflation and with a drive towards being the world's ecological and moral conscience. In particular, Germany is portrayed as a *schoolmaster* (the most important metaphor in the article) whose *teaching and preaching* irritate the French (portrayed as being self-assured and sensitive at the same time). Germany's diplomatic mistakes and self-righteous attitude and towards the French have much to do with the Germans being divided among themselves about

219

the euro, and with political mistakes made with regard to the euro and the D-mark. Gsteiger claims that the German misunderstanding of the French in fact has an adverse effect on the French efforts for change. He concludes by making an appeal to the Germans to make up their minds about the euro and stop nagging the French.

Specific Translation Difficulties

To translate the text and its ideas for the *Guardian* readership, the translator has to take into account that the British readership would probably be less aware of the details of the Franco-German relationship and less well informed about the political situation in Germany than German readers. Gsteiger's appeal will not have the same effect on the British readership as on the German readership, as the Franco-German relationship does not directly involve them. As to the Euro-debate, which was going on at the time when Gsteiger wrote his article, the British position was different from the German one. The German government under Chancellor Kohl was a driving force behind the euro, the conservative Major-government in England was Euro-sceptical.

Translator's Intention and Method

The translator clearly intends to give a 'communicative translation' in Newmark's (1998, p. 47) sense of attempting 'to render the exact contextual meaning of the original in such a way that both content and language are readily acceptable and comprehensible to the readership'.

In the specific case of Gsteiger's article this means that the translator had to adapt the article to the British journalistic style while preserving the meaning of Gsteiger's article and the appeal made in it. Ultimately, the success of the translation will have to be judged by this standard. To begin with, I shall look at the translator's method: how he tries to achieve a better understanding of the situation by the British reader, to what extent he follows the argumentative structure of Gsteiger's text, how he deals with the difference between the German and the British journalistic style, and how he transfers the ideas behind Gsteiger's text.

Accommodating the British Readership

The translator is aware that his readership is less well informed about the subject than the German readership. He therefore adds helpful information, such as the explanation 'the finance minister' to 'Theo Waigel', and 'Hans Tietmeyer' to 'the Bundesbank president'; he translates '3 per cent means 3 per cent' for 'drei ist drei' to clarify the topic (the italics here and in the following quotations are mine)

> (1)Soll man sich Woche für Woche von Theo Waigel belehren lassen, 'drei ist drei' - und sich damit auf eine buchhalterisch strenge Festlegung der gewählten Defizitwerte verpflichten? Darf der Bundesbankpräsident unermüdlich die monetäre Peitsche schwingen und haushaltspolitische Keuschheit fordern?

> Week in, week out, the French are being lectured by Theo Waigel, *the finance minister*, that '3 *per cent* means 3 *per cent'*, and that strict limitations should be imposed on the budget deficit. Should the Bundesbank president, *Hans Tietmeyer*, be allowed to crack the monetary whip relentlessly while unashamedly promoting Germany's budgetary and political ends?

I will come back to further translation problems of this passage later in the article.

Sometimes, however, the reverse happens and the translator under-translates a term, apparently expecting that the British reader knows what is meant. An example of this is the following passage:

> (2) Von einem zentralistischen Interventionsstaat wird ihr Land [= France] jäh zu einer dezentralen, liberalen Marktwirtschaft umgebaut. Dabei war den Franzosen bislang sowohl der politische als auch der wirtschaftliche Liberalismus eher fremd. Liberalisierung und Globalisierung, Deregulierung und Privatisierung gelten als Schimpfworte.

> From a highly centralised state, France is transforming itself into a decentralised, liberal market economy. The French are unfamiliar with political, let alone economic liberalism. Liberalisation and globalisation, deregulation and privatisation: for France, these are dirty words.

The reader is expected to know that a centralised state implies a high level of government intervention. This may probably be expected of the *Guardian* readership, but a slightly more elaborate translation of this term would have made sure that the British reader fully appreciates the contrast Gsteiger creates with his cumulation of terms indicating the opposite.

Argumentative Structure

The translator is not consistent in following Gsteiger's argumentative structure. He does not pay particular attention to maintaining the contrastive expressions or rhetorical questions that support the persuasive character of the text (cf. the first rhetorical question in example 1). The translator also does not always make use of the grammatical or syntactical opportunities offered by the German text, for instance:

(3) Seit fünf Jahren weist Frankreich eine niedrigere Inflationsrate als Deutschland aus, viel länger schon ist der Franc stabil. *Die Nationalbank, früher undenkbar, wurde in die Unabhängigkeit entlassen. Subventionen wurden gestrichen, Unternehmen privatisiert, Beschäftigungsprogramme gekappt. Laxheit braucht sich die französische Republik wahrlich nicht vorhalten zu lassen.*

For five years France has maintained lower inflation than Germany, and the franc has been stable for much longer than the mark. *Until recently, it would have been inconceivable for the National Bank to be independent. Subsidies have been cancelled, enterprises privatised, employment programmes cut back. The French Republic can hardly be accused of laxity.*

The text in the original gains momentum from 'ist der Franc stabil' onwards. The statement about the National Bank being made independent belongs to a list of measures, described in ever shorter clauses, each one of them indicating *action*. The list mounts up to the conclusion that France 'certainly has not been lax'. This rhetorical build-up is not reflected in the translation. Instead of emphasising the fact that it is now conceivable for the bank to be independent, the translation could have foregrounded the action of making it independent, which is what the original emphasises. Similarly, to underline the aspect of activity (vs. 'laxity'), it would have been better to use the imperfect in the translation of 'Subventionen wurden gestrichen' instead of the perfect tense as in 'subsidies have been cancelled'. These shifts in emphasis and in the use of verbs cause the argument to lose coherence and drive in the translation.

The translator very freely changes subjects to objects and passive constructions into active constructions in his translation of sentences. As

Fowler (1999, pp. 70-80) argues when discussing 'transitivity', this has, however, a great impact on how the reader perceives the roles of the participants in the action. Following Newmark (1998, pp. 88-9), we can describe a change in 'transitivity' as a 'modulation', i.e. a 'variation through a change of viewpoint, of perspective and very often of category of thought', as exemplified in the following passage:

(4) Die Franzosen müssen dabei fast über Nacht mit vielen Traditionen brechen und auf manche Sicherheiten verzichten. Von einem zentralistischen Interventionsstaat wird ihr Land jäh zu einer dezentralen, liberalen Marktwirtschaft umgebaut. [...] All das ist für den einzelnen Franzosen oft schwer zu ertragen. [...] Jetzt reicht's mit den Anstrengungen, grollt beispielsweise Serge July, [...] derweil der gaullistische Parlamentspräsident Philippe Séguin kritisiert, [...] Frankreich lasse sich alle Instrumente zur Ankurbelung der Wirtschaft aus der Hand schlagen.

The French have been expected to break with many traditions and dispense with various safety nets almost overnight. *From a highly centralised state, France is transforming itself into a decentralised, liberal market economy.* [...] For the man on the street, this is difficult to accept.

Up to this point in the text, the active role of the French has been emphasised in the German original. However, after the phrase 'Die Franzosen müssen [...] auf manche Sicherheiten verzichten', the author describes the sudden changes with a passive construction. The passive voice is very functional here: it underlines the fact that these changes suddenly happen and that the French are subjected to them ('wird ihr Land jäh umgebaut'). Gsteiger uses this change of voice to shift the emphasis from France as a nation, and the French government as main actors, to the French citizens ('den einzelnen Franzosen'), even gradually narrowed to spokespersons July and Séguin. The translator omits these specific quotations and changes the argumentative perspective considerably by translating 'France is transforming *itself*'.

Gsteiger's argument is supported by the use of an extended religious metaphor, which indicates to his readership how important the Deutschmark is to the Germans:

(5) Sie haben ihren Wählern einerseits *gepredigt,* die D-Mark sei quasi die *Opfergabe auf dem Altar* der europäischen Einigung; andererseits haben sie geschworen, bedingungslos durchzusetzen, daß der Euro mindestens so hart wie die Mark werde. Doch heute erfüllt nicht einmal Deutschland selber die

sakrosankten Kriterien von Maastricht. [...] Es rächt sich, daß die D-Mark zur *Staatsreligion* erhoben wurde - und sei es in der Absicht, nur ja nicht die deutsche Urangst vor der Inflation aufkommen zu lassen. Soll nun aber Frankreich für diese deutschen Obsessionen *büßen*? Muß es sich *abkanzeln* lassen, bloß weil Bonn sich in ein Dilemma hineinargumentiert hat?

On the one hand, they have *preached* to the voters that the deutschmark will have to be *sacrificed* in the interests of European unity; on the other, they have committed themselves to ensuring that the euro becomes at least as strong as the mark. Today, even Germany herself would be unable to fulfil the *sacrosanct* Maastricht criteria. [...]
The mark has become the *state religion*, but should France have to pay for this obsession? Must it accept all the blame, simply because the German government has talked itself into a corner?

The translator does not make a special effort to translate the metaphor consistently, and so part of its impact is lost. Earlier in the article, Gsteiger had alluded to the religious metaphor in a reference to the preparations for the introduction to the euro:

(6) Ausgerechnet jetzt, nachdem die Finanzmärkte von einer fristgerechten *Investitur der Euro-Währung* ausgehen, scheinen sich Bonn und Frankfurt davon zu distanzieren'.

At precisely the time when the financial markets are predicting that *investment in the euro currency* will begin on deadline, Bonn and Frankfurt appear to be distancing themselves from it.

The translator misses the allusion to the religious ceremony completely. He seems to read 'Investition' for 'Investitur' ('investiture') and translates 'investment in (sic!) the euro', which does not make sense (suggested translation: 'now that the financial markets assume that the investiture of the euro as a currency will take place at the agreed time'). Correct and consistent translation of the metaphor would have been very functional in creating a better understanding of German attitudes towards the introduction of the new currency and its symbolism among the British readership.

Accommodating the style of the Guardian

The translator tries to adapt his text to the demands of a British daily newspaper which is read quickly and which puts arguments forward in an emphatic way. This results in several slight over-translations, such as 'clash of personalities' for 'das Zwischenmenschliche' in the following example:

(7) Nicht um das Zwischenmenschliche geht es diesmal.
This time there is no clash of personalities.

This is a beautiful translation, but the rather vague, neutral term from Gsteiger's text has been given a slightly antagonistic aspect in the translation. A slight over-generalisation occurs in (for the context cf. example 4):

(8) All das ist für den einzelnen Franzosen oft schwer zu ertragen.
For the man on the street, this is difficult to accept.

'Oft' has been left untranslated here, suggesting that German criticism is *constantly* difficult to bear for the French.

The translator also changes the text when he translates 'Abwertung der europäischen Währungen' as 'devaluation of the euro over the dollar' — the original speaks about 'European currencies' in the plural.. Using the word *euro* in an English text will have had a stronger effect than the more general 'European currencies'. This was certainly the case in 1996, when there was still a heated debate in the UK about the euro (which did not yet exist at the time).

The translator tries to keep the translation uncluttered with detail. In fact, one of the most striking aspects of the translation are its omissions. As we have seen in example (4), such omissions can concern quotations which serve to underline the argument, e.g. the opinions of two influential Frenchmen, the publisher of the left-wing *Libération*, Serge July, and the President of Parliament, Philippe Séguin. In other cases, omissions concern adverbs of time or connectives which serve to hold the argument together:

(9) *Dabei* war den Franzosen *bislang* sowohl der politische als auch der wirtschaftliche Liberalismus eher fremd.
The French are unfamiliar with political, let alone economic liberalism.

In some cases complete sentences giving explanations (cf. for instance the clause '- und sei es in der Absicht, nur ja nicht die deutsche Urangst vor der Inflation aufkommen zu lassen' in example 5) or rhetorical questions are omitted, e.g.:

(10) Aus Pariser Sicht wächst die Skepsis der Deutschen, je wahrscheinlicher der Beitritt Italiens, Spaniens oder Portugals wird. *Aber verdienen nur die Europäer nördlich der Alpen den Euro?* Ständig werden von deutscher Seite neue Hürden aufgestellt oder alte so hoch gelegt, daß sie schwerlich zu überspringen sind.

Paris perceives German scepticism growing as the entry of Italy, Spain or Portugal becomes more likely. The Germans are forever creating new hurdles and imposing higher conditions which are almost impossible to fulfil.

Transfer of Main Ideas and Appeal Made in the Original

Gsteiger sets the tone for his article in his heading: Der Ton wird schärfer, with a subheading Streitfall Euro: Der Schulmeister Deutschland geht den Franzosen auf die Nerven. Gsteiger thus establishes the metaphor of Germany as a schoolmaster, which will have been familiar to most of his German readership as a basic image that informs his whole argumentation. The schoolmaster tries to tell the French what to do. This irritates the French and causes the relationship between the nations to become fraught:

(11) Die *Regierung in Paris* kann machen, was sie will - stets schallt es besserwisserisch über den Rhein: Jetzt müßt *ihr* noch dies tun und jenes lassen. [...] Wenn dies und das und jenes nicht erfüllt ist, dann kann Deutschland - leider, leider - keine Wirtschafts- und Währungsunion mit *euch* eingehen.

Paris can do what it likes - but *the government across the Rhine* always knows better: it must do this, and abandon that. [...]
If you cannot fulfil this and that criteria then, we are sorry to say, Germany cannot accept you as a partner in economic and monetary union (EMU).

Here the translator moved the element of *the government* from Paris to Bonn. Thus the suggested inappropriateness of the *Regierung* in Paris, being addressed as *ihr/euch* instead of by the polite form *Sie* by the *Schulmeister Deutschland* of the title, is lost in the translation. Yet the element of Germany as a know-all is put forward very clearly.

The translator translates the headings as 'Nerves fray in the Elysée' with a subheading 'Germany's weary carping over monetary union is pushing France to the end of its tether, argues Fredy Gsteiger'. Half-way through the article a further heading is added: 'Must all Europeans now have their economic policies dictated by Germany?' This choice of extra heading reflects the tenor of the translation, even more so because the translator leaves the important metaphor of the *schoolmaster* out of the translated headings. This is unwise, as this metaphor is often alluded to in the course of the carefully crafted German article. It returns for instance in 'schallt es besserwisserisch über den Rhein', 'belehren', 'Schwall von Wahrheiten und Weisheiten aus Deutschland', 'tönt es vorwurfsvoll aus Deutschland', 'Diktat', 'Kritik aus Bonn', and 'schulmeisterlicher Zeigefinger'. In the translation these phrases now seem to dangle in a void. The translator left an opportunity unused and a Leitmotif in the German argument is lost in the translation.

At the end of the article, this leads to an odd situation. As to subtitle and ending, the German text shows a chiastic structure. The title:

(12) Streitfall Euro: Der Schulmeister Deutschland geht den Franzosen auf die Nerven.
Germany's weary carping over monetary union is pushing France to the end of its tether [...]

is echoed by:

(13) Wer hingegen in Deutschland den Euro wirklich will, dem kann man angesichts der *bloßliegenden Nerven in Frankreich* nur nachdrücklich raten, auf den *schulmeisterlichen Zeigefinger* zu verzichten.

One can only emphatically urge Germans who are in favour of monetary union - given *France's clearly frayed nerves* - to refrain from *pointing the finger like a headmaster*.

As the translator has not used the metaphor of the *schoolmaster* in the title, the chiastic structure is lost; moreover, his translation of 'den schulmeisterlichen Zeigefinger' by 'pointing the finger like a headmaster' is not only wrong, but positively odd in the context. (It is wrong because pointing the finger at someone involves an element of accusation, whereas the German expression evokes the image of a schoolmaster who sticks his index finger in the air and says: 'Now listen carefully, children ...'.).

However, the translator accurately maintains the *nerves*-metaphor of the heading, which refers to the French. They are portrayed as a self-assured but also a sensitive nation:

> (14) Frankreich ist eine selbstbewußte, auch eine sensible Nation.
> France is a self-assured and sensitive nation.

and rightly so:

> (15) Indes ist diesmal die Empfindlichkeit berechtigt.
> - but at the moment this sensitivity is justified.

In the text, France's sensitivity offers a nice contrast with Germany's attitude of teaching and preaching.

As to the attitude of Germany, it is significant that this is consistently pictured in slightly stronger terms than in Gsteiger's article. This happens throughout the translation and has a cumulative effect. It starts in the added heading that is an edited quotation from a passage in the translation:

> (16a) Above all, must all Europeans now have their economic policies dictated by Germany?

This serves as a translation for:

> (16b) Vor allem aber: Sollen sich die Europäer, die ohnehin schon ihre liebe Not haben mit den Deutschen als ihrem ökologischen und moralischen Weltgewissen, nun auch noch deren ökonomisches Diktat gefallen lassen?

The translation shows a major shift in focus from 'ökonomisches Diktat' to 'die Europäer'; the translator then changes this into 'all Europeans', thus accentuating the phrase. As to the representation of Germany: the softening aspect of Germany as the world's ecological and moral conscience is left out, leaving the harsh image of Germany as dictator of economic policies.

Another example is provided by the following passage:

> (17) Kein Wunder, daß der Zorn in Frankreich wächst. Soll man sich Woche für Woche von Theo Waigel belehren lassen, 'drei ist drei' - und sich damit auf eine buchhalterisch strenge Festlegung der gewählten Defizitwerte verpflichten? Darf der Bundesbankpräsident unermüdlich die monetäre Peitsche schwingen und haushaltspolitische Keuschheit fordern? Gerade jene französi-

schen Politiker, die für die Währungsunion eintreten, sind zunehmend empört über den unablässigen Schwall von Wahrheiten und Weisheiten aus Deutschland.

Small wonder Germany has become a thorn in France's flesh. Week in, week out, the French are being lectured by Theo Waigel, the finance minister, that '3 per cent means 3 per cent', and that strict limitations should be imposed on the budget deficit. Should the Bundesbank president, Hans Tietmeyer, be allowed to crack the monetary whip relentlessly while unashamedly promoting Germany's budgetary and political ends? French politicians in favour of EMU are increasingly outraged at the torrent of complaints and self-righteous advice coming from Germany.

Here the sentence 'Kein Wunder, daß der Zorn in Frankreich wächst' has been translated as 'Small wonder Germany has become a thorn in France's flesh'. Perhaps the translator did not even recognize *Zorn/thorn* as a faux ami. At any rate, the element of gradually growing anger (cf. 'zunehmend empört') is replaced by repeated stinging, and the element of opposition between France and Germany, with Germany as the aggressor, is put more sharply. This is aggravated by translating the question which follows 'Soll man sich [...] verpflichten?' as a statement; and by translating 'unermüdlich' as 'relentless'. To add further to the cumulative effect, 'Wahrheiten und Weisheiten' is translated as 'complaints and self-righteous advice. This translation is heavily interpreted and very negative. 'Teaching and preaching' would have a similar sound-effect as the original and it would fit in with the metaphor of Germany as a *schoolmaster*.

Another cumulative effect is produced in the following example:

(18) Was in Deutschland fehlt, ist ein angemessenes Verständnis für Frankreich und für die fundamentalen Umwälzungen, die es derzeit durchlebt. Weil man sich nicht genügend für den westlichen Nachbarn interessiert, wird übersehen oder unterschätzt, welche enormen Anstrengungen in der Währungs- und Haushaltsdisziplin der Partner seit vierzehn Jahren bereits auf sich genommen hat.

Distinctly lacking on the part of Germany is a fundamental appreciation of the radical changes which France is undergoing. Because Germany is not sufficiently interested in its neighbours, it is overlooking and underestimating their enormous strengths in terms of monetary discipline and budgeting over the last 14 years.

Apart from the odd false friend — 'Anstrengungen' ('efforts') has become 'strengths' — the singular 'westlicher Nachbar' (i.e. France) is translated here by the plural 'neighbours', leaving 'westlich' out. This has a generalising effect: it suggests that Germany is insufficiently interested in *all* its neighbouring countries. Strictly speaking, this generalisation draws the UK and therefore the British readership into the situation, as does the subheading 'Must *all* Europeans now have their economic policies dictated by Germany?' (see example 16a/b). The German text only says 'die Europäer'). On the other hand, the dominant British discourse does not see British people as Europeans (cf. Mautner in this volume). The generalizations in the translation text therefore probably rather serve to underline the aggressive attitude of Germany. This ties in with the fact that the translation leaves out the phrase 'der Partner'. This again strengthens the element of antagonism between Germany and France in the translation. On top of all this, Germany is put into the active role of *aggressor* in the translation: the vague 'man' and the passive voice ('wird übersehen oder unterschätzt') are replaced by 'Germany' and the active 'is overlooking and [note the slight over-translation!] underestimating'.

Not only Germany's attitudes, but also its intentions are put forward in stronger terms than Gsteiger uses. Twice the translator presents Germany as promoting its own interests where Gsteiger's text does not mention this:

(19) Darf der Bundesbankpräsident unermüdlich die monetäre Peitsche schwingen und haushaltspolitische Keuschheit *fordern*?

Should the Bundesbank president, Hans Tietmeyer, be allowed to crack the monetary whip relentlessly *while unashamedly promoting Germany's budgetary and political ends*?

(20) Zu laut *formuliert* Deutschland seine Interessen
Germany is *promoting* its own self-interest too loudly, [...]

In example (19), 'und haushaltspolitische Keuschheit fordern?' ('[...] and demand a budgetary policy of modesty?') is translated as 'while unashamedly promoting Germany's budgetary and political ends?'. This translation is simply wrong (the translator may have read *fördern* instead of *fordern*). In example (20), 'Zu laut formuliert Deutschland seine Interessen' is translated as 'Germany is promoting its own self-interest too loudly'. This is an over-translation.

As both these cases of promoting are not in the original text, they have been systematically put into the translation by the translator, either deliberately or by mistake. They both convey an added element of German aggression.

In the final paragraph of his article Gsteiger makes an appeal, which is largely omitted by the translator:

(21) Die Forderung muß also lauten: *Wer die Währungsunion verhindern möchte, soll sich offen zu seinem Widerstand bekennen.* Wer hingegen in Deutschland den Euro wirklich will, dem kann man angesichts der bloßliegenden Nerven in Frankreich nur nachdrücklich raten, auf den schulmeisterlichen Zeigefinger zu verzichten.

One can only emphatically urge Germans who are in favour of monetary union - given France's clearly frayed nerves - to refrain from pointing the finger like a headmaster.

The omission here is significant. It would have been important to convey the fact to the British readership that there are people in Germany who are against the EMU, as it would have allowed a more balanced view. The only appeal left in the translation is that 'Germans who are in favour of monetary union [...] [are] to refrain from pointing their finger like a headmaster'. This is a mere shadow of the original appeal.

The above mentioned over-translations, omissions, modulations and cases of added emphasis often have an antagonistic effect and put Germany in the role of aggressor. In the last sentence of the article the translator goes even further:

(22) Müssen sie jedoch so stur darauf beharren, auch *in allem recht zu bekommen*?
But do they have to insist on *being superior* all of the time?

The over-translation 'superior' for 'recht bekommen [wollen]' indicates that the translator taps into a British stereotype about Germans. The alleged sense of or drive for superiority attributed to Germans is a stereotype in British media (cf. Musolff 1997, Mautner, Wittlinger in this volume), together with arrogance, which comes back in various forms in this text. Whether consciously or unconsciously, the translator seems to allow himself to be led by this stereotype. The translator plays down the constructive solution to the euro-problem suggested by Gsteiger (i.e. that the Germans make up their mind about it so that this problem will not have an adverse effect on the Franco-German relationship) by omitting to translate three lines of text (see example 21, italicised passage), but he highlights this drive for superiority: 'Germany wants to win and impose rules on other countries' (cf. Schäffner in this volume). This results in a shift in focus and aim of the text in the translation: whereas Gsteiger portrays Germany as a *schoolmaster*, the translator portrays Germany as an *aggressor*. This is not how Germans generally perceive themselves and it does not cover the ideas and purpose of Gsteiger's text. The exhortative aspect of Gsteiger's text has become a confirmation of a stereotype in the translation.

Conclusion

The translator of Gsteiger's article tried to produce a communicative translation. It is shorter, more staccato, and generally more outspoken than the original. The many omissions result in less subtlety and less nuance in the translation. A reason for this may have been to accommodate the style of an English newspaper like *The Guardian*.

The translator clearly conveys Gsteiger's message that Germany behaves like a *know-all* and conveys Gsteiger's criticism reasonably accurately. However, the translator leaves out important and interesting information on aspects of the Franco-German relationship, which weakens the argument Gsteiger wanted to put across. The omissions also do not allow the English reader to get a better idea of what German media publish on an issue like this and how they perceive Germany. Thus the translation is unnecessarily shallow.

The translator does not always use the opportunities given by the German original to make the translation vivid and to highlight contrasts. He regularly fails to reproduce the careful grammatical and syntactical construction of Gsteiger's article in the translation. Throughout the translation the translator fails to give an accurate translation of the main metaphor (that of Germany as a *headmaster*), which lies at the basis of the whole article and returns in various forms. Instead, he systematically portrays Germany as an *aggressor* with a drive for superiority.

As the translation is presented in *The Guardian* as an article by Fredy Gsteiger and the translator's name is not mentioned, it is suggested that this is what Gsteiger wrote. This is not the case: the translation does not fully cover his words, it highlights different aspects, it omits information, and, moreover, it supports a stereotype not used in the German text. We may conclude that in this respect the translator overstepped the mark.

References

Primary sources

Gsteiger, F., 'Der Ton wird schärfer', *Die Zeit*, 29 November 1996.
'Nerves fray in the Elysée', *The Guardian*, 4 December 1996.

Secondary literature

Fowler, R. (1996), *Linguistic Criticism*, Oxford University Press, Oxford.
Fowler, R. (1999), *Language in the News: Discourse and Ideology in the Press*, Routledge, London.
Mautner, G. (in this volume), 'British National Identity in the European Context. The Dominant conservative Position'.
Musolff, A. (1997): 'Modell Deutschland: Vorbild oder Alptraum? Zur Diskussion um die Rolle der BRD als neue europäische Supermacht in der britischen Öffentlichkeit'. in Disselnkötter, A., Jäger, S., Kellershohn, H., Slobobzia, S. (eds), *Evidenzen im Fluß. Demokratieverluste in Deutschland*. DISS, Duisburg, pp. 87-97.
Newmark, P. (1998), *A Textbook of Translation*, Prentice Hall, London.
Schäffner, C. (in this volume), 'Attitudes to Europe - Mediated by Translation'.
Wittlinger, R. (in this volume), 'Representation of Germany in the context of European Integration in Margaret Thatcher's Autobiographies'.